Secularizing Islamists?

SOUTH ASIA ACROSS THE DISCIPLINES
A series edited by Dipesh Chakrabarty, Sheldon Pollock, and Sanjay Subrahmanyam

Funded by a grant from the Andrew W. Mellon Foundation and jointly published by the University of California Press, the University of Chicago Press, and Columbia University Press.

The Powerful Ephemeral: Everyday Healing in an Ambiguously Islamic Place
by Carla Bellamy (California)

Extreme Poetry: The South Asian Movement of Simultaneous Narration
by Yigal Bronner (Columbia)

The Social Space of Language: Vernacular Culture in British Colonial Punjab
by Farina Mir (California)

Unifying Hinduism: Philosophy and Identity in Indian Intellectual History
by Andrew J. Nicholson (Columbia)

Islam Translated: Literature, Conversion, and the Arabic Cosmopolis of South and Southeast Asia
by Ronit Ricci (Chicago)

South Asia Across the Disciplines is a series devoted to publishing first books across a wide range of South Asian studies, including art, history, philology or textual studies, philosophy, religion, and the interpretive social sciences. Series authors all share the goal of opening up new archives and suggesting new methods and approaches, while demonstrating that South Asian scholarship can be at once deep in expertise and broad in appeal.

Secularizing Islamists?

Jama'at-e-Islami and Jama'at-ud-Da'wa in Urban Pakistan

Humeira Iqtidar

The University of Chicago Press *Chicago and London*

Humeira Iqtidar is the graduate officer in research at the Centre for
South Asian Studies at the University of Cambridge.

The University of Chicago Press, Chicago 60637
The University of Chicago Press, Ltd., London
© 2011 by The University of Chicago
All rights reserved. Published 2011
Printed in the United States of America.

20 19 18 17 16 15 14 13 12 11   1 2 3 4 5

ISBN-13: 978-0-226-38468-9 (cloth)
ISBN-10: 0-226-38468-3 (cloth)

Library of Congress Cataloging-in-Publication Data

Iqtidar, Humeira.
    Secularizing Islamists? : Jama'at-e-Islami and Jama'at-ud-Da'wa in
urban Pakistan / Humeira Iqtidar.
        p. cm. — (South Asia across the disciplines)
    ISBN-13: 978-0-226-38468-9 (cloth : alk. paper)
    ISBN-10: 0-226-38468-3 (cloth : alk. paper) 1. Islam and secularism—
Pakistan. 2. Jama'at-i Islami-yi Pakistan. 3. Jama'at-ud-Da'wa Pakistan.
4. Pakistan—Politics and government. 5. Islam and state—Pakistan.
I. Title. II. Series: South Asia across the disciplines.
    BP190.5 .S35I67 2011
    320.5'57095491—dc22

                                                          2010034634

In memory of my *ami*
(1951–2008)

Contents

List of Abbreviations | *ix*

Preface and Acknowledgments | *xi*

INTRODUCTION
Secularism in Pakistan | 1
A Failed Experiment?

ONE *Colonial Secularism and Islamism in North India* | 38
A Relationship of Creativity?

TWO *Jama'at-e-Islami Pakistan* | 55
Learning from the Opposition

THREE *Competition among Allies* | 98
JD and JI in Urban Lahore

FOUR *Harbingers of Change?* | 129
Women in Islamist Parties

CONCLUSION
Islamists | 156
Secularizing *and* Liberal?

Notes | 163

References | 193

Index | 212

Abbreviations

CIA   Central Intelligence Agency of the United States of America

IJI   Islami Jamhuri Ittehad: a political coalition of nine parties that came to prominence in the 1988 elections against the Pakistan People's Party

IJT   Islami Jam'iyat Tulaba/Talibat: Jama'at-e-Islami student wing for men/women

ISI   Inter Services Intelligence (Pakistan)

JD   Jama'at-ud-Da'wa

JI   Jama'at-e-Islami

JUI   Jam'iyat Ulema Islam

JUP   Jam'iyat 'Ulama Pakistan

LT   Lashkar-e-Tayyaba: militant wing of the Jama'at-ud-Da'wa

NAP   National Awami Party

NSF   National Student's Federation

MMA   Muttahida Majlis-e-'Amal: Joint Action Committee of the Religious Parties that came to prominence in the 2002 elections in Pakistan

PPP   Pakistan People's Party

PTUF   Pakistan Trade Union Federation

Preface and Acknowledgments

Jama'at-ud-Da'wa allegedly masterminded the terror attack carried out in Mumbai in 2008. Although not proven conclusively, this is an entirely plausible allegation, with the proviso that it seems to overestimate the organizational capacity and ambition within Jama'at-ud-Da'wa (JD) alone. Moreover, the lack of demands raised by the terrorists in Mumbai, at least to public knowledge, about Kashmir is an unlikely move for a group that has deep ideological and political commitment to its version of the Kashmiri cause. However, I am not primarily concerned, indeed not even able, to provide a definitive answer to the question of the extent and range of JD involvement in the Mumbai attacks. I bring it up to acknowledge the context in which this research will be received and responded to. The easy conflation of Islamism with violence is promoted most of all by the activities of groups like JD. Yet it hides from view a more granulated account of the multifaceted relationship that Islamists have with the societies and polities within which they operate. This research is an attempt at thinking about the long-term impact of Islamism within predominantly Muslim contexts such as Pakistan.

In the course of conducting the research, and then writing, revising, and refining the argument contained here, I have incurred immense debts of gratitude. My first debt is toward the many individuals within Jama'at-e-Islami (JI) and JD who allowed me to spend time with them, meet their families, colleagues, and friends, and ask them questions, some of them uncomfortable ones. I hesitate to name any of them specifically, precisely because the most helpful are also the most vulnerable in many ways in terms of their roles within the organizational hierarchy. I realize that to some readers my account here may seem particularly sympathetic to the Islamists, but I know that for my Islamist interlocutors it is not a comfortable read either. However, one person I can thank publicly is Mohammed Abbas, who was instrumental in facilitating my initial contact with JD. His own interest in the research process led to many interesting discussions and new questions for me to explore.

I started this research under the guidance of Rajnarayan Chandavarkar, who died unexpectedly in early 2006. I share his loss with many of his friends and students who could be sure of an interested ear and a relentless questioning of our basic assumptions. David Lehmann was kind enough to step in as my adviser at this point. David's unstinting support, self-deprecating sense of humor, and disdain for the more tribal approach to social science research have influenced this research in more ways than he will acknowledge. Pieter van Houten pushed me to clarify the terms used and helped define a sharper focus to the interplay of competition among the Islamists. James Piscatori brought a breadth of comparative knowledge to bear upon this research and raised some critical questions that I fear I still cannot answer. At the Centre for South Asian Studies at the University of Cambridge, Chris Bayly has been an ideal senior colleague, engaging meaningfully with my work at the same time as allowing me space to develop ideas and initiatives. The depth of support that Chris has provided to many younger scholars around him is hard to grasp initially, precisely because of his modesty as a teacher and a scholar. Justin Jones, Kevin Greenbank, Philippa Williams, Barbara Roe, Jan Thulborn, Rachel Rowe, Anna Maria, and Ivan Coleby have been wonderful colleagues at the Centre.

The debt of gratitude I owe Kamran Asdar Ali is made all the more significant by the fact that he did not have any official responsibility toward me. His support of my research through critical readings, suggestions, and exploration of ideas came at a critical time soon after Raj passed away. I can only hope to pass on such intellectual generosity to others. Similarly, David Gilmartin engaged generously with the ideas contained in this research, enriching them with his comments and suggestions. David's work on colonial Punjab has been particularly influential in framing my own understanding, and his questions exposing my assumptions have left an indelible mark on this research. David's wide-ranging support of younger scholars and his willingness to engage critically with their projects is an inspiration in itself. Talal Asad has engaged with this work out of a similar spirit of intellectual generosity. His critique and encouragement, but primarily his own work, have had a profound impact on this research. In a similar vein, I am immensely grateful to Dipesh Chakrabarty, and not just for his support for this book. His work has been deeply suggestive and provocative, and his willingness to continuously question his own previous arguments an inspiration. I owe him also for introducing me to the best editor a first-book author can hope to work with. Alan Thomas and Kate Frentzel at the University of Chicago Press managed to be patient, clear, and supportive at the same time. The two anonymous readers raised important questions about different aspects of this manuscript, and I would like to thank them for their detailed reading.

Gareth Stedman-Jones, Ira Katznelson, and Karen Barkey provided much needed encouragement at a time when I was struggling with bringing some closure to this research. Gareth, John Barber, and Bassim Mussalam have helped to embed me into the stimulating intellectual context of King's College, Cambridge. Gareth has engaged with this work at various levels and also supported it at the Centre for History and Economics at King's College. Farzad Rafi Khan has been generous with his time in discussing the details of traditionalism. Asef Bayat, Joya Chatterji, Akbar Zaidi, Magnus Marsden, Jonathan Steinberg, Marion Kant, Justin Jones, Eleanor Newbigin, Naveeda Khan, and Mohammed Khalid Masud have all enriched different parts of the research contained here through their comments, questions, and support. Aspects of this research were presented at workshops, seminars, and conferences in London, Oxford, Cambridge, Lahore, Karachi, Cairo, Leiden, Sussex, San Francisco, Atlanta, Baltimore, Essex, and Islamabad. I am grateful to many within the audience in these sessions who raised important questions for me to think through.

I would like to thank the Smuts Memorial Fund managers for the generous funding for fieldwork for this research. I would also like to thank Cambridge University Press and Routledge Books, India, for granting me permission, respectively, to reprint a part of chapter 1 (*Religion and the Political Imagination*, edited by Ira Katznelson and Gareth Stedman Jones [Cambridge: Cambridge University Press, 2010]), and a part of chapter 2, which appeared as "Jama'at-e-Islami Pakistan: Learning from the Left," in *Beyond Crisis: Re-evaluating Pakistan*, ed. Naveeda Khan (New Delhi: Routledge Books, 2010), 245–69. Finally, I am grateful to Imran Qureshi for allowing me to use an image from his fantastic series of miniature paintings titled *Moderate Enlightenment*.

How does one thank friends—Madiha, Sadaf, Aisha, Sumaira, Sarwat, Sara, Priya—who listened and argued, laughed and sympathized at (generally) the right moments? But most of all, to try to express how fortunate and grateful I feel for the love and support of my family—ami and abu; Omar, Farooq, and Jawad; Uncle, Amina, Sana, Myda, and Faaiz; and especially Kamal, Zehra, and Taimur—is a gesture that daunts me with its inherent inadequacy.

Secularism in Pakistan

A FAILED EXPERIMENT?

Our parents never had to think about religion. It was just there.
Now it is hard to avoid Islam any where you go in Lahore!

> —Male university student echoing an oft-repeated complaint
> among the secularists of Lahore

Our parents had no idea about Islam. And we did not either.
Now I realize what an un-Islamic (ghair-Islami) *life I was leading . . .*
[it was not] until I made an effort to understand my religion.

> —Female activist of the Jama'at-ud-Da'wa, repeating a
> frequently made remark within Islamist circles of Lahore

Can Pakistan ever be a secular state? How does a country created on the basis of religious identity conceive of secularism? The increasing prominence of Islamists in Pakistani political space, especially over the last two decades, has crystallized a particular reading of Pakistan past and present. It assumes a teleological connection between Muslim nationalism and Islamism. Pakistan, Islam, and fundamentalism—the conflation of the three has become an inescapable focus of media portrayals and increasingly belligerent policy discussions outside of Pakistan. The conjuring up of this trinity has reduced all three to a caricature of the diversity that they exhibit independently. This book is an attempt at disrupting this teleology that denies the possibility of secularism, with all its positive normative associations, in Pakistan. The project of rehabilitating secularism in Pakistan cannot, however, proceed without a critical reexamination of the relationship between Islamism, secularism, and secularization.

Rather than reading the history of Pakistan as a linear move from religious nationalism to Islamism, it is possible, even with just a scratch beneath the surface of popular portrayals and official narratives, to see it as a history pregnant with possibilities and debates. One particular period of Pakistani history that had a tremendous impact on social and political structures but has not received much academic attention is that of the 1960s. This research began with my initial interest in popular protests of the 1960s, with a particular emphasis on labor unions. However, as I looked into this in more detail, and also wrote about some contemporary developments in the Pakistani newspaper *Dawn*, I realized that there were important links between the left mobilizations of the 1960s and the changes in strategies and operations of the Jama'at-e-Islami (JI). The JI has been a particularly influential Islamist group not just in South Asia, with its chapters in India and Bangladesh, but also in the rest of the world through the inspiration its model provided, as well as its links with different organizations. I was able to observe the changes within the JI at close quarters during the time I taught and interacted with students and faculty at the Punjab University in 2002 and 2003. Punjab University had been a fierce battleground in the fight for cultural and political legitimacy between the liberal/left and the Jama'at-e-Islami from the late 1960s onward and particularly during the military regime of General Zia-ul-Haq (1977–88). Among the left/liberal labor and student unions, it seemed that the ones that had survived the wave of mass privatizations and deunionization during Zia's regime were the ones in which Islamists had managed to establish a stronghold.[1] However, close to fifteen years after the end of the Zia era, why had the JI continued its links with these unions? What did the unions gain from their relationship with the JI? Did these links have any impact at all on the JI's policies?

Questions like these, and others, led me to a wider investigation of Islamism. The Islamists are distinguished from the other "Muslim Fundamentalists" by their insistence on engagement with the political structures and state apparatus as a means of establishing a Muslim society (Roy 1994; Fuller 2003).[2] Others, like the pietists, traditionalists, and various types of militants, do not share this emphasis on political engagement.[3] I look at the various kinds of groups categorized under the umbrella term "Muslim Fundamentalist" in more detail in chapter 3. In the course of this research, it became apparent to me that competition among Islamist parties plays an important role, not just in shaping their strategies but also in the impact they have. My engagement with the Jama'at-ud-Da'wa[4] allows me to not just highlight this particular dynamic of Islamism but also to show the diversity that is a constituent element of contemporary Islamism. Like the JI the Jama'at-ud-Da'wa is also headquartered in the larger Lahore area. JD is primarily known through its militant wing, *Lashkar-e-Tayyaba* (Army of the Pure, LT), which has been implicated in a range of violent activities.

Its international prominence has grown since its alleged involvement in the London blasts in July 2005. More recently, the JD has been implicated in the Mumbai attacks in 2008. Since then the group has changed its name to *Tehreek-e-Hurmat-e-Rasul* (Movement for Defending the Honor of the Prophet), but despite that remains popularly known as Jama'at-ud-Da'wa. Access to this group was much more difficult than JI. Initial contact with the men in the organization was made difficult by the fact that at the official level they practice *parda* of the voice as well as of the body. Therefore, conversations between unrelated men and women are discouraged. Nevertheless, the official practice is, as is often the case, defined by its exceptions. Harder still to work around were my own fears in dealing with an organization with strong militant links. Difficult as it was, the interaction with the JD provided a useful contrast to the JI.

The JD is a recent and rather inorganic construct in many ways. It is a product of the Afghan wars, when Saudi and American funding channeled through the Pakistani intelligence services allowed many local gangsters, strong men, and smalltime thugs the opportunity of a larger stage to exhibit their dubious talents. The group was notoriously created to provide a steady stream of jihadis for the Afghan war (Shafqat 2002; Rana 2003, 133–38, 317–27). Its founder, Hafiz Saeed, is putatively a scholar like Maulana Maududi, the founder of JI. He was a teacher of Islamic studies at an engineering college in Lahore. However, his scholarly achievements and intellectual prowess are no match for those of Maududi, who is widely regarded as a pioneering Islamist thinker and writer. Since the end of the first Afghan war, JD had been in the process of defining a new role for itself, initially focusing its attention on Kashmir, although there were episodes of its involvement in sectarian violence within Pakistan too. In 2004, under intense government pressure to disavow its overtly militant leanings, the JD, at least officially, separated from LT and has concentrated on building a network of hospitals, schools, and dispensaries. The separation from LT can only be treated as a line in the sand, but nevertheless it was possible to see a shift within JD toward broader and deeper social engagement. Through my interaction with members and some leaders of the JD, I saw a group that was struggling to define its role in a post–cold war, post-9/11 era. One strand within the organization was increasingly viewing it as a political pressure group, although they still professed a disdain for electoral democracy. Created through foreign funding with a fairly specific aim of recruiting and training young men for engaging in war first in Afghanistan and then Kashmir, the organization was looking for its raison d'être in these changed times. The ongoing American military presence in Afghanistan and its increasing spillover in the Pakistani provinces of Khyber Pakhtunkhwa[5] and Balochistan have presented the temptation of continued militancy to an organization that is only just beginning to engage with domestic social and political issues.[6]

The Jama'at-e-Islami is, by contrast, an organic creation, one that was not founded through external funding or direct official manipulation. Both JI and JD are classified as Islamist but even a quick look at their history and operation would show that there are immense differences between the two, and any political response must be calibrated with this difference in mind.[7] Jama'at-e-Islami is the archetypal Islamist party that was founded in the last stages of British colonial rule in North India. It has been extremely influential in inspiring similar parties as well as loosely affiliated chapters around the world. Maulana Maududi, its founder, was a journalist and a scholar who, in addition to being fluent in Urdu, Arabic, and Persian—languages of the educated middle- to upper-class Muslims—taught himself English and some German. This allowed him to access and engage with Western philosophical works, as well as with Muslim history and Islamic political thought. Despite the violence of its student wing, Islami Jam'iyat Tulaba (IJT), in university and college campuses around Pakistan, and its support for a faction of mujahideen in Afghanistan, it is not, essentially, a militant organization but rather a contender for power operating within the electoral system. The Jama'at-e-Islami has been participating in electoral politics since the early 1950s, albeit without significant success. Indeed, the oft-cited JI failure to translate its street power into electoral strength can be seen as a failure of strategy, but not of commitment to the electoral process. Jama'at-e-Islami activists and leaders often stress that they have been committed to the electoral process despite the problems they have had and not because of easy successes. The recent electoral success of the MMA (Muttahida Majlis-i-'amal, an alliance of religious parties), of which the Jama'at-e-Islami was a key member, is unprecedented for religious parties in Pakistan, and was a fragile one. Nevertheless, it can be seen as part of JI's continued commitment to the electoral system in Pakistan.[8] (I discuss in more detail the context in which the JI originated and the changes in its organization in recent years in chapters 1, 2, and 3.)

Here, I want to emphasize the differences between the JI and the JD. The close relationship between the JI, the Pakistani Army, and US intelligence during the Afghan war has led many analysts and scholars to overlook this difference between an organization funded by the intelligence agencies with the express purpose of recruitment to fight a proxy war, and one that can claim longer roots in the particular intellectual and political turmoil that arose during colonial rule. In fact, it is useful to highlight the differences between the two Islamists groups, JI and JD, to understand the variation in their influence in Pakistani politics and society. There is no doubt that the cold war, and the first Afghan war, brought about a significant expansion in the extent and reach of the operations of all Islamists, whatever their provenance. Islamism in general and JI in particular received a huge boost during this period. Islamist parties were provided funding, organizational support, and legitimacy in countries as diverse as Egypt, Pakistan, and Malaysia for acting as bulwarks against the rising influence of leftist ideology in third-world countries. In Pakistan this strategic decision made at the highest levels of US officialdom meant that CIA funds were available for supporting JI's extended activities, a military dictatorship partial to JI was supported financially and politically, and JI activists were recruited to fight the war in Afghanistan.[9] The moral and political support that the JI received during the Zia regime in challenging leftist elements at primarily institutions of higher learning—colleges and universities in urban centers—but also in various other state-owned enterprises was in addition to a broader shift in public discourse toward Islamic imagery and rationale. After Zia's death in 1988, in what many believe to be a CIA-engineered plane crash motivated by the fact that Zia had outlived his usefulness by the end of the Afghan war, the JI moved close to Zia's political protégé Nawaz Sharif and his Islami Jamhoori Ittehad (IJI, Islamic Democratic Alliance). The decade of the 1990s is significant for the JI's attempts at consolidating a political position for itself in the face of increasing US hostility toward Muslim fundamentalism at an international level, and a turbulent political decade of rapid elections, alliances, and presidential coups d'etat within Pakistan.

An important implication of the JI's visible presence on the Pakistani political scene has been that it has played a critical, though perhaps indirect, role in supporting the rise of groups like JD by providing an organizational role model as well as by opening up the space for Islamist discourse and rhetoric in Pakistani politics. Several JD leaders were introduced to Islamism through their association with IJT (Jama'at-e-Islami's student wing) or through JI literature. Hafiz Mohammed Saeed, who is the most famous of the Jama'at-ud-Da'wa's founders and its current *amir* (commander), was an IJT member and *nazim* (organizer) while he was studying at Punjab University. However, after this initial association with the JI, he and some other JD leaders also spent time in Saudi Arabia, and their brand of Islam has an easily discernible imprint of Saudi/Wahhabi influence.

Lashkar-e-Tayyaba and Jama'at-ud-Da'wa relied for recruitment initially, and to a lesser extent to this day, on smalltime thugs or *gundas*, arms dealers, and other criminals, as well as on those who were groomed by a particular brand of *madaris*, local traditions, and their poverty to embark upon a life of adventure in Afghanistan. (I look briefly into the concept of martyrdom or *shahadat* in chapter 3 and give a more detailed account of its origins in that chapter.) Suffice it to say here that Jama'at-ud-Da'wa, while classified as an Islamist organization by most academic and policy studies, due to its expressed aim of imposing shari'a at the state level and its links to the modern educational system is the product of a very different context from the JI. This difference goes a long way toward explaining the extent and nature of JD's impact on Pakistani society and politics, which is considerably limited compared to the JI.

The important similarity between the two groups that I focus on in this book, however, lies in the overlap in their constituency and the salience of political engagement in their rhetoric and practice. The competition that results from this focus is a critical aspect of Islamist politics, the impact of which has hitherto received little academic attention. I focus in particular on the objectification of religion that has resulted from this competition. Through the ethnographic research discussed in this book, I show the variety in religious practice and its impact on forcing a certain consciousness about the availability of different paths toward leading a pious life. The competing claims of these Islamist groups, and the attempts made by their ideologues and leaders to convince people that the practices suggested by them are correct (*sahih*) while others are not, are forcing a critical engagement with the notion of Islam as a cohesive religion and a deepening realization that there is no single Islam within the predominantly Muslim milieu of Lahore. This engagement in turn has supported a trend toward individuals trying to define the right religious "package" for themselves. I noticed a certain amount of spiritual and doctrinal promiscuity among the members of both JI and JD: many had either been members of other groups or had followed a different *maslak*[10] at different times.

In some ways this is similar to the schism opened up within Christianity by the Protestant Reformation, which was an important precondition for the kind of secularization that happened in Europe. Jose Casanova points out that the hegemony of Christianity within Europe was severely undermined as soon as it was no longer sufficient to say "the church" but to have to specify which one: whether Catholic, Protestant, or other (1994, 21). However, I do not want to stretch this parallel too far, not just because to do that would be to reinscribe the "lateness" of other parts of the world when the European experience is normalized as the ideal, but also because of the very different trajectories that lead up to and beyond this point in the case of European Christianity and Pakistani Islam.

Secularism, *Ladiniyat, Dahriyat*

One of the common ideological foes identified by both groups I studied is secularism. Among the activists of the two groups I studied, secularism is easily conflated with atheism.[11] While the term "secularism" is also used in Urdu and Punjabi, *ladiniyat* and *dahriyat* were used interchangeably to talk about it. *Ladiniyat* means a state of being without religion and *dahriyat* refers to a refusal of religion. Both are closer to atheism in connotation than the Western use of the term "secularism."[12] The ideologues and leaders of the two parties use the terms interchangeably at times, but certainly seem more aware of secularism in distinction from atheism and refer specifically to a policy that relegates religion to the private sphere.[13] However, it is precisely this relegation to the private sphere that they find troublesome, often arguing that this is the first step toward atheism in a society. In arriving at such a conclusion, they are not alone. Many Western scholars, particularly during the 1960s and 1970s, came implicitly and explicitly to the same conclusion.[14] This tendency was stronger among Marxist and Marxian authors, who started with the assumption that religion is a tool for the privileged class to strength its control. What David Martin (2005, 19) has called the "Marxist leap" then projected a future in which religion would cease to exist or at least be of no importance once man was able to engage rationally with all human needs without recourse to religious dogma. My decision to situate my research within the framework of the debate on secularism was driven largely by the emphasis my informants placed on secularism and their relationship with it.

It seems to me pertinent here to pause and disengage secularism from secularization, beyond the commonplace. Most academic studies, particularly in the discipline of sociology, adhere to a clear conceptual distinction between secularism as a policy that mandates and limits the role of religion in the public sphere, and secularization as a process that has two components: the clear demarcation of the public and private sphere within which religion is relegated to the private, and a Weberian demystification of religion. However, what remains unacknowledged in most such studies is that secularism is a *project*. Critically, the causal relationship between the state *project* and the social *process* remains largely unexplored. Vaguely conceptualized, the edifice of secularism is presumed to be standing on the foundation of secularization. It is assumed, based largely on a reified, and perhaps incorrect,[15] reading of the European experience, that secularization at a societal level will lead to secularism as a policy prescriptive at the state level, and once in place the policy will further strengthen the societal process. Yet, in the case of many third-world countries, and certainly in Muslim ones, the relationship is inverted. It was, and still is, assumed that secularism, the state project, will lead to secularization in the society.[16] The nationalist regimes of newly independent Middle Eastern and South Asian states from the 1950s to the 1970s epitomized the ethos of this assumed relationship between secularism and secularization. Although there was support, or at least indifference, toward the policy in other segments of society, the most vehement advocates and self-proclaimed secularists were among the upper classes. Within a framework of modernization and development, it was hoped that the trickle-down effect would apply to social processes as well as to the economic ones.[17]

Important strands of this expectation exist in contemporary Muslim societies. In contemporary Pakistan, the military regime of General Musharaf had undertaken to rid the nation of "fundamentalist" elements by promoting "Enlightened Moderation"— if necessary, by force. In this project General Musharaf had cited Mustafa Kamal Pasha as his role model, and his policies of strict and sudden curtailment of the role of religion in Turkish life as an inspiration (Haqqani, 2005, 2). Most of the academic and media attention has remained focused on the chances of success of such a state policy, often attaching, in the same breath, great normative value to its triumph.

Muslim Societies/Western Categories?

Before I go on to situate the discussion in the context of academic theories of secularization and secularism, I want to explain my use of the terms "Muslim" and "Western" societies while also explicating an epistemological bias that animates this research. When using these terms I do not intend to suggest insular, sealed-off entities. Rather I aim to highlight precisely the implications of a close and continued multistranded entanglement between what is called the "West" and those labeled "Muslim societies." This entanglement has not always been friendly or peaceful, but it has been important in shaping trajectories in both sets of societies.[18] Edward Said's *Orientalism* (1978) has sensitized us to the constructions of the irrational other in the "Oriental" to offset the rational "West" that were as much a justification of colonization as its product.[19] The colonized was inherently lesser than the colonizer in this imagination, but critically, this imaginary is backed by and imbricated with structures of power.[20] While the colonized, including the Islamists, also constructed and continue to construct generalizations and oppositions of the "other"[21]—Occidentalism lives in many guises—these constructions are differentiated by an asymmetry of power.

The intensity and extent of this interaction between the "West" and the "Muslim world" increased exponentially during the "colonial encounter,"[22] which also led to a significant reconfiguration of power dynamics. Since then a rich and multifaceted dialogue that has shaped important trajectories in both these contexts has been ongoing. At the very least it seems rather ahistorical to suggest essentialized, nativist categories that have managed to preserve some intrinsic differences despite the centuries-long interaction that either the critics of modernity or, conversely, most Western critics of Islamic Fundamentalism and its failure to "engage with modernity" seem to suggest. In the case of Islam, this essentialized view assumes that "*Homo Islamicus* will always revert to type under all circumstances and regardless of the nature and depth of the historical changes he may suffer or undergo."[23]

In a perceptive analysis Yael Navaro-Yashin (2002, 8) has suggested that, following Said's influential work, many who have targeted the imposition of Western discourses and categories on Middle Eastern, primarily Muslim, societies (such as Mitchell 1988, 2000; Abu-Lughod 1998) have risked reproducing essentialism in "leaving a precipitation of cultural authenticity or tradition underneath the layers of European costume, thereby overlapping, by default, with cultural revivalisms or nationalisms in the contexts studied." She suggests that in the case of Turkey, at least, it is not possible to distinguish native from the Western points of view because "there is no space where they have not been integrally and historically engaged with one another. Turks like Arabs, and Jews are Europe's internal and not external others" (2002, 9).

While the case is more easily made for Turkey than Pakistan, I do agree with Navaro-Yashin that it would be futile to search for an authentic "native" under the layers of "Western" influence. Yet, I argue, there is some analytical use to the terms "Western" and "Muslim" societies, if only because many within those societies believe there to be a difference. These differences do not stem from inherent, essentialized characteristics somehow common to Muslims across distinct periods in history and living in vastly diverse continents, but from the localized historical trajectories that operate in an interactive, though nonlinear, manner. The interactive, interdependent nature of cultural, political, and economic changes means that there is no "native" core to be separated from the "Western," and yet there is a specific context to developments in each; the two categories do not contain identical entities.

It seems to me that the category "Muslim" is open to greater variation and blurring than the category "Western." More importantly, following Marshall Hodgson it is possible to argue that the sense of rupture is less pronounced within "Western" thought—it is in a sense more "traditional"—given the relatively unbroken and continuous philosophical dialogue, dependent upon largely the same authors, books, and philosophers. Charles Taylor's magisterial *Sources of the Self: The Making of the Modern Identity* (1989) provides a glimpse into this sense of religious and philosophical continuity in Europe. This is not to say that there were no ruptures within the Western context but that the *sense* of rupture is less severe than in the Muslim world. The "West" may now reside in and inform imaginaries around the world, but it draws its strength from a particular kind of universalism that rendered its parochial European origins invisible at one level. The "Muslim," in contrast, is spread around the world, across different tribes, classes, nationalities, and levels of religious commitment with only a fractured imagination of belonging to this category. The "Western" has little difficulty recognizing him/herself; the "Muslim" may as often feel pushed into this category as feel a "natural" affinity to it.

The tension between retaining a perspective on the differences between the "Muslim" and "Western" while also appreciating the layers of continuous interaction that make each of them what they are today can be productive for both analytical and political purposes. In her book *Enemy in the Mirror*, Roxanne Euben (1999, 10) suggests an approach that "builds on the possibility that disparate cultures are not worlds apart, morally and cognitively incommensurable, but exist in conversation with one another, even if they have serious moral and political disagreements." Euben recognizes that the writings of many of the pillars of Western political philosophy, particularly the Greek philosophers, were saved and extensively commented upon during the European Dark Ages by Arabs and Muslims. It was through the writings of Ibn-Sina, Ibn-Rushd, and Ibn-Khuldun, among others, that the Greek writings were reintroduced into European libraries some centuries later.[24] In her attempts to suggest ongoing intellectual influences, Euben shows through a careful historical analysis the various Enlightenment and radical Enlightenment influences on the thought and writings of Syed Qutb, Afghani, and Khomeini. These influences are an important part of the contextualization of the historical juncture at which they defined their uniquely Islamist positions. In illustrating this coimbrication between Western and Islamist thought, Euben is following Partha Chatterjee (1993), who has argued that extensive Western political and cultural influence means that the vocabulary available to postcolonial societies for framing their questions is limited to that defined by a Western experience. This does not mean that the West is the only true subject of history, but rather that citizens of the postcolonial world must choose their "site of autonomy . . . from a position of subordination to a colonial regime that had on its side the most universalist justificatory resources produced by post-Enlightenment social thought" (Chatterjee 1993, 11). Even those who wished, and wish today, to oppose post-Enlightenment thought have had to engage with it, either in terms of the structure of their arguments or through recourse to a particular conceptual repertoire. At the same time, such criticism has highlighted multiple cracks and fissures in the armor of universalism donned by post-Enlightenment social and political thought.

In the disciplines of historical and political studies, the Subaltern Studies collective provided a concentrated jolt to the foundations of this universalist edifice. Dipesh Chakrabarty, who also contributed to the collective, has systematized the underlying theme of some of the work done by the Subaltern Studies group of "Provincialising Europe." By this he means an attempt to understand history and historiography without recourse to concepts that, originating from a specific, namely European, historical experience, have assumed a universal validity. This assumption of universal application is, of course, closely linked to Europe's imperial history, and liberal political theory is particularly implicated in this because of the braiding with imperial ambitions. As Uday Singh Mehta (1999, 37) claims, in empire, liberalism found "the concrete place of its dreams." He does not suggest that liberalism is imperialist but that the urge is "internal" to it (20), asking how liberalism, with its emphasis on individual and communal freedom, justified empire? He argues that it is not just a coincidence that the high tide of liberal thinking in Britain also coincided with the high point of empire, and that liberal thinkers like James Mill, John Stuart Mill, and Henry

Maine lacked the humility to engage in a "conversational" understanding of the colonized people.[25]

The scholars who contributed to the Subaltern Studies collective were not the first ones to present this critique of Eurocentric theorizing, but they did provide a concentrated, geographically specific but theoretically ambitious challenge. The project of "provincialising Europe" is an ongoing one, precisely because of the pervasiveness of this assumption of universalism that sits implicitly or explicitly at the root of many fundamental social science concepts. Even when the conceptual break has been made, operationalizing research in this new framework requires constant vigilance. However, it is also a very exciting project because the process entails not a negation of the universalism but the creation of a new way of understanding our societies. Chakrabarty points out: "The project of provincialising Europe cannot be a nationalist, nativist, or atavistic project. In unraveling the necessary entanglement of history—a disciplined and institutionally regulated form of collective memory—with the grand narratives of rights, citizenship, the nation state, and public and private spheres, one cannot but problematise 'India' at the same time as one dismantles 'Europe'" (Chakrabarty 2000, 43).

The Islamist Challenge to Secularism's Universalistic Pretensions

One concept that has clung to its universalist claims in social scientific analysis, even after others abandoned theirs, is that of secularism. In politics secularism is a doctrine that calls for a separation of the church and state functioning.[26] Yet such an innocuous and seemingly simple statement of separation hides a complex interplay of historical trajectories and political realities that have revealed themselves in vastly variegated interpretations and manifestations of this project. Within much of academic literature secularism continues to have immensely positive normative associations intertwined with a continued assumption of universal application.[27] Although in terms of academic disciplines and their tribal boundaries, theories of secularization have been housed primarily in the field of sociology, their dominance within social science as a paradigm remained uncontested until the 1980s. Until this time, these theories had, with a few notable exceptions (Martin 2005 [1978]) conflated diagnosis with prescription, description with projection. This becomes particularly problematic in studying societies that are markedly different from the contexts in which these concepts took initial shape.

In parallel with the notion of universal application, and in considerable contradiction with it, is the idea that Christianity is somehow particularly sympathetic to secularism (Al-Ali 2000, 131). No doubt this view of an inherent sympathy within Christianity refutes history. The secularism that emerged in the predominantly Christian West was a matter of bitter conflict and struggle over many centuries between different segments of the society and "not just an intellectual exercise rooted in Christian theology and practice" (Keddie 1997, 35–37). Nevertheless, in recent years especially, polemical contrasts are made with the relationship between Islam and secularism—a relationship that seems particularly fraught with tensions. A casual perusal of popular media today would seem to suggest that Islam/Islamism not only poses a serious threat to secularism, it is the most potent threat. Other kinds of religious resurgences have had to a take a backseat to the threat of Islamism. In much of this writing, Islam and Islamism are conflated. Moreover, this view is not limited to popular media, and a stream of scholarly writing focuses on the perceived clash between Islam and secularism. Myron Weiner (1987) and Bernard Lewis (2002, 2003) have suggested that Islam rejects secularism and is intrinsically hostile to it. Samuel Huntington's (1993) polemical "Clash of Civilizations" made explicit what had remained largely implicit in much scholarship on Muslims until then: the idea that Islam as a totalizing worldview could not accommodate liberal values, particularly those of personal freedom and secularism, and thus could not coexist harmoniously with the "West." Ernest Gellner (1991, 2) famously claimed that, "no secularisation has taken place in the world of Islam: that the hold of Islam over its believers is as strong, and in some ways stronger now than it was a 100 years ago. Somehow or other Islam is *secularisation-resistant*" (emphasis added). Others have suggested that Islamism, not necessarily Islam, is a reaction against modernity and unable to accommodate secularism, which is seen as a key constitutive element of modernity (Sivan 1985; Tibi 1988, 1998; Ayubi 1991). Many of these writers follow in Weber's footsteps in terms of defining Islam through its innate absences, as Weber did when discussing why Islam could not give rise to capitalism (Turner 1974).

Conversely, many Muslim liberals have tried to show that Islam per se poses no inherent threat to secularism, and have often pointed the finger at the failed states and authoritarian regimes that have tainted the project with their association in many Muslim countries.[28] Some have pointed out that Muslims could not have understood secularism in isolation from "Christian (Western colonial) supremacy" (Masud 2005, 364; van der Veer

2004).[29] Still others have attempted to show that many Muslim societies were plural and tolerant of religious difference, to make explicitly or implicitly the point that Islam is not opposed to secularism.[30] In the case of Islamism, Irfan Ahmad (2009) has made the argument that Islamism itself is changing, from being opposed to secularism to actually supporting it in the Indian context. These scholars have made many contributions, in particular regarding the lack of a *theological* opposition within Islam toward secularism.[31] However, the discussion in most of these writings revolves around the question: Can secularism be reconciled with Islam and/or Islamism?[32] Very few have interrogated what secularism might mean, or whether the Islamist challenge can be used as a foothold to deepen our understanding of the relationship between secularism and secularization.[33] Such research has not engaged with how a process of secularization may actually unfold in a Muslim society, nor has it looked in any depth at the actual processes that may have resulted from the lack of theological barriers to secularism in Muslim societies. This research attempts to provide a grounded view of the dynamics of this process in the particular context of Lahore in Pakistan.

I draw heavily upon Talal Asad's seminal work in realigning our understanding of the "secular" along with the "religious" as analytic categories. Asad's unique contribution is to suggest that our concept of the secular cannot operate outside our understanding of the idea of religion, or vice versa, and that this relationship is an ongoing, dialectical one (2003, 193–200). While commenting on the standard model of secularization that I look into in more detail later, Asad (2003, 193) points out that: "The interesting thing about this view is that although religion is regarded as alien to the secular, the latter is also seen to have generated religion. Historians of progress relate that in the pre-modern past secular life created superstitious and oppressive religion, and in the modern present secularism has *produced* enlightened and tolerant religion. Thus the insistence on a sharp separation between the religious and secular goes with the paradoxical claim *that the latter continually produces the former*" (emphasis added).

In its attempts at regulating religious influence in the public sphere, the state cannot help but impinge upon the formation of subjectivities, norms, and standards that influence the practice of religion in the private sphere. In this and his previous work (*Genealogies of Religion*, 1993) Asad has gone beyond the criticism of Eurocentric notions of secularization and secularism raised by many others. It is not just that our notions regarding secularization derive essentially from a European experience that was thus universalized in colonial and postcolonial policies. What is critical to our study of Islam and other non-Western religious interactions is also the definition of religion that we employ in this endeavor. Asad's (1993, 29) argument is that "there cannot be a universal definition of religion, not only because its constituent elements and relationships are historically specific but because that definition is itself the historical product of discursive processes." Moreover, religion consists not just of particular ideas, attitudes, and practices but also most critically of followers. Discovering how these followers, "instantiate, repeat, alter, adapt, argue over and diversify" (2003, 194) these practices, ideas, and attitudes in relation to the traditions within that particular religion is a key step in our understanding of how that religion might be secularized in different places and times.

For too long, differences in the modalities of secularization have been linked to levels of development. Modern social theory took secularization as a largely inevitable process, and this inevitability was linked to its relationship with cognate concepts, modernization, and development. Paradoxically secularization was, and continues to be, seen not just as a product of development and modernization but also as a facilitator of the same. Critics of secularization theory contend that with very little empirical evidence beyond Western Europe, secularization theorists made projections and assumptions about processes of secularization in different parts of the world. Indeed some of the first academic criticisms emanated from the "Western" and developed, yet non-European context of America. The dichotomy between steady church attendance in the US during a period of rapidly falling attendance in Europe in the postwar years has led to diametrically opposite responses; some proposed that Europe is the exception, while others suggested that the US is the exception (Davie 2002). In fact, the field of secularization is littered with exceptionalisms, as the continued interference of the state in religious affairs in third-world countries was seen as a signifier of "Third World exceptionalism" (Chatterjee 1998, 345). For decades, the exceptions did not do much damage to claims of universal applicability implicit in secularization theory. Until the last decades of the 1900s, evidence, or lack thereof, regarding secularization in other parts of the world was explained with reference to the "backward" level of those societies, continuing the stagiest view embodied in development and modernization theories. A critical reevaluation of developmental models and modernization theory (Crush 1995; Escobar 1995; Frank 1998; Ferguson 1994; Hobart 1993) has also opened up the theoretical space for questioning established notions regarding secularization.

In historical analysis, secularization as a concept refers to the actual process whereby "a dualist system within this world and the sacramental structures of mediation between this world and the other world progressively broke down" taking with it the medieval three-way classification of "this world" (earth), the "other world" (heaven), and the third sacred-spiritual time of salvation, represented by the church's calendar (Casanova 1994, 15). This sacred-spiritual time was mediated by the church's presence and was separated from *saeculum*, the secular age proper. Indeed, the word "secular" is a derivation from the term *saeculum* that refers to the empty, homogeneous time outside the church calendar. The popularly held narrative of secularization runs broadly along the following lines:

> Once the universal Catholic Church was challenged, and dispersed by various Protestant sects, a unified public authority grounded in a common faith was drawn into a series of sectarian conflicts and wars. Because the sovereign's support of the right way to eternal life was said to hang in the balance, these conflicts were often horribly destructive and intractable. The best hope for a peaceful and just world under these new circumstances was institutions of a public life in which the final meaning of life, the proper route to life after death, and the divine source of morality were pulled out of the public realm and deposited into private life. *The secularization of public life is thus crucial to private freedom, pluralistic democracy, individual rights, public reason and the primacy of state.* The key to its success is the separation of church and state and general acceptance of a conception of public reason (or some surrogate) through which to reach public agreement on non religious issues. (Connolly 1999, 19; emphasis added)

The fathers of modern social theory took secularization to be not just necessary for private freedom and democracy, but also a largely inevitable process. This attitude toward its inevitability echoed down the years so that Alasdair MacIntyre (1964, 7) was able to structure his 1964 essays around three core questions:

1. Why has secularization not progressed any further than it has done, especially among the working class?
2. Whether religious decline is *a*, or *the*, cause of moral decline?
3. What effect has secularization had upon English Christianity?

This inevitability was attributed also to cognate concepts supporting secularization: those of modernization and development. Secularization was, and continues to be, seen not just as a product of development and modernization but also as a facilitator of the same. The fact that in many parts of the world, including those considered the birthplace of modernity, "God has taken her revenge" in the form of resurgent religious movements provides some need to rethink the notion that modernization and secularization are cognate phenomena (Kepel 1995; Berger 1999, 41–42; Bruce 1992). Moreover, the fact that secularism in Pakistan and in many other countries of the world, particularly Muslim ones, has been imposed often by dictatorial regimes does the project no favors. At the same time, it does expose the fallacy of assuming an undeterred relationship between secularism, secularization, and private freedom.

Secularism and Secularization: Beyond the Public-Private Debate

Secularization theory can be seen as a subtheory within the theory of functional differentiation that proposes increasing specialization of each sphere of social life. One aspect of secularization theory that received a severe jolt in the 1980s was the idea of privatization of religion. Secularization theory depends heavily on a clear demarcation of the public and private sphere and the relegation of religious belief to the private sphere. What little debate there was before the 1980s centered on the implication of this privatization rather than a fundamental questioning of the public-private divide or the actual process of privatization of religion. Thus Thomas Luckmann proposed that religion would become "invisible" through this privatization and that precisely because of it, religious belief was likely to flourish and grow (Luckmann 1967). In contrast, several others proposed that this privatization was eventually likely to lead to a kind of atheism. The very public flourishing of religion in the US, Latin America, Asia, Africa, and even parts of Europe, particularly during the 1980s onwards, led initially not to more debate, but rather to a hasty abandonment of secularization theory. Interestingly, the early critics of secularization theory, like Martin (2005), have come to its defense, shoulder to shoulder with some longtime supporters like Bryan Wilson, Casanova, and Karel Dobbelaere, arguing that there is much to be valued in the theory despite its failings. Casanova's (1994) exposition of the fallacies of secularization theory regarding the public-private divide is balanced by a nuanced support for the more defensible propositions contained within secularization theory. In particular, he points out that while many trends within secularization, such as the rationalization of religion, remain valid, it is useful to concede that religion's public presence may provide a critique to the conceptualization of secularization as a universal teleological process (1994, 25).

Contemporary debates about the public sphere remain largely indebted to Habermas's pioneering work. Building upon the empirical situation around the world when religion refused adamantly to remain in the private sphere, Casanova draws on the work of Carole Pateman in feminist political theory, and of Erving Goffman, to unsettle our notions of public and private sphere. Carole Pateman's (1988) work brought to the fore the patriarchal assumptions embedded in a Habermasian "critical-rational" public sphere. Erving Goffman's (1972) perceptive analysis of the "interaction ritual" or the performance carried out in the so-called private sphere of our homes, and among friends and family, also raised questions about the very public nature of the private sphere. To be fair to Habermas, he realizes that his conceptualization of the public sphere cannot be abstracted from the unique developmental history of that "civil society" originating in the European High Middle Ages; nor can it be transferred, or generalized as an ideal typical model, to any number of historical situations (Habermas 1989, xvii). His account also incorporates an understanding of the dynamic nature of the public sphere, and he recognizes that the substantive elements that constitute "public" institutions at one point in history may, at another stage, constitute an undermining of their functions. Thus he notes: "According to the liberal model of the public sphere, the institutions of the public engaged in *rational critical debate* were protected from interference by public authority by virtue of their being in the hands of private people. To the extent that they were commercialized and underwent economic, technological, and organizational concentration, however, they have turned during the last hundred years into complexes of societal power, so that precisely their remaining in private hands in many ways threatened the critical function of publicist institutions (Habermas 1989, 188; emphasis added)."

In more recent work, Habermas has also tried to incorporate the continued and defiant presence of religion in the public sphere (Habermas 2002). However, the relatively uncomplicated understanding of the Habermasian public sphere remains a dominant one in academic debates, but even more strongly in social imagination.[34] What is interesting for my purposes here is to note that the prevailing understanding of the Habermasian public sphere does not analytically unpack the "critical-rational" nature of debate. It is precisely the assumptions about the nature of critical-rational debate that are seen to be under threat from the resurgence of religion in the public sphere. The history of a particular type of secularization in

Europe has meant that religion has been removed from the domain of rational discussion. The suppression of freedom of thought, creative expression, and critical thinking that was closely associated with the Inquisitions, the wars of religion, and the particular relationship between society and the Catholic Church in European countries have conditioned this understanding. Readily available cultural material in the form of stories such as Galileo's fate after placing rationality above church dogma tends to draw attention away from the fact that many of the scientists—representatives of rational thinking—during the Enlightenment era were, in fact, believing men who often attempted to harmonize their findings with their faith.[35] My aim here is not to suggest that religion is inherently rational, but rather that our notions of "rational-critical" debate, particularly with reference to religion, have tended to proceed along relatively strictly delineated, historically conditioned lines.

The relegation of religion, as the illogical and the superstitious, to the private sphere, anchored precisely in this notion of the public sphere as the space for rational discussion and decisions, assumes a public sphere innocent of inequalities in power. However, as Seyla Benhabib (1992) has suggested, a claim to "dialogic neutrality" in rational-critical public debate has blinded us to the actual mechanics of power relations in politics. She points out (1992, 84) that "all struggles against oppression in the modern world begin by redefining what had previously been considered 'private,' non public, and non political issues as matters of public concern, as issues of justice, as sites of power which need discursive legitimation."[36] Moreover, such an aversion to interrogating the mechanics of the public sphere negates the continued importance of religious imagery, values, and political culture of many of the "secular" Western states. William Connolly suggests as much when he points to what he calls "the conceits of secularism": "The secular division of labour between 'religious faith' and 'secular argument,' where faith and ritual are to be contained in a protected private preserve and rational argument is said to exhaust public life, suppresses complex registers of persuasion, judgment and discourse operative in public life. Again these registers continue to operate, even within secularism. But they do so largely below the threshold of appreciation by secularists" (Connolly 1999, 19).

These registers of "persuasion, judgment and discourse" remain hidden in large part due to the fact that the precise relationship between secularism, the *project*, and secularization, the *process*, remains understudied and a matter of implicit understanding. It is critical to disentangle the political project of secularism and its life trajectories from the historical process of secularization in Europe and theories of secularization that relied heavily, although often implicitly, on this particular historical experience. The vague but generally accepted assumption seems to be that secularization in Europe led to secularism, but secularism in the non-Western societies will lead to secularization. The braiding of Western secularization, secularism, development, and ultimately democracy is such that secularism in its current life has become a project whose imposition by dictatorships is tolerated as a lesser of two evils by Western governments and political audiences. Increasingly, secularism is beginning to play a central role in liberal political theory. As Saba Mahmood (2006, 324) observes, "in as much as liberalism is about the regulation of individual and collective liberties, it is the principle of freedom of conscience that makes secularism central to liberal political philosophy on this account." The relationship between Muslims and the West is increasingly being predicated on the ideology of secularism such that "secularism is . . . evolving as a liberal ideology that is crucial in defining the future relations between the West and the Muslim world. It is this rise of secularism as an ideology that vindicates the Islamists' stance of treating secularism as an ideology, and as a threat to the future of Islam" (Masud 2005, 369).[37]

Yet curiously, for a concept with such wide currency, secularism has been very loosely conceptualized, if at all. It is broadly conceived of as a separation of state and religion and left largely at that. In this sense the very looseness of the concept allows it great elasticity; the forms that this separation may take in particular have seen huge variations, almost all involving a very active shaping of religion to fit the state's view of it. Akeel Bilgrami (1998, 395) has called this elasticity "Archimedean secularism" in the Indian context. Just as Archimedes claimed that he could lift the world on a bar if he could find the right leverage point outside of the earth, so secularism as a political project has tended to avoid engagement with substantive issues, attempting instead to bring about a change from the outside. Bilgrami suggests that secularism was an imposition in India, but not in the sense of a modern intrusion into a traditional society, and in this he negates the views put forward by Ashis Nandy (1998) and T. N. Madan (1998), but because of the assumption that "secularism stood outside the substantive arena of political commitments" (Bilgrami 1998, 394). Bilgrami thus suggests that it was not just an *ideological* problem but one of *methodology* in which the state did not adequately engage with the particular modalities of religious practice and political action to separate them out in the Indian context. Bilgrami's fundamental point regarding the possibility of reformulating secularism through a more democratic engagement about the actual substantive aspects of secularism within the state structures of a relatively democratic state is seductive. Yet it seems to me pertinent to caution against excessive optimism resting on the imperatives within the state structures toward such an engagement.

James C. Scott's perceptive analysis in *Seeing Like a State* (1998) of the tendency, indeed need, for modern states to reduce citizens to manageable, simplified categories suggests that it may be wise to locate our hopes for change at a site broader than the state. An alternative reading of secularism would need to recognize that secularism manifests itself in concrete power relations and modes of governance tied to the emergence of the modern state and capitalism (Asad 1993, 2003; Salvatore 2005). In Europe, secularization led to the release of ecclesiastical property into private hands and market circulation. This was a gradual process with many reversals and contradictory thrusts in different parts of Europe. Nevertheless, the increasing sovereignty of states sanctioned by the treaty of Westphalia of 1648 and its control over the property and role of the church led to a critical redefinition of religion and its limits under the modern state. This went hand in hand with a series of intellectual and political ruptures that supported a new version of religious practice, allowing the state to take over many functions that were previously performed by the church, including education, healthcare, and the provision of meaning to collective life substituting the idea of the nation for the religious congregation (Chadwick 1975; McLeod 2000; Katznelson and Jones 2010). Secularism then, following Asad, can be fruitfully reconceptualized not as a one-time separation of religion and state but as the continuous management of religious thought and practice by the state.

Having highlighted the lack of clarity in our understanding of the relationship between secularism as a project and secularization as a process of privatization of religion, I want to look in some detail at other competing conceptions of secularizations that have not received significant attention. Linked to, but not exhausted by, the notion of secularization as the privatization of religion is the idea of secularization as disenchantment and rationalization: not only would the sphere of religion's influence be limited by its relegation to the private sphere, but the sense of enchantment would disappear with it. Weber's notion of the rationalization of religion is one that is often subsumed within the privatization debate. However, I wish to propose here that it is worth separating out the various strands of secularization theory to think about the changes not in the quantity of religious belief and practice but also in its quality. (I discuss some aspects of this strand of secularization theory in more detail in chapter 4.)

In making explicit, and then questioning, our received understanding of the relationship between secularism and secularization, we may hope to come to a more nuanced understanding of the processes that are already underway. It seems to me worthwhile here to ask the question: Are the Islamists facilitating, albeit inadvertently, secularization in predominantly Muslim societies? No doubt, the question sounds counterintuitive, particularly since the Islamists themselves proclaim secularism as a target of their wrath. I hope to show in the chapters that follow that it seems plausible if we are able to critically unpack the alleged relationship between secularism and secularization and recognize that the two may not be related in a linear manner. Moreover, if we are able to disentangle our conceptualization of secularization from the narrow confines of a particularly European history, we may be able to perceive a process of rationalization that has been going on in part because the Islamists have brought questions about the role of religion in modern life into the public sphere, in societies that had no need for the kind of secularization that insisted on a sharp division between the church and the state, the public and the private that occurred in Europe at a particular historical juncture. My attempt here is not to suggest that the Islamists are secular in the sense of consciously identifying with the ideology of secularism—in fact it is very much the reverse of that—but that they are secularizing, that is, they are facilitating a process of secularization as rationalization of religion. I differentiate here between the secular or secularist, and the secularizing. The secular or the secularists are those who identify consciously with some version of the ideology and project of secularism.

This rationalization of religion is discussed in more detail in chapter 4, but here I want to emphasize that it refers to an attempt to view religion as a logical, cohesive whole, erasing out the contradictions that may have been part of religious thought and practice previously. I argue that the rationalization of religion is not exactly the same thing as disenchantment, and certainly does not proceed only along the lines alluded to by Olivier Roy very briefly at the end of his book *The Failure of Political Islam* (1994, 199):

> Islamism is actually an agent of secularization of Muslim societies because it brings the religious space into the political arena: although it claims to do so for the benefits of the former, its refusal to take the true

functioning of politics in society into consideration causes it instead to follow the unwritten rules of the traditional exercise of power and social segmentation. The autonomous functioning of the political and social arenas wins out, but only after the religious sphere has been emptied out of its value as a place of transcendence, refute and protest, since it is now identified with the new power.

This loss of legitimacy in the political sphere, I agree, plays a role. Yet it does not seem to me that this loss of legitimacy proceeds in a linear fashion to the emptying out of the religious sphere "of its value as a place of transcendence." Muslim scholars like Fazlur Rahman warned some decades ago, at the height of the US-sponsored wave of state Islamization in countries such as Pakistan, that Islam was being exploited for political objectives. Rahman (1982, 40) pointed out that "the slogan 'in Islam religion and politics are inseparable' is employed to dupe the common man into accepting that, instead of politics or the state serving the long-range objectives of Islam, Islam should come to serve the immediate and myopic objectives of party politics." The warning has been heeded to some extent, and it seems that a more accurate reading of the phenomenon that Roy is talking about would acknowledge that there is a clearer recognition of the limitations of religious parties in politics in a country like Pakistan rather than a complete emptying out of transcendence from within religion. It seems that the values of transcendence take a different form: rather than complete obliteration, they are subjected to a certain "objectification," a term I borrow from Dale F. Eickelman and James Piscatori (1996). Eickelman and Piscatori are particularly sensitive to the interplay of various long-term trends including the impact of mass education, fragmentation of religious authority, and the rise of ethnicity and nationalism in Muslim politics. I understand this objectification to include the attempted subjection of religious practices and beliefs to the structures of a homogenizing logic insofar as an attempt is made at erasing out contradictions, but more critically to a conscious engagement with the many aspects of religious praxis. Thus, transcendence is not erased but consciously sought through a modeling of subjectivities, behaviors, and praxis.

The following are some brief notes on the challenges of carrying out this kind of research before I present the outline of this book. The research is driven by an interest in investigating concepts and theories through deep contextuality. As an epistemological stance it is sharply at variance with established modes of investigation in social and political theory. The emphasis on lineages, contexts, and intentions of Western scholars in theoretical research is limited in an even more profound manner than the work of historians that Chakrabarty refers to. To break out of this bind, my research is of necessity interdisciplinary and embedded in a particular context.

Interdisciplinarity: Challenges and Rewards

This research makes an explicit claim about the value of using anthropological techniques in analyzing political categories and processes. As a discipline, political science has been relatively slow to engage meaningfully with the place of religion in politics (Bellin 2008; Wald and Wilcox 2006) and has relied on a loosely conceptualized notion of secularism to situate most of the analysis. While the non- and/or antireligious orientation of academics in general (Harding 1991) and political scientists in particular (Wald and Wilcox 2006, 526) may have contributed to a general disregard for the role of religion in politics, an added challenge to critical conceptualization of secularism has been the limitations imposed by the methodological directions pursued in mainstream political science, including the study of comparative politics, that leave little room for interpretive empathy (Gibbons 2006). This becomes particularly problematic in studying societies that are markedly different from the contexts in which these concepts took initial shape. The suggestion here is not that other approaches need to be abandoned, but that our understanding of political processes and categories would be enriched by a deeper engagement with the human beings who are agentive actors. Islamism, in particular, has been studied primarily in terms of the sayings and actions of the leaders and their canonical writings. However, there is often a gap between what leaders write and say, and what followers hear and do; we cannot assume that the leaders are being followed punctiliously or for the reasons they might believe.[38] Leaders play an important role in defining the direction of the movements and organizations that they head, but they alone do not reflect the complexity of those entities.[39]

In the case of literature on Muslim and Islamist politics, the differences between the methodological approaches within political science and anthropology have translated into important variations in conclusions. Influential literature in politics and political history presents the view of a clash between modernity and tradition within Muslim societies. This in turn is dependant upon a relatively rigid demarcation between these two (Roy 1994; Esposito 1997; Hunter 1988). The literature in anthropology shows a very different picture with much more fluidity and creative use of tradition at an individual and aggregate level, primarily by using a more capacious definition of tradition (Asad 1993; Singerman 1995; Starrett 1998; Marsden 2005; etc.). Indeed, it can be said that anthropological research has raised some fundamental questions about the way Muslim societies are studied (Asad 1993; Eickelman 1992; Abou-Lughod 2002; Starrett 1998; Mahmood 2005; Hefner 2005). Some fruitful research has already been undertaken by anthropologists and political scientists working together. In the case of Muslim politics, a particularly important example of such a partnership has been the one between Eickelman and Piscatori. Moreover, some anthropologists have undertaken to directly tackle the political in their analysis (Asad 1993, 2003; Hefner 2000, 2005; Ferguson 1994; Scott 1996, 2003; etc.). The research presented here is suffused with the spirit of these studies that have transgressed disciplinary boundaries, while also recognizing some of the limits of interdisciplinarity.[40]

What then has the use of anthropological methods for political analysis meant in the case of my research? The phenomenological turn in social science generally remained quite weak in political science, and this remains true of the literature on Muslim politics produced during the last two decades.[41] The insights generated by this literature are in many cases highly useful. Yet on the whole this stream of literature has not been able to adequately represent the hybridity that is an integral part of Muslim societies, nor has it been able to show how religious tradition may be incorporated, modified, or rejected on an ongoing basis. More critically, this body of literature has not directly challenged our thinking about the very categories and assumptions of analysis. For instance, in the case of Pakistan, Ahmed Rashid (2000) and Hussein Haqqani (2005) rightly point out that Islamism received a major boost directly from the US government and secret agencies during the cold war era. First, these groups were bolstered as bulwarks against communism in the third world, and then to fight a proxy war as the Russian-Afghan war took hold of American policy imaginations. Their militant origins then form the basis on which the current American invasion of Afghanistan is justified either as a belated cleaning up by the responsible party, or as a lesser of the two evils. However, it seems to me insufficient to leave our analysis at that. We may need to remind ourselves that groups like Jama'at-e-Islami existed before the US support for Islamism propelled them onto the political stage in Pakistan. And of course, the relationship with the US intelligence agencies has changed since the end of the first Afghan war and, if anything, has morphed into an antagonistic one, particu-

larly since the beginning of the ongoing Afghan war in 2002. Simply pointing the finger at their tainted parentage does not allow us to understand the
long-term impact of these groups. But even more critically, continuously
assuming that the category "Islamist" is a black box containing all that
is reactionary and regressive, or that the braiding of the secular with the
democratic is inviolable, does not allow our analysis any flexibility in dealing with the situation on the ground. It seems to me that in such a context
ethnographic research has the potential to provide a wedge toward opening up categories of analysis for reevaluation.

Ethnography beyond Parda

This research is based on an ethnographic engagement with the members
of the two groups studied, across gender, hierarchy, and functional divisions. From December 2004 to December 2005, I spent close to thirteen
months in Lahore, Pakistan, with members of JI and JD. I was able to build
on the contacts established during the time that I had taught at Punjab
University, in 2002–3. Of greater help were my father-in-law's contacts
with students and faculty. He had taught at Punjab University for three decades. Punjab University, as I shall discuss in greater detail in chapter 2, became a hub of Jama'at-e-Islami activists in Lahore from the 1970s onwards.
A large number of the teaching and administrative positions, across different departments, were held in 2003 by current or former Jama'at activists
and sympathizers. Access to Jama'at-e-Islami was facilitated not just by
this prior contact but also due to the relatively large size and open nature
of the organization. However, some among the top leadership had become
particularly wary of researchers from both local and foreign universities.
Initial conversations would often include comments such as "Now they [im-
plying Western governments] are really scared of the Muslims. They have
literally unleashed researchers on us. Not a day goes by when I am not con-
tacted by somebody or the other carrying out research on us."

I have been asked how I can claim to have had ethnographic interaction
with the men in the two organizations. No doubt notions and practices of
parda are important for both groups. I certainly spent more time with the
women in both groups than with the men. However, I find that it is useful
to distinguish between the two groups. Jama'at-e-Islami is a large group
with significant variation in practices across its members. The fact that
members of the Jama'at-e-Islami work in different types of environments
means that there is recognition of the need to interact with people whose

practices may be different from the JI's preference. While teaching at Punjab University, I was initially the only woman in the bus that took university teachers to protests against the privatization of this public university. All the men, bar one, were Jama'at members. Later some Jama'at women also joined us on these trips. Similarly, as I shadowed Jama'at activists during their election campaign for local bodies' elections in Lahore in August 2005, I attended rallies and meetings that were for both men and women. Women's sections were separate from the men's, but men's speeches were relayed through loudspeakers to the women's section. Moreover, I was able to access the men's sections to discuss their reactions and observations. Jama'at men work in government offices, shops, multinational organizations, and own businesses of various kinds, and interaction with some of them was part of my daily routine. Detailed interviews with Jama'at men took place both in their own offices and their homes. Interaction with some of my Jama'at contacts has evolved into a cordial friendship.

Jama'at-ud-Da'wa presented a real challenge in terms of access, and I do not wish to inflate the range of my interaction. This is to my knowledge the first academic study involving significant interaction with the members of this group. Given their ongoing links with militants and my own vulnerability as a person embedded in the context of urban Lahore, I was ultimately quite scared of a deep and continued relationship with members of this group. The organization is quite secretive because of its militant connections, and security is a concern that pervades all meetings. When I walked into the JD headquarters in Masjid Qadsia near Chauburji, in an old lower-middle-class area of Lahore, for the first time, a woman just inside the gate of the women's quarter greeted me loudly with open arms. "*Assalam-a-laikum bahin* (sister)," she boomed warmly as she embraced me thoroughly into the folds of her *chador*. Somewhat confused, and thinking that she must have assumed I am somebody else given my own wrapped-up appearance, I too embraced her. However, I was startled to find that the embrace turned into a very quick body search for hidden weapons, tape recorders, and video cameras. Checking the contents of my bag thoroughly but with expert speed, the woman cast me aside to greet the next entrant with just as much enthusiasm. As I spent more time at the mosque complex[42] I witnessed the procedure repeated for each woman who entered the complex. More importantly, at least officially, JD practices *parda* of the voice as well as sight. This means that not only are men and women to be properly attired and separated physically, but they must also refrain from speaking to each other as much as possible. Some devout women will not answer the phone, lest it be some unknown male. These challenges were complicated by the difference in my class background, and that of the majority of JD's membership. This difference in class background is not an easily surmountable barrier in urban Pakistan. From demarcated neighborhoods and living areas, to highly asymmetrical access to schools, colleges, and job opportunities, the economic apartheid practiced in urban Pakistan is such that it is not easy to find zones of neutral interaction.

Gaining meaningful access to members at different levels of the hierarchy and across gender divides in such a context was a daunting task. Nevertheless, I was aided as much by fortuitous circumstances as by perseverance. The brother of a student at Punjab University was being "wooed" by the JD. This in fact, was a first indication to me of the competition within and amongst Islamists. In any case, the student had become a friend, and his brother, Mohammed Abbas, was extremely helpful in setting up some initial interviews with the JD hierarchy. At the same time, I attended a weekly *dars* (lecture, study circle) led by the wife of Hafiz Saeed, the amir of JD, and held in the home of the mosque custodian at Masjid Qadsia for several weeks before she agreed to facilitate a meeting with the amir. Finally, since some of the men I interviewed could not meet me in their offices or other public places, they invited me to their homes, which allowed me greater depth in interaction. I was able to meet their families, understand some of their dilemmas in conducting everyday life, and observe them negotiating competing claims of Islamic piety from their families and neighbors. In any case, the members' reluctances, their reasons for not meeting, and the creative arrangements for meeting all formed an important part of this ethnographic engagement.

Political agendas linked to categorization were a source of major concern for my informants. The Islamists I interacted with constantly brought under discussion the politics of categorization and representation in academic research. In part due to these anxieties expressed by my informants, I did not record most of the semistructured interviews I conducted, except for those with some Jama'at-ud-Da'wa and Jama'at-e-Islami leaders. Not surprisingly, many of the lower- and middle-level activists of the two organizations were uncomfortable with recorders. In some cases, particularly when interviewing JI/JD male leaders, I found it useful to write while they spoke because the men tended to avoid eye contact as part of their own *parda* practice. Writing gave me something to do while they spoke with their eyes averted. Finally, the JI women's wing activists who accompanied me recorded some of the interviews I conducted with JI leaders in Lahore.

These JI women had decided that the questions I was asking were useful for their own understanding of the organization's history and politics. Most of my interaction within the two organizations consisted of participant observations and unstructured conversations.

One important conceptual issue that I should clarify here pertains to the use of the terms "group" and "organization," and, in the case of JI, the term "party," interchangeably. While both the first two terms are appropriate for describing JI and JD, I have often used the term organization where I have wanted to denote the interplay of structure with politics within an organized entity. The term "group" tends to connote a more amorphous entity and is useful in its suggestion of various directly and indirectly affiliated members. Of the two, JI also operates as a political party in terms of its participation in elections, and hence at times I have used the term "party" for JI. It is worth pointing out that the members of the two groups use the terms *party* (same in Urdu), *jama'at* (group), and *tehreek* (movement) interchangeably when talking about their affiliation. It is interesting to note that while the Islamists tend to view themselves as a social movement, academic literature has only recently started reflecting this self-definition. That they have only recently been conceived of as social movements is due to the combination of a "democratic bias" inherent in the conceptualization of social movements and the view that Islamism is inherently antidemocratic or at least undemocratic.[43]

Angrezi main Urdu: A Note on Translation and Transliteration

I noted down the conversations in Urdu and tried as much as possible to use the same terminology as the informants had. The potential for misunderstanding and misconstruing meaning through reckless and unthinking translations has been highlighted not just by scholarship in different disciplines,[44] but was also noted by many I interviewed when they saw me taking notes in Urdu. Approving of this practice, many commented that the English language just did not have the conceptual repertoire, the vocabulary, to relate to the experiences in Pakistan. The most commonly cited example was of the term *din*. *Din* has been wrongly translated as "religion," my informants contended, when it is really a "way of life" that involves practices infused with a religious understanding but not limited to prayers or other rituals. The ethnographic interaction was supported by the archival research I carried out in Lahore in the Punjab Public Library and the private archive of Mr. Ahmed Salim.[45] Moreover, the Jama'at-e-Islami's own library and publishing unit and the Jama'at-ud-Da'wa library and publishing arm were invaluable sources of print, audio, and video material that allowed me to track and understand their positions and stances. Pamphlets on topical issues, magazines for men, women, and children, books and commentaries in Urdu and sometimes English have been produced regularly by both groups for a long time now, and I used them to support my understanding further. The CDs and audiocassettes produced by these groups and others are rich sites of analysis in themselves, although in this book I have made few direct references to these.

The majority of the published material is in Urdu, and most conversations would also start in Urdu. However, Lahore is a predominantly Punjabi city, and the fact that I could speak Punjabi fluently helped significantly in building a more comfortable relationship with my informants. In urban Pakistan, including in Lahore, everyday conversation is a hybrid of several languages. Many English words are used colloquially across the classes. At the same time, a sentence in Urdu may be sprinkled liberally with Punjabi words and vice versa. Increasingly many Urdu words are written in English script, in a trend promoted by advertising agencies. A typical advertisement for a soft drink marketed by an multinational food conglomerate contains the strap line "*Piyo aur Jiyo*" (Drink and enjoy life), accompanied by pictures of young people of both sexes wearing a mix of stylish Pakistani and Western clothes in vivid colors, laughing and "hanging out" together. *Jiyo* can be translated to mean "to live" or "to exist," but is generally used to connote a richer experience than mere existence: "to live well."

It is possible that this trend toward Romanized Urdu is linked to the rise of a generation of upper-class and upper-middle-class Pakistanis who have studied exclusively in private schools, where the emphasis has been on reading and writing English. Urdu as a medium of instruction has suffered an immense blow with the rise of private schooling since the 1980s, as both parents and school administrators have been focused on students performing well in their A/O-levels, SAT, and GMAT exams, all geared toward accessing higher education outside of Pakistan. Learning English from a young age has been emphasized at schools to the extent that children are forbidden to speak to the teacher or each other in any other language while in the classroom. My children, who moved from a school in England to a private school in Lahore during the course of my fieldwork there, spent some time initially struggling with this particular rule. They were particularly surprised by the injunction issued by the Urdu teacher that they had to answer to her in English. Increasingly since the 1980s, many private-school-educated children have been taking "Easy Urdu"[46] as a subject option in their A/O-level exams precisely because they do not have the reading and writing ability to cope with the prescribed Urdu coursework. Advertising agencies have started catering to this class and age group by writing Urdu slogans in English to suggest a cool yet uniquely Pakistani way of saying things.[47] Colloquial terms such as *aur sunnao*[48] have been appropriated by multinational companies to portray a link to local social context. This trend is further supported by the increased use of mobile phones to text messages in Romanized Urdu. Lahore, in particular, is, as I will elaborate below, a primarily Punjabi city. The Urdu spoken in Lahore has a distinctly Punjabi flavour, which includes a lack of distinction between qāf (ق) and qaf (ک), tōē (ط), and te (ت).

In translating and transliterating conversations, I have tried to hint at this hybridity of expression. Moreover, the use of Romanized Urdu in the way I have outlined above means that I reflect a certain way of writing Urdu in English that is emerging in contemporary urban Pakistan. While the transliterations follow the guidelines established in the widely used Platts's Urdu/Hindi dictionary, I have omitted the use of most diacritical marks for ease of reading, retaining primarily those that are used to denote ع and ء. Another key impact of this decision to reduce diacritical marks is in denoting the letter چ. Rather than adopting Platt's method here, I have written it as *ch* instead, which also corresponds closely with how the letter is transliterated in everyday use in contemporary Pakistan—for instance, as in *Chaudhry* or *Chatkhara* (name of a popular chain selling snacks). In addition, I have indicated where English terms have been used in the sentences quoted.

Lahore-Urban and Punjabi Pakistan

Lahore presents a particular, albeit highly influential, picture of Pakistan through a combination of ethnic and class divisions with upward mobility. Unlike most site-specific ethnographies (e.g., Marsden 2005; Verkaaik 2004, in the case of Pakistan), the research findings are not limited to this particular city. The objectification of religion that I contend is one of the results of Islamist activity over the long term is closely tied to its urban origins and reflected in cities across Pakistan, with some variations.

Lahore is the capital city of Punjab, the largest province of Pakistan. It is among the largest cities in the world in terms of population. The current population of Lahore is estimated at close to ten million, with approximately 86 percent Punjabis, 10 percent Mohajirs (those who migrated from India at the time of partition, some whom may also be Punjabi migrants as Punjab was divided into two parts, one Indian and one Pakistani), and the rest Pashtun, Seraiki, and others.[49] An ancient city that grew in prominence during the rule of Mahmud Ghaznavi in tenth century, it became an important administrative center during the Mughal era, and in 1585 Mughal Emperor Akbar decided to make it the capital of the Mughal Empire. While it only served as the capital for approximately thirteen years, the city received significant attention in terms of its architectural development. As Mughal power dwindled, the city was a site of successive rebellions and attacks, until it was taken over by Ranjit Singh, a Sikh ruler. The British took formal control of the city after the second Anglo-Sikh war that ended in 1849, and thus Lahore and Punjab were relatively late additions to direct colonial control. Nevertheless, in the shape of the canal colonies projects, Punjab was the site of one of the most aggressive campaigns of social and political engineering carried out by the British regime (Ali 1988). In the early twentieth century, that city expanded greatly and was transformed in significant ways by the interests of both the colonial administrators and local populations (Glover 2007). This is a period when the city was a cultural center, manifested in part through its prominence in the incipient Indian film industry—in later years Bombay grew at the expense of Lahore. However, the city was also an important seat of nationalist struggle against the British. During the 1940s, the Muslim League increasingly began to see Punjab as pivotal in its claim for a separate nation (see chapter 2 for details). The first formal resolution asking for the formation of a separate nation for Muslims of India was passed in Lahore, on March 23, 1940, and is consequently known as the Lahore Resolution.

The city is currently overwhelmingly Muslim (96 percent according to the 1998 census). However, this is a recent phenomenon, only since the last sixty years. Before 1947, Lahore's population was almost equally divided between the Muslim, Hindus, and Sikhs. Certain Parsi (Zoroastrian) and Christian communities have been an integral part of the city for some centuries now, and many stayed in Lahore after the partition of India. The partition was a particularly traumatic event for the residents of Lahore, as violence destroyed a city that had remained relatively untouched by intercommunal violence before the partition. Moreover, the mass exodus of Hindus and Sikhs, who had formed the commercial and cultural elite of the city, left a great vacuum. This vacuum was filled in part by the immigrants from the Indian Punjab and other parts of India soon after partition. However, the greatest beneficiaries of Lahore's growth in importance within Pakistan have been Punjabis from the smaller towns and villages of the province.[50]

In terms of ethnic composition, the city is relatively homogenous, and in many ways provincial, with a predominance of Punjabis, unlike the more multiethnic city of Karachi. This close association with Punjabis, who were primarily tied to agriculture, resulted in a self-definition as the *zinda-dillan* (lively, open hearted) among the city's inhabitants.[51] The city is defined by a love of food, festivals, and literary and cultural events. The last of these activities was supported by the presence of a large number of well-known colleges and universities established during the colonial period, while many precolonial educational institutions also continued to operate.[52] Thus, a claim that proud Lahoris continue to make in Punjabi today is that "*Jinay Lahore nain waikhiya au jamya nain*" (He who hasn't seen Lahore, has not been born).

Yet the city is not an easy place to live in. As I mentioned earlier, the economic apartheid that is becoming an increasingly visible feature of urban life in contemporary Pakistan makes its presence felt in the city. Lahore is roughly divided into neighborhoods defined by their social and economic position. From the banks of the River Ravi, where the oldest parts of the city lie, to the eastern reaches of Defence Housing Colony, one can trace a history of a shifting commercial core that had moved from the old city to the Mall Road during colonial times, and from the Mall to Gulberg in the last few decades.[53] The core, then, is associated with the more affluent neighborhoods, and the peripheries map onto a lower socioeconomic status. While it is unusual to see vast slums lying cheek by jowl with the more affluent neighborhoods as in many other large third-world metropolises, it is impossible to escape an increasingly visible poverty even in the richest areas. Beggars maimed and controlled by the begging mafia, drug addicts, the homeless, and contract day laborers return to the sleek main thoroughfares despite ruthless, random removals by the police and the city authorities.

Lahore provides a rich site of analysis for the role of Islamists for various reasons. Punjab as a whole provides an interesting and largely unexplored venue for an understanding of the dynamics of contemporary religious forces in South Asia. Punjab's domination of politics in Pakistan has been a source of tension with the other provinces and an area of some study.[54] While many analysts have focused on Khyber Pakhtunkhwa and Balochistan[55] explicitly or implicitly to understand Islam, Islamism, and militancy in Pakistan, there is very little work explaining the rise of Islamist groups in contemporary urban Punjab,[56] even though the key Islamist organizations are based primarily in Punjab. Lahore, once an important center of left mobilizations, has now emerged as a hub of religious mobilizations, hosting the head offices of some of the most important religious groups, including Jama'at-e-Islami, Tablighi Jama'at, and Jama'at-ud-Da'wa. Scholars of Islamism have long contended that it is a primarily urban phenomenon. Roy (1994, 53–54) places "revolutionary Islam" squarely in the modern and urban domains:

> The masses of revolutionary Islam are also a product of modern society. Islamist themes resonate little in the countryside, where people are often faithful to a popular, marabout-type Islam that includes few clergy. The modern masses are the new urban arrivals, the millions of peasants who have tripled the populations of the great Muslim metropolises in the last twenty years. . . . These urban populations are different from the inhabitants of the traditional Muslim city, contrary to a common analysis that sees Islamism as the bazaar's reaction against active industrialization. . . . everywhere the important families are leaving the bazaar and the centre; they are being replaced by an uprooted class that does not possess urban culture.

Roy's insight is useful, and yet it is important to realize that this "uprooted class" of new urbanites often retains strong links with its extended family and social network in the smaller cities and villages in other parts of Pakistan.[57] These linkages mean that ideas, practices, and beliefs travel quickly to other localities across Pakistan. Moreover, dynamics of mass education, access to international media, and international migration are not limited to Lahore. Therefore, conditions for the ready acceptance and implementation of many of the ideas generated in Lahore already exist in many other smaller cities and towns. In this context, the role that Lahore, as a social and political hub, plays in shaping imaginations in other parts of Pakistan is critical and one that, I believe, makes it possible to extend the reach of these findings beyond Lahore.

Outline of the Book

Earlier in the introduction I laid out the theoretical framework for my inquiry focusing in particular on the literature on secularization, secularism, and Islam. I show that the literature is polarized between a grand narrative

SECULARISM IN PAKISTAN | 35

of the reasons for failure of secularism in Muslim societies, primarily Middle Eastern ones (imposition by authoritarian regimes, lack of modernity, resistance to Western concepts in Islam, etc.), and a focus on the theological aspects of Islam's relationship—antagonistic or friendly—with secularism. This literature does not question the implicit relationship between secularism and secularization at a theoretical level, nor does it interrogate closely the interplay of various social and political forces that operate in a particular Muslim society in a grounded manner.[58] In an attempt to correct this lacuna, I pry apart the implied relationship between secularism and secularization and build on the idea that secularization, in terms of a delineation of the public and private sphere and relegation of religion to the private along the lines of the European experience, may not have been needed in Muslim societies. I shift the emphasis to the rather understudied aspect of secularization where the focus is on the quality of religious thought and practice rather than on the quantity of religious practice, particularly in the public sphere. Critically, I suggest that recognizing the conceptual gap between secularism and secularization alerts us to the possibility that secularization may be supported by the very elements that oppose secularism.

In chapter 1, I take a close look at the origins of Islamism within the North Indian context to suggest that it is an intrinsically modern phenomenon that is closely intertwined with the colonial encounter and is creatively linked to colonial secularism. Islamism mirrors the concerns and claims of colonial secularism in an Islamic idiom. I build upon Talal Asad's insight about the dialectical relationship between "secularism" and "religion," and their emergence as analytical categories to suggest that a specific kind of colonial secularism that attributed universalism to its own substantive aspects and particularism to all others led in part to this innovation in Muslim thought that is called Islamism.

Chapter 2 emphasizes the dynamic nature of Islamism in Pakistan by focusing on the interaction between the leftist groups and Jama'at-e-Islami during the late 1960s. While much has been written about the impact of Islamist groups on leftist groups in the Middle East and other Muslim societies, there has been little analysis of how the Islamists were themselves impacted by their confrontational engagement with the leftists. The chapter traces the shifts in the Jama'at-e-Islami's operational strategies as a response to its opposition to the "secularism" of the leftist groups in Pakistan. Following Charles Tilly (1990), I contend that the radical shifts in JI's policy stances can only be understood if we understand that the organization was shaped by the opposition it faced as much as by the opportunities afforded it. The chapter also allows us to rethink the strict delineation of religious right and secular left as I highlight the use of religious imagery by leftist leaders during the 1960s.

Chapter 3 underscores the impact of competition among Islamist groups. Literature on Islamism has acknowledged the presence of this competition, but there has been no in depth analysis of its impact. I suggest that one important implication of the competition between Islamist groups recruiting from similar constituencies is the "objectification" and rationalization of religion. In their bid to explain their position, both JD and JI carry out various kinds of recruitment drives or *da'wa* activities. A key element of these da'wa activities for each group is differentiating its practices and beliefs from those of competing groups. Building on my ethnographic work as well as archival and print sources, I show how the audiences of these da'wa activities are increasingly having to choose and explain their choice of practices, beliefs, and associations. This, I contend, is an important aspect of the objectification of religion in which religion is not emptied out of its transcendental value but is transformed into a more historically situated, critically analyzed set of values and practices.

Chapter 4 highlights the important role that women play within the Islamist groups that I studied. Both JI and JD have very committed women activists. Here, I address a significant gap in the literature on women and Islam. This literature has looked primarily at the impact of Islamization on women in various Muslim societies. Yet there has been no detailed analysis of the impact that the women who are present in significant numbers within Islamist groups may have on the direction, strategies, and ideologies of these groups. Moreover, by building on the ethnographic examples and through a discussion about rationalization of belief, I point out the existing limitations of social theory in conceptualizing religious belief. Finally, this chapter also engages with aspects of secularization theory that deal primarily with the rationalization of belief. While the focus in this chapter is on women in Islamist organizations, the implications go beyond the gender divide to allow us to think about the longer-term impact of Islamism.

The conclusion brings together insights from the previous chapters to point out that the suggestion of this research is not that the Islamists are wittingly supporting secularization or that they can be seen as liberals. The attempt is not apologetic in its intention either; it is not that "they" are also ultimately like "us." Human beings may be all similar, but human societies are very different. The imagined polity and citizen of this Islamist secularization are likely to be extremely different from the products of secularization in other contexts. The larger implication of this research lies then in recognizing the current limits of political theory in appreciating the difference that must arise from localized historical trajectories and in attempting to theorize about them in ways that would allow these differences to be acknowledged. Islamism's challenge to social science theorizing is no less significant for its obliqueness.

CHAPTER ONE

Colonial Secularism and Islamism in North India

A RELATIONSHIP OF CREATIVITY?

We need to be more thoughtful about the complex, often quite paradoxical, role that colonial rule played in the lives of the different sections of the Indian people at different times. An important ancillary to that process would be an effort on the part of Urdu scholars to recover the life of the mind of that Urdu intelligentsia of long ago—Hindu, Muslim and Christian—who found excitement, and discovered new and creative ways to define and express themselves, in that initial sustained encounter with what eventually became an oppressive colonial rule.

—C. M. Naim 2003, 24

This chapter is concerned with excavating the historical context that gave rise to Islamism, particularly in North India, and the paradoxes that surround its self-defined antagonistic relationship to secularism. Modern state structures, institutions of mass education, and, critically, changes in the relationship of religious identity to political structures are a hallmark of the modern period; secularism is conceived of as an integral and constitutive element of modernity. Yet, as I discuss in this chapter, the very unevenness and variation in the manifestations of modernity require that we recognize it as a project with strong aspirational aspects to it in addition to thinking of it as a historical period. A focus on North India and then Pakistan shows that Islamism is closely related to the secularism that helped define its limits, its contentions, and its focus. My point of departure here is Talal Asad's (2003) insight that secularism is not a one-time separation of church and state, but a constant remodeling and refashioning of religious practice by the state, giving rise to new versions and forms of religion. I propose here that Islamism is closely related to the colonial secularism that helped define its limits, its contentions, and its focus; the relationship between Islamism and secularism is not one of straightforward antagonism, but is rather much more interactive and creative. Critically, I propose that the type of secularism that the British sought to impose in colonial India created the possibility of this novelty in Muslim thought and practice that is called Islamism.

Before we proceed, it would be useful to complicate our understanding of tradition and modernity particularly with reference to Islamism. Islamism is often conceived of as a "traditional" reaction against "modernity." It is helpful to remind ourselves here that in the case of Muslim societies, the *need* for the kind of secularism that took shape, at least in its reified version in Western Europe, with its insistence on a sharply delineated public and private sphere and a clear separation between church and state, did not exist (Brown 2000). There was no single centralized authority such as the pope, and historically the *ulama* (religious scholars) have operated as a diverse, decentralized group of scholars and practitioners (Zaman 2002). The precolonial state evolved other mechanisms for managing the diversity of religious and ethnic communities and supporting mostly peaceful coexistence (Bayly 1996; for the Ottoman Empire, see Barkey 2008). For these predominantly Muslim societies, the rupture in tradition as a result of the colonial encounter was very intense, but, I contend, has been creatively approached by different individuals and groups within these societies in rethinking religious belief and practice—their agency exhibited in the range of responses to the structures of colonialism.

Marshall Hodgson (1974) pointed out at the end of his history of Islamic civilization that Western societies have managed to retain a deeper and more continuous link with their traditions than Muslim societies. Charles Taylor's *Sources of the Self: The Making of the Modern Identity* (1989) certainly suggests a particular religious—read: Christian—and philosophical continuity in Europe. In the sense of a relatively continuous philosophical dialogue, dependence upon largely the same authors, books, and philosophers, Western societies are more traditional than non-Western, including predominantly Muslim, ones. My suggestion here is not of an unchallenged continuity that has seen no shifts in emphasis at various geographical and historical points. Nevertheless, it is possible to discern a thick thread of continuous connections within Western political and philosophical thought, including a strong continued dependence on what must be recognized as theological texts as the basis of modern political and social theory.

At the same time, scholarship on tradition, particularly Eric Hobsbawm and Terence Ranger's widely quoted edited volume (1983), has alerted us to the possibility that many traditions, while retaining some link with past practices and modalities, are very recent creations. In this context, it is important to realize first that "tradition" put to the service of legitimizing competing claims of authenticity, whether by Islamists or others, may be of very recent origins. Second, and more importantly, contrary to a particular stream of scholarship on Islamic tradition, and indeed the claims of many Islamists, "traditional" Muslim society was not rigid and static.[1] Wael Hallaq (2001), Michael Cook (2000), Mohammed Qasim Zaman (2002), and L. Carl Brown (2000) show that adaptive creativity, dissent, and rethinking have been an integral part of traditional Islamic legal and theological thought. The imposition of colonialism and the introduction of a particular model of the state that is called "modern" led to much rethinking and reevaluation within the non-Western, and not just Muslim, societies. While the impact of colonization in terms of its disruptions was tremendous, we can see individuals and groups selectively appropriating and braiding together elements of existing ideas and practices with the newer impositions. Thus, contrary to established understanding, we should see this engagement as one of great creativity through which new schools of thought (such as the Deoband in South Asia) and new forms of organization (such as the Jama'at-e-Islami and the Tablighi Jama'at, also in South Asia) emerged. I want to suggest then that the relationship between "modernity" and "tradition" is not one of linear antagonism but of accommodation, suggestion, and creation. Social actors exhibit their agency through unexpected and unforeseen combinations of existing conceptual repertoires with the new structures and discourses imposed upon them.

Indeed, I sympathize with Akeel Bilgrami (1999, 380) when he suggests that there should be a "moratorium on terms such as 'modernity' and the disputes surrounding them, for they are not categories that enhance explanation and understanding of political and cultural development in contemporary Indian politics and history." What he suggests instead of a rather vague notion of modernity is a more precise periodization that locates specific developments in a particular context.[2] Moreover, the very unevenness and variation in the manifestation of modernity requires that we recognize it as a project as well as a historical period (Asad 1991). I do not suggest a complete abandonment of the term "modernity." However, I want to propose that we abandon associating normative values with the "modern" and instead focus on substantive changes in Muslim practices as a result of the colonial encounter in North India. As I discuss in the next section, the profound impact of this encounter was a result not just of outright rejection or opposition from Muslims, but of negotiation, absorption, and subtle reframing of earlier discourses. In the process, I lend further support to the contention that fundamentalism in general (Lawrence 1990; Eisenstadt 1999), and Islamism in particular, is a distinctly modern phenomenon rather than a traditional response to modernity.

What does it mean to suggest that Islamism is a particularly modern phenomenon? Are the Islamists not, by their own definition, hoping to go back to the glorious first days of Islam under the prophet Mohammed? S. N. Eisenstadt (1999, 2) suggests that fundamentalisms constitute a distinctive form of modern political movements.[3] To him, fundamentalism is a variant of the Jacobin tendencies that are an intrinsic part of modern political movements and that arise in part because of an inherent contradiction within modernity between totalizing and more pluralistic conceptions, between reflexivity and active construction of nature and society, between autonomy and control (62). Bruce Lawrence (1990, 1998) has argued that Islamism would have been inconceivable in any other age but the modern one. His suggestion stems from a view that not only do Islamist groups use modern ways of organizing and communicating, but the very categories, notions, and laws that they hope to defy or modify are modern constructs. In the chapter below I single out the emergence of the modern state and its attempts at managing religious practice and thought within a colonial context in North India as a key development that made Islamism possible.

More critically, I point out that the particular kind of secularism that the British applied to the Indian context was one that created severe impediments to secularization. As I mentioned in my discussion of the theories of secularism and secularization, we do not have a clear roadmap of the relationship between the two. The Western European experience, albeit with much variation internally, was idealized to produce an image of secularization and secularism working in tandem. In the case of colonial India, the universal pretensions of official secularism were instrumental in codifying and highlighting particularistic religious affiliations that defeated any potential for secularization particularly in terms of relegating religion to the private sphere. Religion could hardly be privatized in a public sphere that was structured by the British around religious identities, nor could a process of demystification of religion begin seriously without apparently falling in line with the occupier's cultural framework. I shall focus on two key components of colonial secularism that I believe were critical in supporting the rise of Islamism, itself an innovation in Islamic thought and practice. The first is the structural vehicle of this secularism: the modern state that betrayed its moderness through an invasive interest in categorizing populations, intrusion, and the constant remodeling of subjectivities. The second is the substantive aspects of the project of secularism that were driven by colonizers' preoccupations and that I suggest allowed only particularistic attachment to Muslim practices, attaching universalism to those modes of belief and behavior that seemed secular to the colonial administrators but particularly Christian to the colonized.

The Intrusive Modern State

Even though it proceeded unevenly in different parts of India, the colonial imposition of a modern state, with its constant interference in everyday life, was a major break from the past. Sudipta Kaviraj (1997) has argued that, as in the case of premodern Europe, the precolonial Indian state was of limited significance in quotidian life. "The state had," he suggests elsewhere (1997, 229), "the discretion to tax severely or leniently. It could cause or end wars, but its power to reorder the structure of productive roles which determined everyday destinies of individual men and social groups was severely restricted."[4] No doubt the colonial state built upon previous structures of power, domination, and information collection that existed in precolonial India, especially in the earlier years, and that the transition was not overnight but took more than half a century (Bayly 1996). Yet something new was also being created; this state was different both in the quality and the quantity of its intrusion into individual lives. The colonial state's interference into daily life operated on two parallel and yet intertwined levels. One encompassed the politically motivated, sometimes cynical but mostly self-righteous attempts at social and political "reform." This included the attempts at banning practices like *sati*, the introduction of electorates along religious lines, et cetera. The other and perhaps more critical was the less self-conscious, although admittedly no less self-righteous, ontological remapping of the individual, community, society, and polity (Cohn: 1996; Kaviraj 1997, 231). Included in this is, for instance, census activity that divided individuals into neat and hermetically sealed categories.

This interest in categorizing and shaping individuals and communities is a defining characteristic of not just the colonial state but of the modern state generally. In a perceptive analysis of this inherent compulsion within the modern state, James Scott (1998, 82) has observed:

> The aspiration to such uniformity and order alerts us to the fact that modern statecraft is largely a project of internal colonization, often glossed, as it is in the imperial rhetoric, as a "civilizing mission." The builders of the modern nation-state do not merely describe, observe and

map; they strive to shape a people and landscape that will fit their techniques of observation. . . . I am suggesting that many state activities aim
at transforming the population, space and nature under their jurisdiction
into the closed system that offers no surprises and that can best be observed and controlled.[5]

The intrusion of the modern, albeit colonial, state was not targeted specifically toward Muslims. Rather, this intrusive state touched all religious
practices. Indeed, one of the central planks of colonial sociology was the
codification of diverse practices across the geographical and social landscape of India as a single coherent whole, creating "a religion" as an analytical category. In the case of Hinduism it is often pointed out that Hinduism was not conceived of as a unified "religion" until colonial times (Hansen
1999: van der Veer 2001; Kaviraj 2007). Influential contemporary Hindu
religious nationalist groups are also the result of a similar engagement with
the colonial state (Hansen 1999). Yet until recently a similar analysis had
not been extended to Islam, and the dramatic reconstruction of it during
colonial times had not been adequately recognized. This may in part have
to do with the wider geographical spread of Muslims, some structural similarity to Christianity, and the vague notions of a Muslim *ummah* that per-
colated at various levels in precolonial and early colonial periods as well.
However, recent research is beginning to question this assumption of a co-
herently Islamic imaginary, independent of its Indian connections, as well
as the specific implications of this imagination in the early colonial period.[6]
For the major religious groups, the diverse, regionally specific activities that
were classified, under colonial rule, as one religion were often mutually contradictory.[7]

The idea of a unified religion was closely linked to legal codification.
Not surprisingly, legal codification and homogenization, important for
the modern state's effective administration, was introduced in India by
the British administration in a manner that was shot through with their
own assumptions and perceptions. The contradictions and "looseness"
of Indian textual and customary judicial practices remained a source of
anxiety for early colonial administrators, such that authoritative compila-
tions that would not just represent, but rationalize and reconstruct Indian
jurisprudence were commissioned (Wilson 2007). The early colonial ju-
rist William MacNaghten states that his *Principles and Precedents of Moohum-
mudan Law* was intended to "fix" the many areas "where a contrariety of
opinion has hitherto prevailed" to allow a clear determination of the case

at hand (Wilson 2007, 18). The emphasis, then, was on not just recording but rationalizing and homogenizing. Shari'a had been practiced in India based on a diversified, subjective, and localized interpretation (Masud 1999, Messick, and Powers 1996; Zaman 2002; Kugle 2001). Due to their anxieties as rulers and the precariousness of their rule, the company and colonial administrators started a process of codification as early as the eighteenth century. However, the very process of such codification meant that certain views were excluded and others highlighted, distortions magnified by the interests of the administration and lack of knowledge among the administrators.

The impact of centralized colonial economic policies on Islamic political organization remain largely understudied.[8] Changes in trade and employment options for North Indian Muslims, in particular, led to greater mobility for the middle classes and a need to engage with modern educational institutions. Islamists, it is useful to remind ourselves here, are distinguished from the other types of Muslim Revivalists by their backgrounds in modern educational institutions. Scions of *ashraf* (upper-class) families in North India could no longer expect to make a living from the Mughal court after the war of 1857, and needed to travel to different princely states for careers in their traditional skills. Others had to change their occupation and move into new professions, often with the help of modern education.[9] Maududi's own career is a useful illustration of this very trend as he moved from Hyderabad to Jabalpore to Delhi in search of employment variously as a journalist/editor, tutor, and college lecturer. Toward the end of the nineteenth and early twentieth century, entering the colonial bureaucracy was a much-valued option but dependent almost exclusively upon a modern education. Muslim entrepreneurs and industrialists were a source of financial support to different local political parties, religious groups, and social causes, even as their manufacturing and trading activities were deeply entrenched in the international system. Various competing trends existed and contributed to the fissiparous nature of the Muslim community. The British policy of strengthening feudalism in West Punjab, through increasing the size of landholdings for loyal *zamindars*, a large majority of whom were Muslims, was mediated by the formation of the canal colonies that tied Punjab closely to an international export market (Ali 1988; Gilmartin 1988). This policy also led to a significant difference in the levels of education and political participation between East and West Punjab. Groups like Jama'at-e-Islami and Tablighi Jama'at were founded within or around the northeast of Punjab, and enjoyed some support there among the more literate Muslim population and a relatively egalitarian landholding pattern.

A Religious Public Sphere: Paradoxes of Colonial Secularism

In terms of an explicit policy regarding religious belief and practice, the colonial administration was concerned, particularly in the latter half of the nineteenth century, with maintaining an official distance from religious identities that were seen as particularistic in the Indian context. Of course, the policy went through several reversals and modifications, as well as regional variations in how it was implemented.[10] However, even as secularism was broadly conceived of as a position of equal distance from the different religions, the very constitution of "religion" was different from the administrator's own experience. The boundaryless and pervasive nature of practices and norms, alien and strange to the British sensibilities, demanded, nevertheless, some recognition. The resulting codification of religious laws, political constituencies, and census activity meant first that religion emerged as a unified cohesive category of identification, and second that it attained a political prominence it had previously lacked. Much of this line of reasoning is familiar to scholars, particularly historians of South Asia, in the context of a rich collection of research on communalism and religious nationalism, particularly Hindutva. In the context of Islam, this literature is largely concerned with the demand for a separate Muslim homeland, Pakistan.[11] However, Islamism has not been analyzed by embedding it in this context, nor have the insights generated in the study of communalism been carried over to think through Islamism.[12] My argument about the creation of Islamism in relation to colonial secularism goes beyond the claim that the British introduced politicized religious identities in India to entrench their own rule; not because the British did no such thing—"divide and rule" was a policy prescriptive,[13] and not just in India—but because colonialism was a variegated multidimensional relationship that resulted in many unplanned and unforeseen developments. I want to suggest that as a result of a multilayered, long-term, and multidimensional interaction certain processes were set in motion that have resulted in Muslims, among others, having to define, rationalize, and engage with aspects of their belief and practice in ways they did not need to before. Of the various responses generated, Islamism mirrors the key concerns of colonial secularism most closely, but by shifting the focus on Islam rather than Christianity.

Recent historical research (Metcalf 2004b; Gilmartin and Lawrence

2000) has shown that religious identity was one of the many in a hugely diverse India. Indeed, the idea of an integrated India should be treated with some caution, and it is useful to remind ourselves here that under the Mughal Empire its population was only nominally unified under an empire, with different languages, ethnicities, princely states, castes, class positions, and religious practices exerting competing pressures. For instance, Vasuda Narayanan (2000) has shown in the context of South India that Muslim invaders from the north were distinguished not through their religious beliefs, but on the basis of their ethnic origins—as Turks rather than Muslims. Similarly, Catherine Asher (2000) has pointed out through an analysis of the construction of "Muslim" mosques by Hindu rajas and "Hindu" temples by Muslim rulers the fluidity of religious identity in precolonial political matters. C. A. Bayly (1996, 27) points out that "pre-colonial social enquiry and representation were never communal[14] in the sense that they saw India as a field of conflict of two irreconcilable faiths." This is not to imply that Indo Muslim political practices or "governing principles" were secular in that there was a conscious separation of religion and the state, but rather that they were a matter of indifference.

The colonial administration's stated policy of neutrality toward religious "belief," negated by an active practice of highlighting and utilizing religious difference where it seemed beneficial to the interests of the East India Company and later the British Empire, created a tension that, at the very least, did not exist previously. In a suggestive paper, Ayesha Jalal (2002, 235) presents a rather understated case:

> The colonial state's avowed policy of neutrality based on political indifference toward religion was easier to proclaim than translate into practice. As a moral stance, it clashed with the imperatives of ruling a culturally alien society. The British needed to appropriate existing symbols of cultural legitimacy, so for them religion could never be a matter of political indifference. Intrinsic to the search for collaborators and the organization of social control, religion was in the service of the colonial state's political purposes and thus had qualitatively different consequences from the political treatment of religion in the preceding centuries.

In addition to a distinct equation of Christianity with modernity, which I discuss later, the colonial administration made sometimes contradictory, often temporary, but nevertheless discernable shifts in its dealings with particular religious communities. After the rebellion ("mutiny" in British records) of 1857 against the increasing British imperial presence and under the nominal patronage of the last Mughal king, Bahadur Shah Zafar, Muslims were treated by the colonial administration as a potential threat. Such a view tended to gloss over the very real and deep divisions that existed between Muslims of different regions, classes, and ethnicities to highlight the threat posed by their putative allegiance to the same faith. Governor General Mayo deputed W. W. Hunter to investigate the possibility of a religious duty binding Muslims to disloyalty to the British rule. Hunter's report, *The Indian Musalmans*, published in 1871, denied such a link but highlighted that there were "fanatical" elements that, unless checked, would lead to greater uprising among the ignorant Muslims (quoted in Jalal 2002, 237).[15] This report, and policies that flowed from it, had an impact in shaping *ashraf* Muslim perceptions of their victimhood, as well as a separate identity (Mufti 1995: Shaikh 1989).

A related and critical development was the shift from qualitative notions of dominance to quantitative ones (Kaviraj 2010). Democracy and secularism are, as mentioned above, often intertwined in liberal theory and popular rhetoric. Yet the contradictory pressures that the notion of democracy exerts on identities and communities remain important—on the one hand, there are pressures to distinguish groups, and on the other, to expand membership within that group to be able to claim a majority.[16] Moreover, the type of democracy that the colonial administration finally conceded to in the Indian context requires further analysis, and we need to distinguish between the "representative" forms of government that the colonial state established to strengthen its own power and the "democratic" forms that would have entailed transferring significant power to the elected representatives (Washbrook 1998). These representative forms were designed to co-opt elites through engaging them in an advisory and administrative role rather than a policymaking and directional role. David Gilmartin (1998) has rightly argued that we need to analyze the very structure and concept of elections, understood to be the vehicles of democracy, as introduced under colonial rule to understand the formation of Muslim identity and nationhood in modern South Asia. Rather than an unproblematic structure for the expression of popular views, elections "as a result of their distinctive position in the structuring of relations between the state and society, called forth a distinctive pattern of community rhetoric—a pattern whose analysis . . . gives new insight into the relationship between religion and nationalism" (Gilmartin 1998, 416, 417). The introduction in 1909 of Minto-Morley reforms, which introduced the principle of separate electorates to Muslims at all levels of representation, can be seen not as the culmination of a process that started in 1880 with the introduction of religion-based electorates in municipal elections, but one more step in a rather long process of defining communities along religious lines. Once started, the process created an impetus for individuals as well as communities to sharply define their allegiances, practices, and beliefs, at the same time as claiming members from different parts of India. Existing in a twilight zone between the two starkly defined identities of Muslim and Hindu was no longer possible for those who had previously done so.[17] Their identity had to be defined, enumerated, and ultimately rationalized.

Critically, the norms associated with their lives in Britain became the standards through which religious belief and practice and their relationship to modernity were measured by the colonial administrators. Van der Veer has argued that there was a distinctly religious aspect to modernity as it was presented to Indians during the colonial rule and through establishment-supported missionary activity; the Christian way of being was presented as the modern way of being (1999a, 39; also 2001, 2004). Moreover, the colonial administration's policy proclamations regarding secularism aside, the rhetoric of civilizing missions was not inaccessible to the increasingly literate Indian population; they could not fail to grasp at least intuitively the contradictions inherent in this policy, nor the thinly veiled contempt toward their own practices and beliefs. The colonial administration's support for missionary activity in India and Africa has received some scholarly attention recently (Masud 2000; van der Veer and Lehmann 1999, 2001; Mani 1998). Many of the groups collectively associated with religious fundamentalism in South Asia today, like the Arya Samaj (Hindu), and Jama'at-e-Islami and Tablighi Jama'at (Muslim), not only started in direct response to the activities of the Christian missionary groups, but also adapted many of their techniques and operational strategies (Masud 2000, xlvi–lvi; Metcalf 1982; van der Veer and Lehmann 1999). The key difference was that these newly founded Hindu and Muslim groups focused primarily on their coreligionists with the idea of reintroducing a true religion to them and bringing them back to a purified mode of practice and belief.[18] Certainly, Jama'at-e-Islami, founded in the last years of colonial rule in India, was originally conceived of as a da'wa or proselytizing organization by Maududi, but organized on the lines of a Leninist party.

Thus, a central tension within the colonial administration's policy of secularism was that even as local religions were proclaimed parochial and particularistic, the traditions of Christianity informing its reading of secularism were raised to the pedestal of universal values. That British and European secularism was the result of a particular historical trajectory in which a structured, hierarchical church conceded its control over property and society only after a protracted, often violent struggle with the emerging modern state (Salvatore 2005) did not seem to distract the colonial administration from imposing its notions of "religion" and "secularism" in a very different context. It is this rendering of all other religions as particularistic that made it difficult for them to aspire to the secular-universal. David Gilmartin (1991, 125) has quite correctly pointed out that "the meaning of 'public' has to be understood in the Indian colonial politics not primarily in contrast to the sphere of the 'private' but in contrast to the sphere of the 'particular.'"[19]

This tension is particularly apparent in the legal and juridical norms that the British established in colonial India. At the initial stages of colonial rule they assumed that all Indians acted out of "inherent religiosity and orthodoxy, so the codes of religious law were sufficient to adjudicate in all their crises" (Kugle 2001, 270). At the same time, they attributed to their own legal traditions the "principles of universal jurisprudence" (Kugle 2001, 281). This provided the backdrop to the persistent attempts at codification of Islamic laws, binding their practice through the use of precedents and increasingly limiting their application to the point that by early twentieth century, the religious law could rightly be termed static and out of date. Thus, in the process of codification, what was a dynamic and variegated practice was stunted so that it was of little use in contemporary life.[20] More critically, public matters and those of universal application were to be adjudicated by laws of an English provenance. The earliest British codifiers and reformers had indeed imagined "that 'India' would be a mirror of England: Indian constituted the nemesis of English rationality, yet it was also the arena in which this new class of civil servants could fulfill its urge toward centralization and order" (Kugle 2001, 278). Indeed, while the general assumption is that Indian law was primitive compared to British law, this simply is not the case. The English legal system was no more "modern" than the Indian one, and struggles to modernize the legal system in England were more easily realized in India, illustrating that "imperial powers were often able to do in their colonies what they were unable to do at home"(Skuy 1998, 514).[21] It is this very claim to universalism made by colonial secularism embedded in legal practices, cultural norms, and political structures that Maududi and the Islamists destablized by their insistence on the universalism of Islamic laws. In a mirrored reversal, they claimed the compatibility of Islamic cultural norms, legal practices, and political concepts with the modern state and its effective running.

Muslim Responses to Colonial Secularism

This multifaceted interaction with a new way of conceptualizing religion and its relationship with the political and public spheres led to a plethora of responses from the Muslims of India. I hesitate to use the term "Muslim community," lest I give the impression of a coherent, internally unified group. The huge variety of responses from Muslims is not surprising if we keep this diversity in their social positions, educational backgrounds, regional affiliations, and cultural trajectories in mind. From Syed Ahmed's emphasis on modern education to the Nadwa ulama's insistence on a stronger base in Islamic education before allowing modern education to "corrupt" young minds, from the Indian nationalism and "secularism" of the traditionally trained *alim*, Maulana Azad to the religious nationalism of the uncommonly modern Mohammed Ali Jinnah, from the political opportunism of Punjabi feudal lords to the pan Islamism of Mohammed Iqbal (Pakistan's national poet), the variety of ways in which Muslims responded to the changes brought about by new legal, political, social, and economic changes under colonial rule makes sense only if we recognize this internal diversity within the "Muslim community."

Most discussions of the Muslim response to the colonial encounter have underplayed the dynamic nature of this interaction, and the dimension of time has been a much-overlooked aspect of responses generated within the Muslims of India.[22] The longer the interaction with the colonial state and, in particular, its repression of local demands for self-rule, the greater the disenchantment with the "Western." However, this dimension comes to the forefront when we think not just about the differences between the various Muslim leaders, but also the changes in the stances of the same leader. Thus Mohammed Ali Jinnah started his career as the "ambassador of Hindu-Muslim" unity and ended it as the founding father and governor general of a nation-state founded on the basis of religious nationalism. Mohammed Iqbal was initially a staunch supporter of Muslim nationalism, after his sojourns at Cambridge and Munich universities, but toward the end of his life he became increasingly disenchanted with the "Western" notion of nationalism and sought a reconfiguration through pan-Islamism. Maududi himself started out as a nationalist who then grew increasingly fearful of the consequences of democracy for Indian Muslims and began to see the world in communal terms.[23]

Even as Muslims formed a diverse and internally fractured group,[24] the very homogenizing impulse of the modern state structure operative during British rule facilitated an emergent imagery of Muslim community and nationhood that gained momentum during the early years of the twentieth century. In particular the shift from a qualitative notion of dominance to a quantitative notion of minority and majority was critical in underpinning this new political imagery. Academic writings of the late 1980s and 1990s (Jalal 1985; Gilmartin 1988; Mufti 1995; Shaikh 1989) that focused on Muslim nationalism leading to the formation of Pakistan convey the reluctance with which the Muslims of North India rose to appropriate a collective identity; there is a sense of having exhausted other options, of being pushed into a corner. In his article "Secularism and Minority: Elements of a Critique" (1995), Amir Mufti brings to the fore the particularly difficult dilemma faced by the Muslims of North India by juxtaposing their situation with the "Jewish question" in Germany. He suggests that "'German Jew' and 'Indian Muslim' are names not merely of social groups but of entire cultural and political problematics and trajectories; names, furthermore, of the respective torments of European and Indian modernity" (1995, 78). He uses Gotthold Ephraim Lessing's play *Nathan the Wise* to situate this dilemma. Nathan, a Jewish moneylender, is asked by Saladin, the Muslim ruler, to declare which of the three great monotheistic religions is the true one. As Nathan agonizes over his answer, he realizes he must tread carefully, for:

To be a Jew outright won't do at all—
But not to be a Jew will do still less,
For if no Jew, he might well ask, then why
Not Musulman? (Mufti 1995, 76)

Mufti traces the formation of the Muslim subject in colonial sociology as primitive/religious/antimodern and connects it to the crisis of representation within Indian nationalism, where the nationalist claim for the existence of a singular Indian nation seeks to accord the "Muslim" the role of the national minority. Thus, Mufti claims (1995, 85), it asks the Muslim to explain himself, and the question is experienced as a trap: "If 'Muslim outright' then how can he be an Indian in the modern sense? And if 'no Muslim' at all, then why not a 'bare and blank' citizen?"[25] Thus, if nothing else, this body of writings from the late 1980s that I mentioned above sensitizes us to the dilemma faced by Muslims in first recognizing themselves as a group and then defining their role in the emerging polity of a modern Indian state.

Islamism: Modern and Rational?

Islamism is a particularly modernist take on defining this relationship between belief and the state. Islamism's focus on the state is generally understood to be the result of an internal compulsion within Islam. This has been a result of taking at face value the Islamist's claim that in Islam there is no distinction between religion and state. The vast majority of Muslim opponents of the Jama'at-e-Islami have tended to prove the contrary through recourse to Qur'anic texts and Hadīs (sayings of the prophet). Irfan Ahmad (2006, 12) rightly points out that both the academics (Ernest Gellner, Bernard Lewis, Bassam Tibi, Myron Weiner, etc.) and the Muslim critics of Maududi's focus on the state rely on theological arguments to explain or criticize Islamism. Quite clearly though, the centrality of the state in Islamist thought is a result not of a theological compulsion within Islam, but the context in which Islamism was founded.[26]

Formation of Islamist groups like Jama'at-e-Islami is part of the multifaceted response generated as a consequence of the "colonial encounter." The response, as I have attempted to show above, was not limited to Islamism, but included a variety of positions taken up by different, and sometimes the same, Muslims, including those of Indian nationalism, communal nationalism, traditionalism, and socialism. That these various responses should operate in an intersubjective, dialectical manner, refining and redefining their positions based on the interaction with others should therefore come as no surprise. Maududi himself went from espousing secular nationalism to religious nationalism, and then to radical organization. He operated in a period that was particularly thick with debate and discussion. His interaction with socialists (particularly the Khairi Brothers in Delhi), mostly nationalist traditionalists such as Jam'iyat-ulama-Hind, and communal political forces in Hyderabad constituted a context in which he was able to articulate a particular vision of political engagement. It was in part a result of these influences and the context of his involvement that the structure of Maududi's ideology is radically different from the traditionalist ulama and the organization of his party is based on the modernist notions of the Leninist party. His conception of history is very much a modernist one, and the JI was formulated as a "vanguard" party primarily to engage in the project of modernity.[27] My argument here, however, goes beyond Maududi to highlight that Maududi's ideas gained popularity precisely because of the context in which they found resonance within a certain segment of Muslims of North India: those who were determined to be part of the project of becoming "modern," of running a modern state, but without letting go their "Muslimness" in the public arena. Maududi in his writings and the JI in its organization and activities aimed to provide a rationalized, logical Islam, compatible with modern lifestyles. He made an explicit effort to decrease the role of spirituality and miracle in Islam and was vehemently opposed to various traditional practices. These included saint worship, visits to cemeteries to pray for the deceased, and extended social ceremonies surrounding lifecycle events such as marriage, death, and birth. A key element of Maududi's innovations was his opposition to the role of the ulama. Maududi insisted that a 'Muslim needs only the Qur'an' to understand Islam. His *tafseer* (exegesis) of the Holy Qur'an is extremely popular even today for its accessible style and beautiful language.

Maududi's modernity was a source of contention with the traditionalists. Many of the ulama who criticized Maududi believed that he was stripping Islam of its spirituality.[28] At the heart of Maududi's endeavor was an effort to make use of modern arguments to support Islamic conclusions, to present it as a rational religion that was not outdated as the "naturists" (or *nechari* in Urdu) claimed it to be. In attempting to rebut the secularist *necharis*, Maududi nevertheless had to take on the structure of their arguments and their thinking and to thus reproduce it to some extent. Little wonder then that Maududi's writing appealed to the first-generation college-educated, socially conservative Muslims of North India. The rational approach to religion and its practice then translated into several innovations at various levels. At the level of political engagement, Maududi's vision of the Islamic state duplicated, assimilated, and reproduced Western political concepts, structures, and operations, producing a theory of statecraft that, save for its name and its use of Islamic terms and symbols, showed little indigenous influence (Nasr 1996, 90). At the level of daily life it has included innovations in dress, such as the tailored headscarf and *niqab* that was the trademark of JI women in Pakistan until the 1980s. While offering complete *parda*, this differed markedly from the relatively impractical *chadors, burqa's*, and other forms of veiling practiced previously by urban women, allowing them greater ease in the use of their hands (not occupied anymore in holding up their *chador*) and visibility (unlike the *burqa'*).[29]

The traditionalists claim (Cook 2000; Winter n.d.; Nasr 1975; Usmani n.d.) that in his attempt to provide logical reasons for following Islam and in his engagement with the modern state, Maududi and the Islamists innovated spirituality out of the religion. The opposition between Maududi and the traditionalists should not blind us to the fact that Maududi built on a reformist tradition in South Asian Islam that covered a range of movements from Syed Ahmed Barelvi's armed resistance to the changes within sufi tariqat, as well as Wahabism (Metcalf 1982, 2004b; Robinson 2001). Reform movements in the precolonial and early colonial period were concerned not so much with the European presence but with the perceived decay in social and political life within Mughal India. Maududi's approach to religion and its practice translated into innovations at various levels, while building upon earlier vocabularies and "traditions" of reform. The invention of Islamism, however, is closely tied to the secularism that created its possibility.

The discourse of containing the "irrationality of religion" through the policy of secularism has been a particularly strident one in postcolonial South Asia. This vehemence on the part of the secularists has produced an equally zealous response among the "religious." In suggesting that the Islamists are modern and secularizing, I do not want to reinforce the view that there is no other way to be modern, or that the modern person is inevitably secular. Rather my argument is that if we do not impose a teleological conclusion upon our analysis of secularization, we may perceive that religious practice is constantly changing and reflecting the context in which believers operate. Some aspects of religious practice in contemporary Pakistan, particularly urban Lahore, where I based my fieldwork, can be seen to be secularized in terms of a shift from largely unthinking inherited belief to objectified, critically analyzed belief. Islam in this context is certainly not secularized in the sense of abandoning its claims on the public sphere, yet a far-reaching debate has been initiated on not just the role of Islam in the public sphere but also the meaning, limits, and uses of the public sphere in contemporary Muslim societies.

CHAPTER TWO

Jama'at-e-Islami Pakistan

LEARNING FROM THE OPPOSITION

During the 1960s everything was political. Qayyum Nazar[1] came back from Paris and told us how he had met Jean-Paul Sartre. He had gone to the café where it was known that Sartre spends time. So he went to Sartre and told him, "I am a writer and I am from Pakistan." He [Sartre] said "What do you have to say about Algeria?" Qayyum said, "I am a writer, and nonpolitical." Sartre said, "Then you are a member of the French occupation, get out!"

—Aziz ud din Ahmed, interview

This chapter presents a historically embedded view of the emergence of Islamists as the opponents of "secularism" in contemporary Pakistani politics. The Islamists continue to define themselves in opposition to secularism in Pakistan, contrary to the developments in neighboring India, where the Jama'at-e-Islami India is increasingly making appeals to the state to "enforce" secularism to protect the minority Muslims (Ahmad 2009). Yet this self-definition and popular projection masks a much more complex and variegated relationship with secularism and its various aspects. Secularism has meant slightly different things at various points during the last six decades in Pakistan's turbulent political history. Examining the dynamics of the relationship between secularism and Islamism, in this chapter I focus on the emergence during the 1960s of the JI as the key religious party opposing socialism on the basis of its purported secularity. To liberal, secular urbanites, including those in Lahore that I interviewed, the JI epitomized the "fundamentalist," the "religious zealot," and the "antisecular." The close relationship between Zia's military regime (1977–88), especially in its early years, and the JI has been instrumental in solidifying its credentials as an antidemocratic, antisecularism party while attributing a cognate relationship to secularism and democracy. Yet it is useful to remind ourselves that both Bhutto and Maulana Bhashani, leaders associated with the left movement and democracy in Pakistan, spoke of an "Islamic socialism."

Moreover, some of the major ulama parties, Jam'iyat-ulama-Pakistan (JUP) and Jamiat-ulama-Islam (JUI), sided with the left, "secular" parties. How then do we read the opposition that JI mounted against the leftists primarily on the platform of an antisecular stance?

Hussain Haqqani (2005) provides a succinct and updated view of the increasing co-option of Islamic rhetoric, and the JI, during the late 1960s by the military establishment in Pakistan. Although it is not the focus of Haqqani's book, the trend that emerges from his evidence regarding the army's manipulation of Pakistani politics is one of policies of secularism shot through with ambivalence toward Islam. Undoubtedly the establishment of Pakistan in the name of Islam created the basis for a secularism that was unsure of its remit and unsteady in its grounding, both within the ideology of the new nation-state and the masses that came to inhabit it. Yet there was a significant amount of debate about whether this religious identity could be used creatively to support democracy. Indeed, the proponents and supporters of "Islamic socialism" claimed that religion provided the very foundation on which to build a tolerant and just society.

The notion of "Islamic socialism" gained ground within a certain political and intellectual context enthused by the experience of socialism in China and East Asia. Literature on Islamist groups has tended to focus on the impact that these groups had on the left, secular groups (Kepel 1995, 13–27; Zubaida 1997; Esposito 1999a, 657). Some have looked at the absorption of leftist protest within the Islamist fold.[2] However, the impact of the leftist groups on the Islamists has not been studied in any detail. The actual process and details of this conflict-ridden interaction have not been explored to understand the influence it had on the Islamists in terms of their strategies, operations, and policies. In this chapter I address this gap in the literature by looking at the changes in Jama'at-e-Islami Pakistan's stances and policies since Pakistan's formation. I point out the subtle interplay of ideology, personal ambition, and political context that shapes Islamism. In so doing I also raise important questions about the continued use of political and social categories, particularly those of the "religious right" and the "secular left" that are rooted in the context of almost half a century ago.

A related lacuna exists in the literature on Jama'at-e-Islami in particular. The Jama'at-e-Islami is admittedly one of the most influential Islamist groups in the world. Maududi's writings have been instrumental in inspiring similar groups, and chapters of the JI itself, in different parts of the world. S. V. R. Nasr (1994, 1996) has provided a comprehensive and thoroughly researched analysis of the JI Pakistan up to the early 1990s. Others like

Abdul Rashid Moten (2003), Rafiuddin Ahmed (1994), and Irfan Ahmad (2009) have also provided useful insights into the organization and its official ideology. However, with the exception of Ahmad (2009), most of these studies have not engaged with the activists and members across the different levels of the organization. As I argued earlier, the official proclamations and leaders do not represent the complexity of motives and actions of the activists that allow us to understand the organization and its impact better. Moreover, these studies have not followed the significant changes that have occurred within the Jama'at-e-Islami since the mid-1990s.

JI Pakistan: Against Secularism and Democracy

The JI's powerful position in one of the oldest and most important educational institutions of Pakistan, the Punjab University, is explained in part by the JI's close relationship with authoritarian regimes (Haqqani 2005; Nasr 1996). The JI had provided the most ferocious and organized opposition to populist, progressive agendas from the 1950s onward, as had other such Islamist parties in many Muslim states during the cold war era (Esposito 1999b, 657; Kepel 1995, 13–19; Zubaida 1997). In Pakistan, left-leaning student unions clashed with the IJT on many university campuses, particularly those like Punjab University, which were highly politicized, and JI was instrumental in bringing down the most popular political leader, Bhutto. Nasr (1996, 88–106) has suggested that the Jama'at-e-Islami's ideology tended to support authoritarianism and contained a powerful critique of both the left and Western democracy to the advantage of Pakistan's military dictators. The JI had been the main ideological adversary of the left since the 1960s, and Zia, the military dictator who overthrew Bhutto's regime, depended heavily on the religious groups for legitimacy (Nasr 2001). He placed Jama'at leaders in charge of sensitive cabinet portfolios and on prominent state-sponsored organs. Further, in February 1979 the military regime promulgated the Hudood Ordinance, to lead toward an Islamic legal system. Ostensibly dealing primarily with theft and robbery, the laws were used to control dissent and resistance to Zia's regime. Significantly, these laws were exclusively implemented against the poor (Faruki 1987, 53–78). That many religious groups in Pakistan have been funded and set up by the US and CIA has been amply documented (Ali 2001, 248–70; Gardezi 1991, 113; Rashid 2000; Cooley 2000) and is often held as further proof of their antidemocratic credentials.

However, in 2003, when I started lecturing in the political science department at the University of Punjab, I noticed important changes in the workings of the Jama'at there. The introduction of a Board of Governors scheme in public universities by the Musharaf regime triggered fears of privatization, layoffs, and increased social polarization among the students and faculty of these universities. At this point, the most organized resistance to this privatization was provided by the staff and students affiliated with the Jama'at-e-Islami. While there was no doubt an element of wanting to protect their turf, it was interesting to note the rhetoric that they utilized in this process and the alliances that they were willing to make on an issue basis. This chapter outlines some of these changes and attempts to explain how they may have come about. To understand the JI today, I argue, we need to understand the dynamics of its opposition to the "left" in Pakistan. The Jama'at's oppositional engagement with the left had a deep impact on its strategies, constituencies, and ultimately stances on various issues; as a result of this engagement with the left, the JI extended its operations and interacted with segments of Pakistani society it would not have otherwise. As a consequence of these strategic and operational decisions, the JI has more grassroots links than other political parties in Pakistan today. At the same time, many of the liberal/left elements have been depoliticized, thus opening up further space for political mobilization by Islamist parties like the JI.

Two decades (the 1960s and 1970s) of often violent and certainly rancorous confrontations between the left and the Jama'at often obscure the fact that it was only after the mid-1960s that the Jama'at began to define itself almost exclusively in opposition to socialism through a focus on secularism. Maulana Maududi's earlier writings and Jama'at's work prior to this period have been premised on a critique of modernity and the West in general, of colonialism and its impact on Muslim societies, without particular emphasis on communism and socialism. This critical engagement with the left shaped the Jama'at in important ways. The Jama'at learned critical lessons about its own organizational capabilities and limitations, picked up strategies, and issues, and extended its operations among groups like student and labor unions—its continued engagement with these groups distinguishes it from other political parties in Pakistan today. All of these have, over time and in combination with other factors such as changes in the international political order and changes in JI leaders and their aspirations, led to significant modification in the Jama'at stance on various issues including democracy, imperialism, feudalism, and women's rights. I explore these changes in three constituencies of JI activism—students, labor, and peasants—to highlight respectively the changes in their position toward "democracy," "imperialism," and "feudalism."

Olivier Roy is correct in suggesting that there has been a certain de-intellectualization of the Islamist parties given that none of the current leaders matches the intellectual capabilities of Maududi, Syed Qutb, and Ali Shariati (Roy 1994, 60). In a similar vein, I find that these changes in JI stances do not reflect deep insight into aspects of these overarching, broad categories of social and political analysis. For instance, the denunciation of "imperialism" in contemporary JI political language is not accompanied by any substantial inquiry into the different types or meanings of "imperialism." Rather, they represent pragmatic decisions made by the most internally democratic national political party in Pakistan. Significantly, while this Islamist group is bereft of an outstanding ideologue equivalent in stature to Maududi, it provides a structured environment for some broad-based intellectual engagement with social and political issues for its activists in direct contrast to the other national political parties in Pakistan. It has thus facilitated the production of "organic intellectuals."

This chapter focuses on the late 1960s, arguing that this period was important because it was during this period that the categories of the "secularists" and the "fundamentalists," the "modern" and the "antimodern" were sharply delineated to encompass the characteristics that are still used today, half a century later, to define the members of these categories. This analysis is based on research in Lahore and focuses primarily on the interaction between the left and the JI in that city. The dynamics of JI and the left interaction in Karachi, the other major center of both JI and leftist mobilizations, are similar in broad terms, but with an important difference: the JI's core constituency in Karachi split along ethnic lines in the 1980s with the formation of the Muttahida Quami movement.

Radical Times: The Late 1960s in Pakistan's Political and Social History

A critical period in Pakistan's history, the mobilization of the 1960s and early 1970s has, so far, received very little scholarly attention. The impact of the mobilizations that started during the 1960s has been immense, not just in the formation of various institutions and changes to the laws, but also, and more crucially, in signaling a shift in political and social relations. It is not uncommon to come across the comment in upper-class households that before the '60s, the *haris*/servants/peasants knew their place in society. This shift included not just a change in the expectations of the public, but it also defined the limits of government actions in some cases and certainly prescribed the context in which government actions had to be justified. What Bhutto called the "awamification" of Pakistan was not, as has been alleged (Jones 2003), only the result of PPP (Pakistan People's Party) policies, but part of a larger change that was sweeping through the country.[3] In his book *1968: Marching in the Streets,* Tariq Ali (Ali and Watkins 1998, 13) reminisces that every single month in the year saw an explosion of questions, ideas, politicization, and movements around the world and contends that "in fact, the biggest success was achieved in Pakistan, where the student movement triggered off a gigantic popular upsurge which led to the overthrow of the military dictator." Akbar S. Ahmed (1997, 210) notes that:

> There has been a distinct "awamification" in Pakistan in so far as ordinary people have gained power, wealth and rights as never before in history. Their expectations are high and the changing social structure allows them greater say than they have ever had before. . . . After the establishment of Pakistan the governors and ministers would be the Nawabs, Khans and Chaudhrys (the first Prime Minister, Liaquat, was Nawabzada, or the son of a Nawab). It is significant that the leaders of Pakistan—the governors, generals and secretaries—in the last two decades belong mostly to the lower middle classes, brining with them their world-view. Their fathers would have been junior clerical staff or junior army officers.[4]

That this mobilization was successful in toppling a long-standing military dictatorship was, then, the least of its achievements, while remaining its most immediate and easily counted success. The potential for a change in the system that many glimpsed in these mobilizations led to a significant sociopolitical shift in expectations. A student activist[5] of the time recalls,

> We really thought that there was going to be a change in the system. We really thought that feudalism (*jagirdari nizam*) was going to end. This is why people in my village and others voted against their feudal lords for the first time, because they really thought they could change it all. We would walk into the commissioner's office and kick open his door . . . it was an immense liberation. People used to cower in front the bureaucracy before that. . . . And, of course, we thought we had put the *maulvi* in his place (*auqat*). . . . They [implying religious groups including JI] had passed a fatwa against Bhutto and the *qaseeda khawan/mirasi* (rural/semiurban storyteller/singer) would go around singing "Ai *fatwa main chaj ich*

pa kay chatan da / tay gali gali wich watan ga."[6] He would get a lot of money from people with this song.

The tradition of democratic politics was not very strong in the regions that constitute present-day Pakistan. The Muslim League, which was the political party that led the call for the formation of Pakistan and became the ruling party after independence from British rule, did not rely on grassroots mobilization in the four western provinces that became Pakistan. Instead the Muslim League formed alliances with local landlords and tribal leaders to gain the electoral victory of 1946 (Waseem 1987; Gilmartin 1988; Jalal 1985). This was a continuation in the pattern of governance established by the British. Particularly in northwest India the British ruled through intermediary power brokers, princes, and landlords who maintained control over local populations (Barlas 1995). In his comparative analysis of Pakistan and Malaysia, Nasr declares that "Both Pakistan and Malaysia lack a strong notion of nationalism born of a sustained struggle for independence against colonialism. In both countries the ruling elites closely collaborated with the British to the very end. . . . The close connection to colonialism in both cases made for states that were not forged through the crucible of the struggle of independence but were rather handed down—created—at independence" (Nasr 2001, 25).

The leadership of the Muslim League emanated predominantly from Muslim-minority provinces, where Muslims felt threatened by the specter of a Hindu-dominated independent India. Paradoxically, Pakistan was created by combining the Muslim-majority provinces, where the demand for a separate homeland had less resonance. On the formation of "a moth ridden Pakistan," as the father of the nation, Mohammed Ali Jinnah, is reported to have said, this leadership moved into the unfamiliar territory of a state they had helped create (Jalal 1985, 271–93). Since the Muslim League leadership was not confident of its constituency in Pakistan, provincial elections were not held in the country for seven years after its formation, or general elections until 1959. The lack of grassroots mobilization for its creation, the unrepresentative nature of its key political party from the very inception, and the relative institutional stability of the civil and military bureaucracy all paved the way for a state where left activists faced an uphill battle. In East Pakistan, present-day Bangladesh, leftist political mobilization had historically been much higher than in West Pakistan. In the 1954 elections for the provincial assembly in East Pakistan, the communists won a total of twenty-six seats while the Muslim League won only ten (Ali 2003,

182). However, the communist party was not able to make serious inroads in West Pakistan, given its lack of local linkages and organizations: its top leadership was, like the Muslim League, imported from India.

The peak of left mobilization in Pakistan is generally believed to be the student-led protests that started in November 1968 against the military dictatorship of Ayub Khan. Ayub Khan had focused on economic development under the tutelage of Harvard economists like Gustav Papaneck, who advocated a "trickledown" economy and publicized Pakistan as the miracle economy, even as real wages deteriorated sharply. In retrospect, Ayub Khan's era was indeed a period of rapid industrialization and economic growth. However, this growth was achieved at great social and political cost (Amjad 1978). The authoritarianism of Ayub Khan's regime weakened institutions of civil society. Furthermore, glaring inequalities in income led to increasing unrest. According to economist Mahbub-ul-Haq, "by 1968, 22 families controlled 2/3 of Pakistan's industrial assets; 80% of banking, 70% of insurance . . . 82% of total advances made in Pakistan were concentrated in just 3 accounts" (Mahbub-ul-Haq in Gardezi 1991, 31). The disparity in the distribution of wealth between the provinces and between the propertied classes and the masses became major issues (Jahan 1972). Left-leaning intelligentsia and ethnic parties were critical in mobilizing industrial labor and the urban poor in demonstrations against the regime (Sayeed 1980). The demonstrating students were joined by workers, lawyers, doctors, and teachers. The movement exerted such pressure on the government that Ayub Khan was forced to resign in 1969. Bhutto, a minister in Ayub Khan's government who had resigned a short while earlier, seized the moment and launched a populist political party called Pakistan People's Party with the slogan "*roti, kapra aur makan*" (food, clothing, and shelter).

Some analysis of the mobilizations during this period (Rashiduzzaman 1970; Ahmed 1972; Misra 1972; Ali 1983) was carried out at the time, but often from partisan positions and to a large extent focused upon the divisions within the various "left"[7] groups, which was of course a more contemporary preoccupation. In a more recent commentary, Marvin Weinbaum (1996) recognizes that the mobilizations during the late 1960s and early 1970s were the closest Pakistan came to mass democratic action, but dismisses these as primarily motivated by frustration and anger. He may be correct in part in this analysis of its causes, but that should not lead us to underestimate the influence of these mobilizations. The impact of a political education goes much beyond the protest attended. Political study groups, teach-ins, and easy access to radical literature defined the consciousness of a whole generation of Pakistanis. Wilcox (1970, 73–74) rightly realized that "while the style and circumstances of the martial law government of General Yahya Khan appeared to be a carbon copy of the 1958 Ayub Khan regime, Pakistan had radically changed and the whole political society was 'once again at the starting point.' 1969 was a year in which the Pakistanis attempted to come together to decide what that starting point was, and in which direction they should together or separately move."

There can be little doubt that the left in Pakistan was not very entrenched. Moreover, the intellectual leadership, in particular, was part of the educated elite.[8] However, the mobilizations of the 1960s and 1970s, generally conceived of as leftist, with all their limitations, had a significant impact on the state and society in Pakistan, and remain a key milestone in the country's political history. Jama'at's contentious engagement with the left was a response in many ways to the potential inherent in these mobilizations, involving, as they did, a broader cross-section of Pakistani urban and rural society than ever before (Weinbaum 1996, 639–54). I would argue that this period was important also because it was during this period that the categories of the "secularists/progressives" and the "fundamentalist/conservatives," the "modern" and the "antimodern" were sharply delineated in Pakistan, as in many other Muslim countries around the world. The social and political characteristics attributed to members of each of these groups were demarcated, and it is these characteristics, highlighted almost half a century back, that are relied upon in policymaking and academic analysis today. There were, as we shall discuss briefly below, moments of collaboration between some elements of the Islamist stream, and particularly the JI and the left before the 1960s, but it was after this period that they became increasingly hostile to each other. It is also important to note here that not all religious groups defined themselves in direct opposition to socialism. Many ulama and religious leaders like Maulana Hazarwi and Maulana Rehman supported leftist mobilizations.

The Relationship between the Left and the Jama'at-e-Islami before the 1960s

The acrimonious and contentious relationship between the left groups, the "progressives," and the Jama'at, "the fundamentalists," defined during the late 1960s and sharpened during the 1970s and 1980s, obscures a period when the differences were not so intense as to prevent a coming together by some groups for specific aims. Ironically perhaps, given the sharp dichotomy between the "secular" left and the "religious" JI, the earliest Muslim communists in Punjab were in fact members of the religious *Hijrat* movement. After the defeat of the Ottoman Khilafat by the British, these Muslims declared India a *Dar-al-Harb* (Land of War against Islam) and decided to move to the Muslim state of Afghanistan to be able to live their lives in close accordance with Islamic principles.[9] The Afghan government was suspicious of their motives and the group moved to Tashkent, where it was welcomed by the Soviet Union. However, fearing that they may be forced "to become atheists or to eat pigs," the group moved onto Turkey, where they were arrested by the republic's army. They were then "rescued" by the Red Army and some among them joined the famous Indian communist M. N. Roy's training camp in Tashkent; twenty-eight of the group went to the University of Eastern Toilers. Some of them returned during the 1920s to set up and expand the Communist Party of India (CPI). Prominent Lahore communists from this group include Ferozeuddin Mansoor, Fazal Elahi Qurban, Abdul Majid, and Akbar Khan.[10]

The Communist Party of India's role in the formation of Pakistan remains controversial. Pakistan, a state founded on the basis of religion, would seem the antithesis of the "secular" leftist ideology that JI would focus on in later years. Nevertheless, there seems to be significant evidence that points toward some level of collaboration between the Muslim League and the Communist Party in Punjab. Punjab was an extremely important province for the Muslim League leadership, most of which hailed from areas that are now India. The dream of a Pakistan, whether as a separate geographical entity, a bargaining chip, or a constitutional entity within a federated India, needed the support of the Punjabi Muslims. Up until the 1937 elections, the Punjabis rejected the Muslim League. In 1943, the Communist Party of India, in a thesis proposed by P. C. Joshi, the new party secretary, supported the Pakistan nationalist movement as the right of minority self-determination (Zaigham 2004, 15). Some communists in Punjab worked very closely with the Muslim League after 1940.[11] During the 1945–46 elections, the communists arranged rallies and meetings for the Muslim League leadership, particularly among the rural communities. They helped the ML leaders with their speech writing and also delivered speeches at the league rallies.[12] Danyal Latifi, a member of CPI who worked very closely with Mumtaz Daultana, wrote the Punjab Muslim League Manifesto.[13] This manifesto supported full employment, nationalization of key industries, graduated taxation on land holdings, and state land for landless peasants. It seems that the mass mobilization that took place in Punjab, particularly rural Punjab, for the idea of Pakistan just before partition was given a major boost by the inclusion of the communists in the campaign.[14]

In his novel *Ghaddar*, Krishan Chandar points toward this role of the communists while focusing on the chaos and violence that was unleashed upon ordinary Punjabis as a seemingly arbitrary and ambiguous boundary was imposed on them. The novel covers three days in the journey of the protagonist of the story, a young Hindu man, fleeing Lahore at Partition. He is attacked by some Muslims, but: "Suddenly I raised my hand as if to stop him and smiling, looked into the eyes of the horse rider (who seemed to be the leader) and said laughing, 'I have such luck! All my life I worked as a communist carrying out propaganda for Pakistan, for the right of Muslim self-determination, and today, when Pakistan has been created, this spear is being placed on my chest.' I don't know why I said that, which power it was that made me say these words, because I had never been a communist and had never participated in any political movement."

In any case, his tactic worked and his Muslim captors let him go. Unlike the communist supporters of Muslim league, Maududi had been against the Partition of India and the formation of Pakistan. Later, in the 1960s, the Jama'at distanced itself from those comments as it built its campaign against the left as anti-Pakistan. Instead, the Jama'at highlighted the allegedly close relationship between Mohammed Iqbal, the national poet credited with first suggesting a separate homeland for Indian Muslims, and Maududi.

In the specific context of the Jama'at, we see in Maududi's writings, in the various issues of *Tarjuman ul Qur'an* (lit. translator of Qur'an), and in important essays such as "Musalman aur Maujooda Siyasi Kashmakash" (Muslims and the Current Political Struggle) that the menace of socialism is not separated from the overarching threat of Western modernity during the early period of JI stretching up to the mid-1950s. Maududi's earlier writings built a critique of modernity and Westernization in general, not focusing exclusively on socialism or communism. Nasr (1996, 25) argues that Maududi's own view against communism was crystallized during his stay in Hyderabad, where the largely Hindu peasantry was challenging the Muslim Nizam's rule during the Telengana movement. Maududi viewed communism through the lens of communalism, seeing in it the seeds of the destruction of a Muslim ruler and a Muslim way of life. The main focus of his writings and activism at that time remained the impact of colonialism, modernity, and non-Muslim cultural influence, Western and Hindu. Nevertheless, Maududi also associated with and attended many sessions hosted by the famous Khairi brothers of Delhi between the years 1929 and 1931 (Aziz 1987, 88–92). The Khairi brothers were influenced by socialist thinking, and if nothing else, Maududi seems to have developed an appreciation for the Leninist party model. It might be said that, in fact, JI is the best Leninist party in Pakistan with its strict membership rules, cadre-based organization, continuous ideological training, and centralized decision making. Nasr (1996, 40–42) asserts that Maududi viewed the Muslim League as JI's main competitor among the Muslims of North India, and that Maududi also saw Mohammed Ali Jinnah as his nemesis in providing leadership to the Muslims of India.[15] After the formation of Pakistan, Maududi saw the Communist Party of Pakistan as a tactical ally against its main enemy, the Muslim League. C. R. Aslam, a veteran left leader in Pakistani Punjab, recalls: "After the partition, Muslim Leaguers would not allow anyone else to hold a rally or a demonstration. Jama'at-e-Islami's Maulana Maududi was also very annoyed with this situation. He said to me, 'Think of something.' I spoke to Ferozeuddin Mansoor and then the first demonstration we held in 1948 in Mochi Gate [in Lahore]. This rally was a joint Jama'at and Communist Party of Pakistan rally. On the stage, Ferozeuddin Mansoor and Maulana Maududi sat together."[16]

Later on, in 1965, the leftwing NAP (National Awami Party) and Jama'at were both members of the broad coalition that supported Mohtarma Fatima Jinnah's candidacy against Ayub Khan.[17] However, the differences between these groups were already beginning to surface. Chaudhry Rehmat Ilahi, a key JI leader leading the negotiations at that time, as much of the JI leadership including Maududi was in jail, recalls a period of some confusion regarding these elections.

> This was a difficult decision. Ayub Khan's regime was dictatorial and far from Islamic . . . in fact to a large extent it was secular. Different groups and political parties were dissatisfied and so were we. The opposition consisted of different parties and elements, but because the elections were now in front of us and he [Ayub] was going to run for the post of president, we wanted to do something. . . . Alliances are a product of the context . . . When there is a flood even man and snake take shelter in the same place.[18]

Abid Hasan Manto recounts: "We worked for her [Fatima Jinnah] in Punjab but mentally there was a vacillation. In spite of the fact that Bhashani had suggested her name, we were not sure. . . . What are we doing? Jama'at is also in this coalition and we are campaigning for them in Punjab?"

This was the last national-level alliance between the left and the Jama'at.[19] The strength of the leftist mobilizations in Pakistan during this period was increasingly forcing Maududi to engage, politically and intellectually, and in a sustained manner, with socialism. His response eventually was to define the JI in opposition to the left. I focus below on three constituencies of mobilization through which the JI directly confronted the "leftist/secularists": students, peasants, and labor unions.

Politicized Students: Agents and Articulators of Change

Besides the communists, the key vehicle for pre-partition Muslim League mobilization, however limited it may have been in Punjab, were the students, particularly those organized under the banner of the Muslim Students' Federation (MSF), the student wing of the Muslim League. There was some overlap between the two groups, and some communist leaders were actively involved in setting up and organizing the MSF. That the Muslim League leadership saw this student federation as a key vehicle for amassing support in a critical province of what was to be Pakistan is demonstrated by the fact that from 1941 onward, the top leadership of the Muslim League, including Mr. Jinnah, attended Punjab MSF conferences regularly. No other student union received such a high level of attention by the ML leadership during this time (Ahmed 2000, 39).[20] The Hamood-ur-Rehman commission, set up in 1964 as a result of student-led protests against Ayub's University Ordinance, not only recognized the important role of students in contemporary politics, but also traced the prominent role for students in the country's politics to the nationalist and independence movement in British India. It recognized that students had been "utilized" by the Muslim League for its campaigns in "the Frontier Province against the Red Shirts, in the Panjab [sic] against the Unionists, in Bengal against the Krishk Praja Party, and later for the referendum in Slyhet" (Commission on Student Problems and Welfare, 1965, 178). The report writers comment that "naturally" the students felt proud of their work and felt that they had become a political power. Student leaders had the ears of ministers; while the professors cooled their heels in the anterooms, student leaders walked straight into the private chambers of ministers. Student wings of political parties were given great importance, and students sought election on a party basis in educational institutions. Campaigns were run with as much fervor and resources as campaigns in the wider political world, with placards, banners, speakers, and "even refreshments for supporters" (Commission on Student Problems and Welfare, 1965, 179).

The first two decades after Pakistan's formation saw significant expansion in educational facilities. This was in part due to the developmental focus of the state. Moreover, new opportunities were created by the eradication of competition with Hindus and Sikhs from within educational institutions as well as the various sectors of economy and bureaucracy. With the expansion of educational opportunities to many previously marginalized communities, rural or lower-middle- and middle-class areas, students of the time became the link between those communities and the urban political sphere. A large majority of the students in universities and colleges at that time were among the first in their families—or even villages or urban neighborhoods—to attain higher education. A class of students emerged that was more diversified ethnically, as well as in terms of class, gender, and social and political links, than the largely upper-class or feudal elite to whom education had been limited in previous years. Students were not just passive recipients of ideologies from above, from the various political parties whose student wings they formed, but were active articulators of the diverse backgrounds that they represented. As such, they acted as a critical channel of communication between the public political sphere and the society, particularly in urban Pakistan. Looking back at this link with the students and universities, labor leader Hanif Ramay[21] says:

> At one point trade unions and several other sections of the society were intrinsically linked. Students and trade unionists held joint rallies, for instance. In their elections in Punjab University or NCA [National College of Arts)], we would go to support our allies. Similarly they would support us workers. There were also several organizations working with peasants. There was a movement for larger social change. We had a combined struggle. If one was suppressed then we all supported that section of the society. The problems of one were felt by all others. (Aik ka dukh, sab ka dukh tha.) That link has been broken. The worker is alone now. It is very difficult to organize without the moral, financial support of other sections of the society.

The diverse social background of the students was complemented by an international debate on competing ideologies. The 1960s were a period of renewed intellectual enthusiasm as the Chinese model rekindled energies and ideas. Chinese help to Pakistan during the 1965 war generated great public goodwill toward China.[22] At the official level, the government turned a blind eye to the influx of Chinese literature in the country.[23] Access to this literature was not limited to the three or four major cities of Pakistan, as had been the case for Russian literature, but permeated the smaller towns as well.[24] Unlike the Soviet Communist Party, which established a top-down relationship with the local party members,[25] the Chinese party preferred very much to let the local players decide their course of action. After the [pro-Russia] Communist Party of Pakistan was banned in 1954, the National Awami Party (formed in 1957) emerged as the main political platform for left activists, with an increasingly Maoist presence.[26] By the mid-1960s, Mao's philosophy and the ideas from the Chinese experience began making a discernable impact in Pakistan; a new generation of leftists had arisen. The enthusiasm and energy generated by the younger generation also acted as an inspiration for an older generation of leftists; many among those had lost interest after the Communist Party of Pakistan had proved unable to connect to the masses. Professor Aziz ud din comments on his own experience (Aziz-ud-din Ahmed 2005)[27]:

> I was greatly inspired by the student movement. When in 1962–63 the movement started in students, I was union in-charge (at Islamia College, where I taught). I heard that some of our students had been arrested and were in police custody. We went to meet them; the conditions they were being kept in were horrible. Even when they were picked up [arrested] by the police, they had just been thrown into the jeep with their legs and arms this way and that. Somebody had hernia, others had various injuries. . . . We pleaded with the police to open up his cuffs, but they did not. Later on the police started firing at the student demonstrations and killed many of them.

This new generation of leftists was typified by the Professors' Group and by the Young People's Front in Lahore. The Professors' Group was a group of left-leaning lecturers and teachers based primarily in Punjab University with members from various colleges affiliated with it. The group operated on various fronts. They dominated the Punjab University Lecturers' Association and were active in student politics through the Nationalist Students' Organization. In addition they formed a *Dehati Mehnat Kash Mahaz* (Rural Worker Front), *Mazdoor Mahaz* (Labor Front), and later in the 1970s a mass front called *Jamhoori Mahaz* (Democratic Front).[28] Some of the prominent members of the Professors' Group include Aziz ud Din Ahmed, Khalid Mahmood, Ijaz ul Hasan, Kamil Khan Mumtaz, and Munir Ghazanfar. The Young People's Front was another group, started by Dr. Aziz ul Huq, who articulated a critique of both the pro-China and the pro-Moscow old left in Pakistan, of their factionalism and mechanistic policies, and their lack of linkages with the masses. He presented some of his writings to a group called Halqa Arbab-e-Zauq and involved students and young activists in his group. The Halqa had many previously left writers and poets as well as several who were critics of left politics. Iqbal Leghari (1979, 132) contends that a key accomplishment for Huq was that he managed to rid the left groups of the stigma of being anti-Pakistani.[29] "Huq projected a strong appreciation for Pakistani nationalism and the Pakistan movement. While the old left was stuck with the image of looking upon the creation of Pakistan as a conspiracy of British imperialism, Huq on the other hand emphasised the creation of Pakistan as a political and economic necessity for survival of Muslims in India" (Leghaari 1979, 132). The Awami Fikri Mahaz, in which Raza Kazim and Mahmood Kasuri were involved, typifies efforts in that era to create an open forum in which issues could be debated and discussed from various perspectives. Study circles held in schools, colleges, universities, villages, and industrial sites, as much as in upper- and upper-middle-class drawing rooms, became a source of politicization as well as networking.

And this indeed was the defining attribute of the period; it was a time when space was created for debate and discussion of ideas and alternatives. In terms of numbers and certainly in terms of organization, the left was still very weak in Pakistan. The mobilizations spearheaded by students against the University Ordinance and other issues were supported by various segments of the society, which were disgruntled by Ayub Khan's regime, including the feudals whose power had been reduced by Ayub Khan's support for rapid industrialization. That they eventually led to the fall of Ayub's dictatorship often obscures the fact that other than the feudal interests, perhaps, no other group had the organization to replace Ayub. In fact, Bhutto's success in building a party within a year, almost out of nowhere, is explained only by understanding the particular context in which he was operating. His enormous personal popularity based on certain antiestablishment stances he had taken, combined with the lack of an organized platform for the left in West Pakistan, meant that he was able to channel the energies of various groups previously working independently of each other.[30] He also represented a faction of the elite, the disaffected feudals, which was at that time willing to support the student-led mobilizations to destabilize Ayub's regime. Although PPP is often credited as spearheading the 1969 protests against Ayub, in fact PPP only entered the agitations after they had been started by autonomous student groups in different cities. Qasim Anwar, a student of Forman Christian College at the time, recalls:[31] "Nobody planned it, we heard the news, we had political discussions and study circles, and finally we reacted. One day, when we heard of protests in other parts [of the city and country], we started marching out of our college. The number of students and others who joined grew, and the police cracked down on us. . . . It was totally out of proportion to what we could do."

Dr. Mubashir Hassan, one of the ideologues and founders of PPP, comments:[32] "No particular group had started the agitation. The situation was ripe, and as Mao Tse Tung said, the spark was enough to light the prairie fire. Everyone made a contribution. PPP became active after the arrest of Bhutto on 13 November 1968, from a bedroom here in my house [in Lahore]. . . . PPP gave no call for agitation before 13 November. Students were agitating, and I think on the 10th and 11th a journalists asked Bhutto, 'Why don't you ask the students to stop the agitation?' and Bhutto said 'Why should I stop them?'"

Indeed, Bhutto was not in a position to order the students to stop; cleverly, though, he decided to show support for them soon afterward. This made the PPP the only political party that was openly in support of the students' agitation. PPP then provided the political platform for continued agitations that might have died out if the student groups that had started these agitations had been left to themselves. In return, these students supported the PPP election campaign during 1970–71, creating the impression of an organization that did not, in fact, exist. PPP's later organizational chaos and electoral misfortunes are in part explained by this meteoric rise unsupported by an organizational structure. No doubt many PPP leaders, including Bhutto's daughter Benazir, were, in the absence of any long-term interaction with various segments of society, right to be puzzled by the fickleness of public loyalty. Mubashir Hassan, too, never able to repeat his electoral victory of 1971, reflected on the relationship between the leader and the masses:[33] "Really the leader is like a mother, the masses like a baby. The baby cries, and the mother has no idea what he wants. She tries different things, food, kisses, sleep, et cetera, and eventually something clicks and makes the baby happy . . . for a short while at least. And the mother does not know what clicked now, and what will click the next time the baby cries."

The *Narsury* of Jama'at-e-Islami and the Menace of Socialism

"If JI is the garden, then IJT has been our *narsury* [plant nursery]. . . . IJT is where we get the vast majority of our new members and leaders from."[34]

It is significant that the large majority of JI leaders today are those who played an active role in student politics during the 1960, '70s, and early part of the '80s. Their training in the rhetoric and to some extent practice—albeit not unsullied by the use of violence—of democratic politics, including the ability to organize and motivate individuals and carry out campaigns,[35] leaves them with greater belief in their own capabilities than any other major political party in Pakistan today.

Formed in Lahore on December 23, 1947, IJT has the distinction of being the longest-running student body in Pakistan's history. Twenty-five students from Lahore, Gujranwala, Faisalabad, Sargodha, Sialkot, Multan, Dera Ismail Khan, and Sahiwal organized the inaugural meeting, which was addressed by Maulana Maududi, Prof. Abdul Hameed Siddiqui, Ch. Ali Ahmed Khan, and Naeem Siddiqui (Anas 1989, 113). The Islami Jam'iyat Tulaba (IJT) was seen by some of its founders as the inheritor/continuation of MSF. They drew an explicit link between MSF's religious-nationalist orientation and IJT's religious orientation. Prof. Ahmed Anas, explaining the ideological background for the formation of Jam'iyat, points out that "once Pakistan was formed MSF was directionless, because what it had been agitating for, a separate country, had been achieved, and so it died a natural death" (Anas 1989, 111). He goes on to explain that in the place of a student body working toward carving out a Muslim homeland, the IJT was needed as the student body for *inhabiting* a Muslim homeland. The IJT attracted the religious, socially conservative student, and there was some continuity in members from MSF to IJT (Khalid 1989, 106).[36] According to the IJT narrative, MSF was not able to provide adequately for "ideological training and character building," and thus IJT emerged as a successor to MSF. In fact, to some Islamist critics of the MSF, like Dr. Malik, MSF had been permeated successfully by communists, and IJT was required to continue the original charter of MSF in the newly created Muslim homeland (Khalid 1989, 107).

By the 1960s, the Jama'at was particularly perturbed by the strength of populist and leftist ideas within the college and university student population, because this created certain important challenges for the JI, much more so than for any other religious group or party in Pakistan. The reasons for a high level of anxiety about the strength of leftist influence among students may be traced in part to Jama'at's own ideology and organization. As mentioned earlier, Islamism posited a break from the traditionalist approach, including the *madrasa*-based (religious school) educational system. The Jama'at aimed to build a mass of "pious" people in the *mu'assir tabqa*—the influential class—that included educated professionals and officers. Jama'at's commitment to the influential class was also reflected in its organizational structure, where unlike the other religious groups and parties such as Jam'iyat Ulama Islam, the Jama'at did not have a network of madrasas to draw upon. In a bid to influence the *mu'assir tabqa*, the Jama'at had focused on institutions of higher education rather than building madrasas of its own, which would have most likely drawn in candidates from the lower classes. Consequently, the IJT focused on colleges and universities, where it came in direct competition with the leftists. Moreover, the background of the Jama'at leadership in those early years of Pakistan's formation also played a decisive role. The Jama'at leadership tended to belong to Muslim *ashrafiya* migrants from India, often with technical and professional degrees.[37] Their inclination was to talk to people like them. While the Jama'at leadership did not go as far as the leadership of another Islamic group to claim that "Islam is not a religion to be studied while sitting on a mat/rag" (*Islam tat par bhet kar parhanay ka mazhab nahin hai*),[38] the organization catered to and was designed for educated members.[39]

In its initial years, the IJT stayed away from active involvement in politics, but by the 1960s the "menace of socialism" had galvanized the IJT into a more activist role. Dr. Israr Ahmed says that the IJT was "like an association (*Anjuman*) of pious young people (*nek taba' log, nek sīrat naujawan*) with one taste (*mizaj*)" (quoted in Al-Rehman and Khalid 1981, 98). The second nazim, Dr. Mohammed Naseem, reminisces: "None of us were in the union. I thought that in normal circumstances students should not take part in politics. They should acquaint themselves with the situation, form their opinion and when they are done with their education and enter the practical life, then in political and social terms whatever they can do, they should" (quoted in Al-Rehman and Khalid 1981, 30).

However, an increasing competition with the left-leaning groups for the hearts and souls of the *mu'assir tabqa*, the students who would later become the leaders of the nation, forced the IJT to first take stock of its shortcomings and later to plunge into action. Khurram Ja Murad (quoted in Al-Rehman and Khalid 1981, 43–44), a key JI ideologue and one time Nazim, emphasizes that the increasing strength of the leftist ideology among students and teachers, their (university-level) electoral success, and organizational capacity in confronting the administration all made the IJT realize its limitations. The IJT, he contends, feared not just marginalization, but complete annihilation, and so was galvanized into extending its operations to a wider group of students and competing in the university and college elections. Like the left groups, the IJT started organizing study circles, debates, and book fairs. Like them, the IJT expanded its welfare activities to include admission support (accessing and filling the correct forms, and negotiating the arcane bureaucracy many public universities are saddled with) and introduction tours for new students (including getting their university ID cards made, registering for courses, allocating hostel rooms, etc.). All this in addition to a general role as student representatives: negotiating exam timings, contents, transportation issues, et cetera with the university/college authorities.

In keeping with its focus on the educated segments of Pakistani society, the JI's response to the threat of socialism also built on its strength in writing and publications. The JI produced large numbers of pamphlets about socialism. With titles like *Socialism ki Nakamiyan* (The Failures of Socialism, 1969), *Mohammed, Qur'an aur Islam Roosi Mushriqeen ki Nazar Main* (Mohammed, Qur'an, and Islam in the Eyes of the Russian Infidels, n.d.), and *Alam-I-Islam aur Socialism ka Challenge* (The World of Islam and the Challenge of Socialism, n.d.), these pamphlets positioned Islam and socialism in direct contradiction with each other. Often such pamphlets would point out that "atheism is the religion of socialism"[40] and that socialists were pretending to sympathize with Muslims to create a new brand of Muslims who were like "melons—green on the outside and red on the inside."[41] Left/secular activists raised questions about Jama'at's ability to fund the publication of such pamphlets in large numbers.[42] For instance, one pamphlet entitled "The Failures of Socialism," authored by Saeed Asad Gilani, was first published in January 1969 in a run of ten thousand copies, in February 1969, three thousand more copies were published, followed by five thousand more the next month and another five thousand in April 1969.[43] Left-leaning union workers joked that "There is more Islam in the sea than on land in Pakistan, because the Americans bought Maududi's books and pamphlets (to provide financial support to the Jama'at), and had to throw them in the sea by the cartons."[44]

Another avenue for combating socialism was the mass-front magazines like *Zindagi*.[45] Perusing through the pages of the magazine, one gets a palpable sense of an increasing animosity against the left. This animosity and fear that started off relatively mildly in the 1950s with jokes and words of caution about the *la diniyat* promoted by socialism turned into a fulltime occupation as almost the whole magazine was dedicated to detailing the failings of socialist and communist regimes, updates from various campuses about the activities of the left and the IJT, "analysis" of leftist politics in other parts of the world, and strategies for strengthening the religious, particularly the Jama'at's, response against this menace. By the 1970s it had turned into an all-out war in which *Zindagi* literally dogged every step of the left, particularly the PPP, which had become a mass platform for left mobilizations during 1969–71.[46] At the same time, one can also discern a trend for discussing issues highlighted by the leftists, for example, problems of students and industrial and agricultural laborers, of concentration of wealth in the country, and of social hierarchies now couched in Jama'at's vocabulary. *Zindagi* set up a special campus and university watch, naming individual professors and lecturers who questioned religion or showed leftist tendencies. For instance, in its December 29, 1969, edition, the magazine named several professors in Islamia College, Lahore, who had criticized Islam or promoted a materialist view of religion. These included Prof. Minhaj ud din, Amin Mughal, Zahoor Ahmed, Eric Cyprian, and Zafar Ali, among others. In such articles, conversations between the professors and their students are reported as if verbatim, creating an impression of documentary authenticity. This process was repeated for different departments of Punjab University and for other colleges in the city in other issues of the magazine.[47] Many of these lecturers were then physically attacked by IJT activists, and during Zia's regime many were singled out for early retirement or harassment through suspension or postings to smaller towns.

IJT: From Violence to Antiglobalization Movement

In universities and colleges, identification with either IJT or its opponent groups was increasingly forced on students, and by the mid-1970s the IJT had already built a reputation of clashes and violence with the other student organizations. This was a radical departure from IJT's initial years, when the IJT stayed away from active involvement in politics. It is possible that the IJT first started using violence against the nationalist and left elements in East Pakistani colleges and universities. Particularly at the time of the civil war preceding the formation of Bangladesh, IJT's violent tactics won it the support of the army establishment (Nasr 1993). This alliance with the army counted as a success within some parts of the Jama'at, and this success allowed IJT a greater measure of independence from the parent body in West Pakistan in the following years. From disrupting discussions and debates organized by left/liberal groups on campus, to breaking up mixed-sex parties and beating male students who were seen in the company of female students, to "disappearing" opponents, breaking joints, and pulling out nails in Male Hostel Number 1 of Punjab University, IJT is popularly accused of being the terror arm of the Jama'at, reaching beyond the left/liberal groups to any individual student who dared challenge IJT activists on any issue.

State support to the IJT through police cover in fights, delayed registration/follow-up of cases against IJT activists, and access to political and bureaucratic officers was more blatant during Zia's rule. However, IJT leaders contend that the organization expanded most during Bhutto's regime.[48] Certainly under Bhutto's rule the number of all types of student and labor unions increased dramatically. But many leftists complained that in fact Bhutto did provide tacit support to the IJT to create a counterbalance to the radical students' mobilization, on which he had capitalized before elections, but to whom he was now reluctant to fulfill his promises.[49] Violence in Lahore's university and college campuses continued during the 1990s under Benazir and Nawaz Sharif, turning into territorial wars between gangs of students without much ideological direction, until the IJT found a new purpose in organizing against the Board of Governors scheme introduced by General Musharaf. Widely seen as a move to privatize the education sector and open it up for international players, the IJT, along with other student's groups, is a key member of the antiglobalization movement in Pakistan. Its critique of privatization of national education is based primarily on the principle of equal access to health and education. The public universities where IJT is strong and which provide it with the bulk of its membership have, for the last three decades, been catering primarily to lower-middle-class men and middle-class women. The vast majority of upper- and upper-middle-class men tend to either attend private universities or move outside of Pakistan in pursuit of higher education. Waqas Anjum, IJT national Nazim from 1995 to 1998 and now a JI *rukn* (member), explained:[50] "The government is only increasing the segregation in society through these measures. Those who sit on a *taat* [jute mat] in their school will have one board [of education, for curriculum and examination, etc.], the army has its own, and then the Agha Khan Board. They are creating different types of people—those who rule and those who are ruled. It is only the organizational capacity of JI and my involvement in it that sustains me, otherwise the situation in Pakistan is truly depressing (*dil shakista karnay walay halat hain*)."

IJT's violent practices, muted now but still present,[51] have been justified internally as the response of a group besieged by violence initiated by the state or IJT's political opponents. Hafiz Salman Butt[52] insists that:

IJT is nothing short of a miracle. For youths of 17 to 24 to organize them-selves, and to exhibit control, to put up with each other (*bardasht karna*) and to run campaigns . . . it is all a miracle that *there is not more violence* [emphasis added] . . . our members have taken part in *Jihad* in Afghani-stan and Kashmir, and even after returning from there they have not acted irresponsibly. If they wish to act irresponsibly, even today, hun-dreds of armed students with various kinds of weapons can come out, especially in Karachi. After *Al-Badar* and *Al-Shams* [in the then East Paki-stan], after fighting India and Russia, the MQM and common citizens of Pakistan are nothing in front of IJT.

This quote typifies the general JI response to questions about IJT; vio-lence is not completely denied but justified as a "courageous" response to violence instigated by the opposition. Running through this response is a veiled threat of potential for greater violence, withheld for now—out of re-sponsibility, not cowardice. Nevertheless, within some parts of JI, including the women in particular, who are, as I shall discuss in chapter 4, playing an increasingly important role in changing the organization from within, there is increased questioning of the use of violence. A. Ghani, Convener Women's Commission of JI, observed:[53] "I really want this cleared up. If this happened [IJT-led torture and murder campaigns in Punjab Univer-sity, Lahore], then we should know this, admit it, and understand why. If it didn't, then we should be able to say so conclusively. I am really suffer-ing from this in my *da'wat* work. There are many educated women who are willing to join us but their husbands or brothers who were in colleges and universities at that time stop them, saying, "Their [JI] women may be ok, but you don't know what their men are like.'"

As is often the case with such mass-front organizations for closed cadre parties like the JI, the IJT enjoyed significant leeway from the parent body in experimenting with violence; this leeway was unlikely to be completely incidental, and more likely to be a matter of design. However, this relative independence was a double-edged sword, allowing IJT to take stances at variance with the parent organization. When the JI central leadership under Mian Tufayl was still enthralled with Zia's martial law takeover, the IJT in Punjab University passed a resolution against martial law regime, urging a return to democratic politics.[54] For the IJT, which had just consolidated its control on several important university campuses through a mix of violence, persuasion, and organization, a democratic environment held greater promise than for the JI at a national level. Today, through the IJT, the JI has an institutionalized link with the middle- and lower-middle-class students who use the public universities that IJT has access to.[55] I have attempted here to discuss both the limitations and the potentials embedded in IJT today. Kandiyoti's warning about Islamist movements whose "tolerance of pluralism is undemonstrated, and whose intolerance of opposition is quite evident" (quoted in Abu-Lughod 1998, 25) demands serious attention. But so does the dynamic character of political and social players. The IJT is unlike any other student body in Pakistan's history. While the other student bodies like PSF and MSF have degenerated completely into local gangs operating with little or no ideological training and with only sporadic access to political parties with which they were affiliated at some stage, the IJT, the longest-running student union in Pakistan, is a body of relatively organized students who act as a bridge—imperfect, flawed and not fully representative, but a bridge nevertheless where none other exists—between the least-represented segments of Pakistani society and one of the major political parties in the country.[56]

Jama'at and Peasant Groups

When the Okara[57] peasant movement, a cause célèbre among liberal/left circles in Pakistan, began in mid-2000, the movement's leaders originally approached the Kissan Board in their area. The Kissan Board is closely associated with the Jama'at-e-Islami, whose amir Maulana Maududi famously opposed land reforms in the 1950s on the grounds that they were un-Islamic. The Okara movement started when the military agencies, which own close to seventy thousand acres of land in Central Punjab, attempted to introduce a contract system to replace the traditional *batai* (sharecropping) system that had been in place for more than a century. Peasants working on these military lands rebelled against the contract system, protesting that this was the first step in a plan to eventually evict them and pave the way for corporate farming. That the Kissan Board was their first choice for highlighting their predicament implies a relationship between the board and the small farmers and peasants. Critics of the Kissan Board and JI have admitted this much.[58] The board helped organize the initial protests, to which the military responded as the military is trained to; six peasants have been killed, dozens injured, and the leaders of the movement jailed several times.

By 2005, the movement had split along issues of tactics and leadership, some elements remaining close to the Kissan Board and others moving closer to NGOs. The Kissan Board's role in the Okara uprising remains controversial, as does the role of other players; critics claim that the Kissan Board was too conciliatory toward the military, as well as too opportunistic in its zealous proselytizing missions among the peasants, more than 80 percent of whom are Christians. Nevertheless, it is important to realize that no other national political party in Pakistan has institutional links, however tenuous, with peasants or small farmers; the movement's other choice for an alliance were NGOs,[59] not any of the other national or regional political parties. No other national-level political party in Pakistan currently raises the issue of feudalism in its rallies.[60] How did the Jama'at-e-Islami, a party whose ideology focused on transforming the *mu'assir tabqa* (the influential class) to take over the state, develop linkages with the small farmers and the peasants of Okara?

The term "feudalism" has received much academic criticism over the last four decades. In the case of Pakistan, some have made the case that feudalism does not exist except in small pockets, and that the agricultural economy has been deeply enmeshed in capitalist production since colonial times.[61] My intention here is not to provide an analysis of the *kind* of feudalism present in Pakistan. Here, I find it useful to keep in mind what Dipesh Chakrabarty notes regarding Orientalism: "The phenomenon of Orientalism does not disappear simply because some of us have now attained a critical awareness of it."[62] Put differently, critical analysis does not make a problem go away. Regardless of the definition of "feudalism" used and its applicability to Pakistan, the term *jagirdari nizam* remains important in Pakistani colloquial use to denote a broad experience and understanding of severely unequal land holdings and the social and political relations that surround this unequal access. My intention here is to point toward some of the changes in the rhetoric and strategies of JI in raising certain issues and using a particular language. I turn now to the leftist mobilizations of the late 1960s and early 1970s among the peasants and the JI's response to them.

Toba Tek Singh Kissan Conference and *Yaum-e-Shaukat-e-Islam*

The Toba Tek Singh Kissan Conference and the Shuakat-e-Islam demonstrations in response to it serve as useful illustration of the Jama'at tailoring its responses to the strategies of the left. The Toba Tek Singh Conference epitomizes in some ways the peak of broad multiparty leftist political mobilization in Pakistan. The PPP became the political platform for most leftist mobilizations in West Pakistan soon afterward, so that the PPP and the left became synonymous for many of the activists and for their opponents. The eventual disillusionment with the PPP because of Bhutto's authoritarian style, and the persecution of PPP activists under Zia's regime, had a significant impact on leftist mobilizations in the country. That the JI organized the Jalsa Shaukat-e-Islam in direct response to the Kissan Conference provides some insight into the way the JI was increasingly defining itself primarily in opposition to the left. A joint history of Toba Tek Singh and Shaukat-e-Islam is also useful to highlight the different slogans of the time and to trace changes in the JI position since then.

Toba Tek Singh is a small town, a *qasbah*,[63] in Pakistani Punjab. There were important symbolic and practical reasons for holding the conference there. Saadat Hasan Manto, onetime member of the Progressive Writers Association, has immortalized the name Toba Tek Singh through his eponymous masterpiece.[64] Criticism of religion-based nationalism in that particular story combined with Manto's body of work defying social structures, and his association with the Progressive Writer's Association, came together to endow Toba Tek Singh with great symbolic resonance for left activists. The Toba and its surrounding areas had also been home to some of the key communist leaders of pre-Partition Punjab, including Sohan Singh Josh.[65] Toba Tek Singh comprised primarily small land-holding peasant farmers, but lay close to the periphery of the large feudal lands of Jhang. The inhabitants of the town were relatively well off and educated. All of these factors probably contributed to a higher than average level of political organization and awareness in the qasba. As many writers in left-leaning magazines like *Al-Fatah* and *Lail-o-nahar* reminded readers, Toba Tek Singh was the only qasbah in Punjab in which Ayub Khan had only two more votes than Fatima Jinnah. Much prior to the Kissan Conference being held there, it was known as Pakistan's own Leningrad.[66]

Hajra Masroor,[67] writing in *Al-fatah* (September 24–October 1, 1970, 13), notes that: "Since the Kissan conference was held in this qasba, Toba Tek Singh's name has certainly reached the nation's newspaper readers.

According to our newspapers the mentioned conference was a huge failure. Nevertheless all the leaders of our time have started to believe it is essential that they give a speech in Toba Tek Singh."

This gives some indication of the strength of reaction to the conference that was held from March 23 to 25, 1970. The decision to hold the Kissan Conference was made in 1969, and hectic mobilizations in Punjab (primarily in Faisalabad, Jhang, Sargodha, Multan, Khanewal, Dera Ismail Khan, and Sahiwal) laid the foundation for the conference.[68] There was significant contention regarding the number of people who attended the conference, the organizers claiming close to two hundred thousand and the opponents as low as seventy-five thousand.[69] Nevertheless the conference was important enough to receive continuous coverage on the front page of national dailies like *Dawn* and *Pakistan Times*[70] for a few days. Maulana Bhashani, Bengali leader of the NAP, traveled in a special train from Lahore that also carried students, laborers, unionists, and other activists. While the NAP was the sponsor of the conference, the PPP, Labor party, Islam League, Khaksars, Jam'iyat Ulama Pakistan, Pakistan Trade Union Federation (PTUF), Sind Hari Committee, National Students Federation (NSF), Awami Fikri Mahaz, and West Pakistan Students Union were among the more prominent participating organizations. A large number of journalists, both local and foreign, were also present to cover the event.[71] The train, covered in red banners and flags, stopped at various stations en route, including Sheikhupura, Sangla, Chak Jhumra, and Gojra; Maulana Bhashani addressed the crowds gathered at each of the stations briefly. At Toba Tek Singh, the conference organizers had set up tents for the participants, but many of the houses in the qasba were also open to conference attendees. The main conference area was a converted playground that the organizers claimed could seat approximately 150,000 people.[72]

The slogans and the demands raised at the conference reflected local concerns enthused by an international context of leftist and nationalist struggle in China and Vietnam, in particular. Maulana Bhashani demanded that the government hold a referendum to ask if the people wanted "Islamic socialism." If the military regime failed to do that, he claimed, "We might have to resort to guerrilla warfare."[73] Bhashani pointed out that the Ayub government had alleged that thirty thousand guerrillas were operating in East Pakistan; questioning those numbers, he nevertheless insisted that if the government failed to hold the referendum on Islamic socialism, there would be many more guerrillas. This threat and the passionate cry at the podium of another leader, Masih ur Rehman, that "Yahya Khan is a traitor to the country" became the most-cited quotations from the conference, particularly in Jama'at and government-sympathetic newspapers and journals. As a consequence, the key demands raised by the conference received much less media attention; the primary demand highlighted by almost all the speakers was for the restructuring of National Assembly representation on class basis.[74] Land redistribution and changes in the system of *batai*, or division of produce, were important demands in keeping with the theme of the conference, which, of course, was focused on the peasants and farmers of Pakistan. The cry that emanated most frequently from the crowd was "*Jera vahvay, ohoi khavay*" (He who tills should be the one who eats).

The eighty-year-old Bhashani's formulation of "Islamic socialism" was a combination of religious symbols with socialist demands. At the conference, Bhashani claimed that his party, the NAP, was not a communist organization, but that "My party wants to nationalise the means of production in the name of God Almighty, because God is the real owner of every thing in the world." Claiming that it was the order of God to fight for rights, Bhashani declared war against the "30 monopolists, and 5000 feudals" who controlled Pakistan. In fact, Bhashani said that he believed Pakistan was ready for Islamic socialism and it could be imposed within two years, stating, "No power on earth can prevent the establishment of *Hakumat-i-Rabbani* [government of God]."[75] Continuing the use of Islamic imagery, Bhashani presented jihad as struggle against injustice and pointed out that the red cap was not the monopoly of China or Russia but a symbol of jihad against all injustices. Bhashani's use of Islamic symbols and the participation of some members of ulama, like the JUI's Maulana Hazarwi and Jama'at's own dissident Maulana Kausar Niazi, were a clear threat to the Jama'at's monopoly over religious discourse—a threat that JI was quick to perceive, and react to, as we shall see later.

There can be little doubt that all the participants, the "leaders" and the "followers," the intellectuals and the farmers, were not always talking about the same things. The gap between the farmers and the middle- and upper-class speakers could be immense. Aziz ud din Ahmed recounts, "As Faiz [Ahmed Faiz, renowned Pakistani poet] read his Persian laden poem at the Kissan conference, there was a part in his poem which went something like 'tum hi Nazeer bhi aur Basheer bhi.' The farmer sitting next to me asked what is he talking about? Who is Nazeer and which one is Basheer?"[76] At the political level, while the NAP was a major organizer of this conference, the PPP emerged as the more organized and vocal political party. PPP banners, flags, and activists were present in sufficient numbers and with ample enthusiasm to leave many journalists with the impression that the PPP had the most representation at the conference. Bhutto did not attend the conference, not wanting to be associated too closely with a movement demanding an immediate end to feudalism, but he sent instead a delegation of various PPP leaders with Malik Miraj Khalid. Nevertheless, the Kissan Conference was a remarkable achievement in bringing many different elements of the left together and articulating some common program of demands. Ultimately, it does seem to have become a campaign in which, as the members of the Kissan Committee claim, the other left and liberal democrat movements could not afford to not participate. For many of the younger left activists, like those involved with the Professors' Group and the Pakistan Youth Forum (both based in Lahore), this also presented the first opportunity for mass mobilization and contact.

This coming together, however momentary and fleeting, of the left parties was not lost on the Jama'at-i-Islami. As Maulana Maududi announced that the *Islam Pasand* (Islam-loving) forces in the country would give an answer to the Kissan Conference on May 31 in Shaukat-e-Islam rallies across the country, with a major one in Lahore, Jama'at activists went to work to portray this movement as larger than Jama'at's own political agenda. The editorial in *Zindagi* asked:

> Why is it that a small minority [the left] is able to succeed in its plans? In our view, the answer is clear, and it is that although the socialist elements are divided in many groups and fronts, they come together for common aims. . . . When, on March 23rd the Toba Tek Singh Kissan Conference was held, none of the socialist fronts and parties refused to join it by saying that it is a show of power by M. Bhashani, making it successful would establish the greatness of Bhashani. . . . The reaction of some Islamic circles to celebrating 31st March as *Yaum-I-Shaukat I Islam* indicates that they are deluded into thinking that a show of power by the Islamic forces of Pakistan will provide the credit to a particular person or party. (*Zindagi*, June 1, 1970)

This editorial highlights the predicament in which the leftist mobilizations had placed the JI. Not only were they losing control over Islamist discourse to the left, given Maulana Bhashani's, and increasingly Bhutto's as well,[77] populist formulation of Islamic socialism, they were facing intense competition from within the ranks of the other Islamic parties, particularly ulama parties.[78] Ultimately, the JI was able to organize a fairly large demonstration in Lahore[79] and significant others in cities like Multan. The publicity for the *jalsa* (public meeting) was aided by sympathetic newspapers like *Nawa-I-Waqt* and *Chatan* (edited by Agha Shorish Kashmiri, a well-known journalist sympathetic to the Jama'at-e-Islami). Of more immediate and practical help were the local mosque custodians, or *maulvis*, who were given the text of their Friday sermon by JI activists to rouse public opinion and participation. In Lahore, a procession winding its way through different parts of the city's main financial area culminated in speeches at the Mall Road, which "highlighted the dangers of socialism to Pakistan."[80] The official JI reason for holding Shaukat-e-Islam was explained by Salim Ahmed Salimi, a longstanding Shura member: "We organized Shaukat-e-Islam to highlight the bankruptcy of socialism to the people. We undertook a campaign in mosques and in neighborhoods, through pamphlets and articles, to tell people that there were no mosques any more in Russia."[81]

Information about the closure of mosques in the USSR had been filtering into Pakistan since the early 1960s. As a policy, it was only undertaken in the USSR toward the mid-1950s (Malashenko 1993, 65). It is interesting to note that even as JI focused most of its attention on discrediting the revolution in Russia, it was actually the Chinese experience that had galvanized much of the second wave of leftist mobilization in the late 1960s. The first wave of Russian-influenced mobilization, particularly under the Communist Party of Pakistan, had petered out by the late 1950s. China's support for Pakistan in the 1965 war against India had paved the way for public affection and official leniency toward the influx of Chinese literature in Pakistan.[82] Significantly, leftist influence in the cultural arena and in centers of higher learning, universities, and colleges was felt much more acutely by JI than any other religious group because of JI's reliance, in the absence of its own madrasa network, on universities and colleges for membership, expansion, and influence. This focus on "secular" universities and colleges was not incidental to the JI's strategy but central to it. Jama'at's focus on creating a vanguard organization meant that the JI was heavily dependent on colleges and universities—where the "leaders of tomorrow" were being educated—for its membership and activism. The strength of left mobilization in the centers of higher education was a serious threat to JI, and the first site of its engagement with the left in the early 1960s (Iqtidar 2006). Ch. Rehmat Ali,[83] a key member of JI *shura* and *naib amir* (assistant commander) at that time insists: "Yes, we [the JI] had focused on working against socialism at that time. . . . You have to think of it from our perspective then. We were truly worried. . . . There was a real danger from the socialists, with the international environment as it was, and Russia so close by. In universities and colleges you would find students and teachers wearing Mao badges. It might not be something that seems very important today, but at that time we were really worried."

Pitting the "secularism" and "atheism" of socialism against JI's Islamic program, portraying the debate as one about religion, the campaign was nevertheless rooted in the political situation of the country. Party-based national-level elections had not been held in the country since the beginning of Ayub's martial law regime. The JI hoped to participate in the forthcoming elections in 1970, and leftist parties like the NAP and PPP were providing a greater challenge than the JI had contended with before. Indeed, it seems that the JI leaders and activists, buoyed by their success as a pressure group over the last two decades, had overestimated their electoral strength. In part due to this expectation, as yet untested, of their popular appeal, JI had fielded the second highest number of candidates (151 candidates for 300 National Assembly seats) of all the political parties that contested the 1970 elections. JI's dismal performance in the elections was a shock to the organization, with important implications for the leadership, which I discuss below.[84]

As much as the slogan of the Kissan Conference was "*Jera vahvay ohoi khavay*," the slogan of the Shaukat-e-Islam was "*Socialism ka qabristan-Pakistan, Pakistan*" (Pakistan—the graveyard of socialism). It was this lack of an alternative plan, this resort to "Islam is a complete way of life," and the negativity of the Jama'at campaign that led to allegations of it being the government's arm. Many within the left also claimed that JI was funded by the US to obstruct the path of "progress" in Pakistan, and the lack of a clear program other than its opposition to socialism was proof of this.

Ideological Commitments; Practical Challenges

Even as the Jama'at continued to publicly decry socialism, internal discussion and debate was influenced by the demands raised by the left activists. It is no coincidence that the Jama'at manifesto, passed by *shura* in 1969 and published in 1970, incorporated a stance, however weak by left standards, on land redistribution. This manifesto, passed by the *Markazi Majlis e Shura* (Central Consultative Committee) on December 20, 1969, made some concessions to socioeconomic realities by noting: "Due to the imposition of a wrong system of agricultural ownership for a long time, many inequalities may arise. To end those we should act on the *shari'at*'s principle that unusual measures (*tadabir*) that do not clash with the principles of Islam can be adopted in unusual circumstances" (Jama'at e Islami Manifesto/Manshoor 1970, 23).

This was a significant change in JI policy, keeping in mind that Maududi had publicly opposed the land reform by Prime Minister Liaqut Ali Khan in Punjab during the 1950s. He had justified large landholdings in Islamic law and claimed that such a measure would pervert the establishment of an Islamic state in Pakistan.[85] Thus when the 1969 manifesto (Jama'at e Islami Manifesto/Manshoor 1970, 23) recommended "ending all those new and old properties that have been accumulated through wrongful means during any government," it was a radical departure from the JI's established stance. However, its emulation of leftist strategies had limits. The JI *manshoor* (manifesto) suggested that "traditional ownership" be limited in West Pakistan to one hundred to two hundred acres and accordingly where production was low due to the condition of the land. More land than that should be bought on fair (*munsifana*) terms by the government. Finally, this innovation had to be seen as a temporary measure only; it could not be given a permanent position because constant innovation/application would clash with not just the Islamic law of inheritance but also various other shari'a norms (Jama'at e Islami Manifesto/Manshoor, 23). The list of caveats to the proposal of land redistribution highlights the JI leadership's reluctance at having to address the issue at all, as well as the pressure exerted by the competition with the leftist mobilizations.

In a move to infiltrate the opposition, the JI made some organizational extensions into the very heart of leftist mobilization—among the students, labor unions, and peasants—through the Kissan Board. In relation to its stance on feudalism, the Kissan Boards were to play an important role in later years. Maoist literature and influence in Pakistan had risen significantly since the 1965 war in which China had assisted Pakistan and reaped immense gains in popular support as a result. The Maoist model was particularly inspirational in its seeming suitability for a predominantly agricultural country such as Pakistan. The Russian model depended too heavily on the existence of an urban working class that was largely absent in the Pakistan of the 1960s. Left mobilizations were not limited to cities and industrial workers, but were also beginning to impact rural areas. The Jama'at organized the Kissan Board in 1976 to deal specifically with the concerns of the peasants and the small farmers, and in response to the leftist mobilizations in this field. The scope of its work among peasants has remained limited, but over the years it has formed strong links with small farmers in certain areas, particularly the Punjab.

Jama'at Islami and Labor Unions

The Jama'at's move to create a presence in various labor and professional unions is of particular interest because it demonstrates sharply not just the impact of leftist mobilizations on JI strategies, but also that there is significant elasticity within Islamist ideology. The JI India expressly decided against a move to build a presence in unions,[86] even as the JI Pakistan started several initiatives in that direction. Currently JI has affiliated unions working among different professional groups including college and university lecturers, doctors, homeopathic doctors, lawyers, agri-scientists, and the business community. Here I shall focus on the National Labor Federation, the Jama'at-affiliated labor federation working among the industrial and service sectors, which comprise primarily lower-middle-class and working-class laborers.

Given the relatively low levels of industrialization and increasing deindustrialization as existing industries close under the pressure of structural adjustments, the extremely limited sphere of labor organization, and active repression in Pakistan, one could reasonably ask why the JI bothered at all to start mobilizing in this arena.[87] It is important to realize that at the time that the JI seriously extended its operations in unions, in the late 1960s, labor unions were part of a larger movement and could quite justifiably expect to play an increasingly important role in the Pakistani state. Perusing the Jama'at-affiliated magazine *Zindagi*, one notices, in the late 1960s, a trend of increasing concern for the conditions of "the worker" in industry, in the service sector, and in the informal sector.

Having played an important role in toppling Ayub Khan's regime, labor unions received considerable attention from Bhutto, as well as Zia. Bhutto learned from the example of Ayub Khan and moved swiftly after his own victory to curb the power of the unions.[88] One can easily imagine the parallels Zia must have drawn with Ayub's military rule, after he himself imposed martial law. Recognizing the role that students and unions played in toppling Ayub Khan's regime, he sought to prevent a similar fate for himself by banning all unions, including student unions in colleges and schools, right after assuming power.[89] In later years he cultivated the Islamist unions as an antidote to the influence of the left-leaning unions of the time. In the public sector in particular, where the government had greater say, the Zia regime was able to provide patronage to Islamist elements in the form of official recognition of and concessions to JI union demands, resources for organizing and holding rallies, police cover in fights with rival unions, and police negligence in registering or following up on cases registered against the JI activists. At the same time, specific laws were passed to break the strength of existing left/liberal unions, as in the case of Pakistan Railways.[90] State support for JI during this period also meant that JI members were often parachuted into positions of responsibility in organizations, leading ultimately to changes in the constituency of the unions. This was compounded with the grassroots work that some JI labor workers had been doing for a decade or so already. In a bid to rid important enterprises of leftist influence, Zia's regime provided support in expanding the JI base in most public-sector enterprises so that by the 1990s, the key enterprises that faced privatization under increasing pressures from the IMF and the World Bank were the ones in which JI unions were strong.

The National Labor Federation (NLF), which is the current form of Jama'at's labor wing, boasts of having the largest number of unions affiliated with it. In addition, the NLF claims to have the key unions in Pakistan's public sector (like WAPDA,[91] KDA, National Shipping Yard) as well as in the biggest enterprises, like Pakistan Steel Mills, PIA, and most banks. Many of the Islamist unions formed and nurtured during and after the Zia regime became used to playing a critical role in the organizations they were part of. Thus, in the Pakistani case, many of the organized labor groups that managed to survive the low level of industrial activity, the repression, and the co-option include predominantly Islamist middle management and leaders.[92] And now it is within these sectors that the pace of privatization and liberalization has increased over the last decade, but with increasing resistance from the previously "pocket unions."

Significantly, the liberal elite has welcomed privatizations as a means of getting rid of the Islamist influence, without much concern for the decreased access this would lead to for the middle and lower-middle classes in critical sectors like healthcare and education.[93] The Islamists in unions are thus facing the double pressure of privatizations and the Musharaf regime's public resolve to root out Islamist influences. This intensified pressure is forcing many Islamists to abandon their previously close relationship with the army and the state. At the same time, this oppositional stance of the Islamists holds an attraction to those who feel the state has reneged on its promises of healthcare, education, and employment to them, and they are brought into the folds of Islamist groups even when they may not feel much affinity with the religious rhetoric. The JI today is the only political party with a direct and official link to labor unions; JI central leadership meets at least once a year[94] with the NLF leadership, and NLF headquarters at Mansoorah provide relatively easy, informal access to JI leadership. This link, among others, has played a role in changes in the JI's stance towards "imperialism," a term that JI literature, leaders, and members use with increasing frequency now. By "imperialism," these JI activists and leaders mean the economic, political, and cultural influence of the US government. Multinational companies, the US government, and the Israeli state are perceived as linked and supportive of each other. Their use of this term has not led to any internal theorizing about the differences between imperialism (*Samraj*), and colonialism (*Nau-abadiyati Nizam*), nor to any sustained analysis of how this imperialism may be substantively different from imperialism of the 1960s, when leftists accused the JI of supporting imperialism by aligning themselves with the US against the USSR. In addition, the desired goal is not the eradication of imperialism, even if theoretically, but a substitution of US imperialism with Islamic imperialism. Nevertheless, JI remains the only political party that continuously raises issues of economic, political, and cultural independence in its training sessions, political rallies, and literature.

Allan Bloom's polemical and problematic *The Closing of the American Mind* (1987) has, at its core, an intriguing idea that merits further discussion. He has suggested that America's social and political problems stem from a "loss of narrative"—a narrative that had helped individuals mold their lives, and in the American case, a narrative that "relativism" destroyed by making the search for excellence obsolete. A narrative itself may be problematic, and certainly in Bloom's formulation the American narrative seems to have no space for nuances in gender, race, religion, or class, but it is the power of a narrative in shaping individuals as well as communities that interests me here. As I interviewed and met with labor unionists, it seemed to me that the most important difference between the JI and the liberal/left activists was that the JI activists had a definite narrative about their purpose, while the others were floundering with theirs. Given a history of repressions and almost continuous setbacks, especially in the recent past, it is not surprising to witness signs of increasing despondency among all union organizers. However, I was struck by a surer note among the JI union organizers. For instance, after he had recounted a long history of facing repression at his personal level in the form of jail sentences, I asked Mr. Saqib[95] why he and the NLF would want to be involved with organizing labor at all—why fight this losing battle? This was a question I had asked all the other union organizers as well, and at this juncture they had provided formulaic answers regarding commitment and wanting to improve the conditions for workers, with a lack of conviction that was at odds with their words. Mr. Saqib, however, had a fairly simple answer and a stronger sense of conviction. He claimed that he and the NLF felt a need for "continued politicization of workers. Under the current circumstances, this is the most important thing we can aim for." For the left-leaning union leaders, the key reference point was the level of union activity in the late 1960s and early 1970s. All of them repeatedly emphasized the loss of the link that workers had with students and teachers of the Punjab University and National College of Arts in Lahore. While this link has been broken for the left activists, the NLF continues to benefit from educated and committed organizers, within a dwindling space for labor organization in present-day Pakistan.

Working with the Islamists against "Imperialism"?

The last decade has seen a renewed interest in federation formation in Pakistan, bringing together unions that had previously competed against each other. There are ten major federations in Pakistan now. The largest two are the Pakistan Workers' Federation (PWC) and the National Labor Federation (NLF).[96] In its earlier stages, the PWC also invited the NLF to join in. In fact, the question of working with the Islamists is currently a much-debated one within the other unions, precisely because of the presence that the NLF has been able to establish. The union leaders I interviewed admitted significant soul searching within their organizations regarding this issue. This soul searching seemed to be triggered by the increasing dominance of the Islamists in the unions, and the consequent usefulness of forming an alliance with them when holding protests and rallies. Often the non-NLF union leaders would start off by recounting the previously close relationship between the army and the Jama'at, the fact that the Islamists were given state patronage to subvert "true" worker representation, and the many acts of violence perpetrated by the Islamists against the left activists. This would then lead to the question: "How can we trust them?"

One left-leaning union leader who had realized the potential of such an alliance and had used it was Nazim Husnain.[97] It is probably also fair to say that the mobilization that he has led has been the most successful in recent years in terms of getting its demands accepted by the government. Nazim Husnain, a self-professed leftist, contested for the position of the president of All Pakistan Lecturers Association against a Jama'at candidate. However, over the period from 2002 to 2005, when I conducted these interviews, they had been working together against further privatization of the remaining public universities and teaching hospitals by the Musharaf government through an act passed in 2002. Mr. Husnain formed alliances with the various Islamist student and staff associations across Pakistan to mobilize against these privatizations. In his own words, "We forged an issue-based alliance with anybody who had a stake in this . . . with the labor party, religious rights groups, Christians, Jama'at-e-Islami, Muslim Student's Federation . . . everybody. . . . So of course they publish these demands under their own name with their own spin sometimes, but what do we care? The issue reaches many more people than we can afford to involve on our resources."

In working with the Jama'at, he found that it stands out not just because of the number of people it can mobilize, but also in terms of the quality of its resources. "The IJT is the most well organized and politically trained of all the student unions. . . . Also we must admit that their women are extremely well trained politically, very vocal and very articulate. You can see that they must conduct regular study circles etc. . . . Within APLA too, their party discipline is quite strong. We have a working relationship with the Jama'at in APLA. If they agree with us they work with us, if they don't they just remain quiet . . . for now."

A key issue that emerges out of his experience is that the Islamists are now interested in publicizing the issues that Nazim Husnain, for instance, is raising: privatizations, lack of access to public health and education facilities, the influence of World Bank and IMF policies on Pakistan. This is not something that he or indeed many others on the left had imagined the religious groups would want to do in the last decade. Abid Hassan Manto, leader of the Nationalist Socialist Party and a veteran left politician and intellectual, claims that he was approached by Qazi Hussain Ahmed, amir of the JI, to organize antiglobalization rallies together. The fact that Manto declined to form this issue-based alliance is by his own admission due to a history of left/liberal relationships with the JI that he cannot move beyond. A key worry, as Ramay points out, is that "Now Jama'at has started writing on the walls: end the class system, end feudalism, end imperialism, end US hegemony. These are tactical changes on their parts. Their history is otherwise."[98]

But underlying this is also the concern that "we may end up being used instead of using them. There is no doubt in my mind that their organizational capability is much more than ours. . . . The only reason the fundamentalists bother with the trade unions is because they want to expand their social base, want to attract new people to their own groups by talking about peace, democracy, and in promoting populist policies."[99]

All of this contains elements of truth. But the question here is why has the JI concluded that this is the best way of expanding its social base? Why has it even bothered with a strategy to expand its social base at a time when the other political parties are not making any significant moves in that direction? Moreover, if these are really legitimate and pressing concerns, and the JI is trying to engage with them, why should the JI not be viewed as a legitimate political player? Nothing stops the other political parties like the PPP or the PML (Pakistan Muslim League—Nawaz group or any other faction) from raising similar issues or expanding their base in this way—and yet they do not.

The criticism that the Jama'at leadership is opportunistic and will renege on promises made to the rank and file is a valid one. This may happen just as it happened in the case of Bhutto, whose PPP provided a platform at one point to the peasants and workers in Pakistan for a potentially larger stake in national decision making. Once in power, Bhutto worked systematically to curb the very elements that had supported his rise, and formed alliances with those he had spoken against. However, the impact of that mobilization remained with a generation of Pakistanis and had a decisive impact on many aspects of Pakistani society, not least of which was some openings for the marginalized, albeit not as many as they had been led to expect (Jones 2003). Similarly, the JI's role in opening up space for debate on issues of national sovereignty and independence is acknowledged by all sides, even if the intention of its leaders is doubted. The success of the anti-Ayub mobilizations can be explained in part by using Sydney Tarrow's framework. Tarrow (1998) contends that movements[100] are successful when "divisions among elites not only provide incentives to resource-poor groups to take the risks of collective action; they encourage portions of the elite that are out of power to seize the role of 'tribunes of the people'" (1998, 79). Sustainable collective actions are those that build on dense networks of social groups and on common cultural norms, and are able to benefit from divisions within the elite through alliances with some part of it. Bhutto represented a disgruntled faction of the elite, the feudals who felt left out of the rapid industrialization policy under Ayub and so provided some support to the leftist mobilizations. It is useful to remember that the large majority of PPP ticketholders in the 1971 elections were in fact feudals, and certainly, shortly after coming into power, Bhutto sought to replace the more left-leaning advisers and ministers within the PPP with feudals. In fact, PPP policy choices, once in power, are easier to explain and understand with this in mind rather than their election manifesto.

The Jama'at-e-Islami, with its grassroots work among lower-middle-class constituencies, coupled with the upward mobility of some of its original members into the economic upper class, has significant potential to leverage its position as a bridge across these groups (Tarrow 1998). Yet the increasing heterogeneity of the JI's social base also creates tensions within the organization. In this regard the situation is likely to be similar to that observed by Joel Benin and Hossam el-Hamalawy (2007) in a recent MERIP report.[101] They report a convergence between elements of leftist unions and the Muslim Brother (MB) in organizing strikes within Egypt, although not without creating tensions within the MB.

Leadership Styles; Political Opportunities

JI's turn toward populism is both reflected and aided by Qazi Hussain Ahmed, the third amir. Qazi Hussain Ahmed, son of a Jam'iyat ulama Hind *alim* (scholar) from Khyber Pakhtunkhwa, may have carried over some of the JUH's nationalist zeal to the JI. With an MA in geography from the Peshawar University, he started out as an academic, lecturing at the university for three years. Nevertheless, his association with JI was longstanding even by then, as he had been associated with the IJT since his school days. At the end of the tenure of Mian Tufayl, who was the second amir of JI Pakistan, with Maududi as the first one, the JI *arakeen*[102] could choose between Prof. Khurshid Ahmed, a JI ideologue, Jan Mohammed Abbasi, amir of Sindh, and the then relatively youthful and more populist Qazi Hussain Ahmed. Qazi Hussain Ahmed's election signaled a desire for change among the JI members, moving away from the style and politics of Maududi.

Maududi had resolutely refused to engage with socioeconomic issues, seeing Western dominance and threat primarily in cultural terms. Even when the vigor of leftist mobilizations during the 1960s forced Maududi to engage with leftist analysis,[103] he remained unwilling, and unable, to place the economic before the cultural. With regard to feudalism in particular, JI under Maududi was unable to adequately reflect the aspirations of its social base. The Mohajir community that formed the bulk of JI members in its early years was resolutely antifeudalism. The US intelligence personnel in Pakistan suspected several JI leaders, like Maulana Islahi, of communist sympathies,[104] but Islahi and others who supported him were purged in a leadership battle early on in Jama'at's career in Pakistan.[105] Ultimately this inability to represent the Mohajir interests cost the JI dearly when the Mohajir Qaumi movement (MQM), formed in 1983, was able to woo away a large segment of JI's supporters in urban Sindh, leading to a crumbling away of JI hold in the cities of Karachi and Hyderabad. Within Punjab, the JI's initial support base composed primarily of petty government officers, small shopkeepers, small farmers, and local intellectuals (school and college teachers). In Lahore, its members were mostly new arrivals in the city from Punjab's smaller cities and rural areas—by and large all excluded from Pakistan's feudal-dominated political system. Antifeudalism was an instinctive cause for its constituency that the JI never mobilized under Maududi, who initially envisioned the JI as an elite group of accomplished and pious Muslims. JI's crushing defeat in the 1970 elections seems to have led to some soul searching both within the party ranks and on the part of Maududi himself. *Tarjuman ul Qur'an*, the party organ, printed several letters suggesting reorganizing the party and also proposing Maududi's substitution by a younger amir.[106] Such pressures, combined with Maududi's own apparent regret at the high level of JI politicization in the preceding years,[107] eventually led him to step down as amir in 1972.[108]

The JI under Mian Tufayl, a trusted Maududi aide and follower, was an organization in crisis by internal accounts.[109] This crisis is generally explained internally as precipitated by the Jama'at being initially fooled by the pious behavior of Zia. In this version, the JI agitated against martial law soon after it became clear that Zia had no intention of reinstating democracy, and its relationship with the military dictator soon turned confrontational. It would seem that the crisis was, in fact, deeper than this. JI's close relationship with the army, although denied by most JI leaders now, and at best a confusing episode for the activists, created unprecedented opportunities for organizational reach and personal gain for members at almost all levels of the party. The opportunities for corruption, at a personal and organizational level, alarmed many, and those within the Shura motivated by ideology, ideals, and differing political interests (e.g., the Karachi Jama'at, which turned against Zia due to his role in the creation of MQM) argued against continued cooperation with Zia.[110] Nevertheless, many JI leaders and some of its various affiliated bodies, like IJT, NLF, and *Anjuman Usatiza* (University and College Teacher's Association), worked closely with the regime and grew in importance during Zia's tenure. The balance between ideology and personal gain, precariously poised anyway in the "ideological political party" that the JI claims to be, tilted more heavily toward personal gain during Zia's regime, leading some members to worry about the survival and purpose of the organization. Mian Tufayl, to some extent, embodied this close relationship with the military. He hailed from Jallundhur, as did Zia, and seems to have valued a personal relationship with the general, taking pride in the consultations Zia solicited from him and the JI.[111] He is not known for doctrinal insights and organizational skill; his claim to leadership may have been mediated by his close relationship with both Maududi and Zia. Ultimately, it was the structure of the party, codified and institutionalized during the Maududi years, the presence of many with varying political interests, and a tightly knit social fabric of activists inhibiting blatant personal opportunism that prevented the JI from complete capitulation into Zia's arms.[112]

Qazi Hussain Ahmed had also grown in importance during Zia's regime, when he acted as the JI's contact for the Afghan Jihad. After being elected as amir, Qazi Hussain Ahmed has instituted some of the most far-reaching organizational changes in the party's history. Resolving, in a way, the long-standing debate within the JI about the indeterminately long and arduous selection process for becoming a rukn,[113] Ahmed has created a new category of "member" to cater to the JI's political aspirations. With a target of five million members Pakistan-wide, in parallel to the current approximately twenty thousand arakeen, this is meant to greatly extend the reach of the JI. The end of the Afghan Jihad, the harsh realities of the changed policy priorities of JI's onetime ally in Afghanistan,[114] and the introduction of a form of democracy in Pakistan allowed, or perhaps forced, Ahmed to expand on his populist tendencies and explore the grassroots links that the JI had made in response to the leftist mobilizations of the late 1960s and 1970s. Today the JI's stance on feudalism is almost indistinguishable from the slogans raised at the Toba Tek Singh Conference. The MMA, in which the JI plays a prominent role, provides in its manifesto for "the abolishment of all chronic and new feudal systems with forfeiture of illegal wealth and its distribution among the poor; and to provide lands to peasants and farmers for their livelihood; and guarantee reasonable prices for their produce" (MMA Manifesto 2001). Later on (point no. 14), the manifesto also declares the aspiration to "rid the country and people of influence of imperialist forces and their local agents."

Hussain Ahmed frequently speaks against feudalism and imperialism, and for democracy in his *jalsas* and rally speeches.[115] The JI party literature and activists are increasingly touching upon it in education and training sessions.[116] The 2006 Shura resolution notes that the general public is suf-

fering from "the growing curse of price hike, unemployment, inflation, social disparity and disappearing purchasing power, while on the other hand
the tillers, labour and government employees are being deprived of their
due rights. . . . The worst kind of western capitalist system has been practi-
cally imposed on the country, while corruption has reached to its peak."[117]

This radical change in JI policy from its active resistance to land reforms
in the 1950s to inclusion of antifeudal slogans in its rallies and manifestos
today is made more significant by the absence of even rhetorical mentions
against feudalism by the other political parties, even as the importance of
land redistribution in the still largely agricultural Pakistan remains undi-
minished.

The JI's members and activists—antifeudal in sentiment, upwardly mobile when upward mobility was more feasible given the expansion in employment and economy, and now struggling to preserve their lifestyles in
the face of increasing economic polarization in Pakistan[118]—are not trained
nor inclined to bring about a revolution. JI literature, activists, and leaders use the term *inquilab* (revolution) often enough, but what they actually
mean is evolution in the political context,[119] and a revolution, if at all, at the
personal level.[120] A share of the political pie, changes in laws and constitu-
tions, the instigation of social change, and the ultimate transformation of
the individual are JI's main aims, conceived of within the existing electoral
structure. The recent changes in US policies, placing Islamist groups under
domestic and international pressure, have forced JI leaders to explore the
potential within the links with the lower and lower-middle class that they
had formed in response to the pressures of leftist mobilizations during the
1960s and 1970s. This exploration has led the JI leadership to discover a
source of strength in their political ambitions: the potential for independent popular support. JI leadership seems to be increasingly aware of the
potential of populist themes and is in closer and more systematic contact
with various sections of the popularly termed "grassroots," including small
farmers through the Kissan Board, than any of the other political parties.
Quite apart from the challenge of building support among the rural voters, where local landholding families continue to hold considerable sway,
there are internal obstacles that hold the JI back from electoral success.
Their inexperience in mass representation and the political opportunism of
some leaders who rose to prominence particularly during Zia's regime is
not easily overcome. Ideology, a stumbling block in the past limiting the
JI's will to form mass links as a political party, particularly under Maududi's

leadership, may be its saving grace now by placing limits on the personal opportunism of its leadership.

In this chapter I have attempted to provide a historically embedded view of the emergence of JI as the foremost Islamist party in Pakistan opposing "secularism." Yet I hope to have also shown, first, that secularism was an easy target in a country with an extremely ambivalent relationship with religion and the political sphere; and second, that while the argument may have been defined in theological terms, the concerns that drove the JI and other players in their decisions have often been determined by the political context in which they operate. This cynical use of both "religion" and "secularism" by the military, the political elite, and by the Islamists has been critical in bringing the Islamists firmly into the domain of the non-sacred. In part as a consequence of this, the invocation of Islam in politics and public life is not received within contemporary Pakistan without a certain skepticism or cynicism on the part of the audience (Khan 2003). While much has been written about the legal and geopolitical implications of Islamization in Pakistan, its biggest impact has been in the realm of intellectual discourse—all public arguments and debates since the 1970s have had to engage with the role of Islam in Pakistan's state and society. It is the impact of this continued engagement about the role of religion in public and private life, in a landscape of fierce rivalry and competition among the Islamists, that I turn to in the next chapter.

CHAPTER THREE

Competition among Allies

JD AND JI IN URBAN LAHORE

[General] Musharaf says "Pakistan First,"[1] *and we go along because we have no view of what comes first.... We can't even impose Islam in a five-*marla[2] *house, we can't even it impose it on our four-feet-tall bodies, how can Musharaf impose Islam in Pakistan? What kind of Islam will he impose? How can we judge which is the right Islam?*

— JD leader addressing a meeting

In the previous chapter I discussed some of the changes that occurred in Islamist parties, particularly in the JI, due to their interaction with left groups in Pakistan. However, since the mid-1980s, the more significant challenge to the JI's ideological and political position has arisen from other Islamist parties in the country, as the left/liberal groups and parties succumbed to eleven years of pressure from the Zia regime and the dynamic adaptations of the Islamists. A changed international context, with the fall of the Soviet Union and the rise of the unipolar world, has also had an impact. More critically, within the increasingly Islamized public sphere, the JI has had to face mounting competition from other Islamist groups and carve out a niche in the ever more crowded market of Islamist parties in Pakistan. Negotiating the space between the state and the society, between the traditionalists and the Muslim modernists, between democracy and jihad, the Jama'at-e-Islami had to preserve its identity as well as grow its constituency. While attempting to balance itself on this tightrope, the more critical challenge to the JI came from other Islamist groups, particularly the more militant ones. In this chapter I argue that it is important to understand aspects of competition among Islamist groups to grasp the dynamics of their long-term impact. One such implication of this competition, fluid and interactive in nature, is an objectification of belief and practice.

Literature on party competition has tended to model and analyze the changes within parties (Bernholz and Vaubel 1998; Kitschelt, 1989; Roemer 2001) and their policies (Laver and Hunt 1992) in the context of elections. However, Jama'at-e-Islami and Jama'at-ud-Da'wa do not compete directly for electoral support. In fact, while Jama'at-e-Islami operates as a political party, Jama'at-ud-Da'wa does not participate in elections. Yet both are in competition with each other for popular support and acceptance. They cannot be classified as lobby groups; neither can the two groups be defined solely as social movements. Here I do not disagree with those who have suggested that Islamism needs to be seen as a social movement (Burke and Lapidus 1988; Ahmad 2009; and Bayat 2007), but suggest that individual groups within the larger Islamist movement should be assessed also as parties or organizations in their own right. This is useful, in particular, to understand the dynamics of change in the direction or emphasis of the movement.

Analysis of competition between political parties has depended heavily on the model introduced by Anthony Downs (1957), in part because of its simplicity. Downs's model reduces various aspects of the political process to aspects of a race for acquisition of power between two political candidates, disregarding the role of activists and policy preferences within the parties. As Roemer has perceptively suggested (2001, 2), "the price of its simplicity is the elimination of politics from political analysis." Roemer's own attempt at developing a theory of competition is intended to introduce some of this complexity back into the modeling process. While useful at some levels, it is a largely static model, lacking a nuanced understanding of the long-term implications of the competition among these players, not just for themselves, but also for the society at large. Herbert Kitschelt's (1989) detailed and fairly descriptive study of the emergence of green parties from the larger social movements of the 1960s provides many interesting and useful parallels with the changes taking place within Islamism. Kitschelt (1989, 42) points out that scholars have explained party organization, programs, and strategies in terms of four variables: (1) the ideology of the core constituency; (2) prerequisites and consequences of organization coordination; (3) imperatives of the electoral marketplace; and (4) institutional constraints on party competition. However, he finds that "most classical theorists have treated imperatives of electoral marketplace as the decisive determinants of party structure and strategy." By shifting the emphasis away from the electoral marketplace, Kitschelt (1989, 46–62) extends our understanding of intraparty competition in shaping the strategies and structure of a political party. However, he too does not focus on interparty competition in much detail, nor on the long-term impact of that competition on the social movement and society at large.

Literature on "Muslim fundamentalism" is beginning to recognize the complexity of the various groups operating within this umbrella term. Competition between these groups has been pointed out, but its implications have not been studied in any detail. In this chapter, I shall first provide an overview of the diversity of groups classified under the generic term "Muslim fundamentalist" as well as some idea of the extent of competition between these different groups. I then give a brief historical overview of the Jama'at-ud-Da'wa's origins and political role by focusing on key concepts of da'wa and *shahadat* (martyrdom). This leads into a discussion of how the competition between Jama'at-e-Islami and Jama'at-ud-Da'wa is generated and played out at a local level. Finally, to highlight the impact of this competition in terms of an objectification of religious practice and belief in urban Pakistan, I point out Islamism's key differences with traditionalist Islam.

"Muslim Fundamentalist": Too Broad a Category?

The term "Muslim fundamentalist," while being used almost synonymously with "medieval, reactionary, militant and oppressive of women" (Metcalf, 1994, 706), is a vast umbrella term that covers a range of different groups, often with conflicting agenda and strategies.[3] Some groups, like the Tablighi Jama'at that Metcalf (1994, 2002) has studied, focus on personal change and profess an apolitical stance; others, like the Jama'at-I-Islami, openly advertise their aim of controlling the state apparatus. Groups like Lashkar-e-Jhangavi and Sipah-e-Mohammed are militant organizations that aim to annihilate each other.[4] Rafiuddin Ahmed (1994, 670) draws a further distinction between *fundamentalism* as "shorthand to gain entry into some more compelling and discrete reality" and the *conservatism* of many ulama, *pirs* (sufi saints), and *mullahs* (religious teachers) who seek to return to the laws of Islam but reject militant and political stances. Many fundamentalists in turn are contemptuous toward the conservatives, who tend to support forms of popular religion.

The editors of the "Fundamentalist Project"—a multiyear study of world fundamentalism that resulted in the publication of five volumes— found the term fruitful in terms of generating research across a broad spectrum of religions, and not just Islam, but the wide range of movements and organizations studied within the project has led to significant controversy.[5]

Increasingly scholars are making a distinction between the "fundamentalists" and the "Islamists";[6] the Islamists are products of modern, secular educational institutions but are drawn to initiatives aimed at radically altering their societies and states. Mohammed Qasim Zaman (2002) alerts us to the differences within Muslim scholars, highlighting the different roles that the ulama, Islamists, and Muslim modernists have played and continue to play. In the case of Pakistan, he highlights the different approaches of the Islamists, the modernists, the militants, and the ulama in terms of their relationship to the state; the ulama have been the most skeptical of the power of the state.[7]

Critically, the various groups claiming Islam as their raison d'être do not always see each other as working in complement. The ulama have traditionally distanced themselves from militant organizations, even when providing the intellectual justification for militancy; political parties like Jama'at-e-Islami have tended to distance themselves from apolitical groups like the Tablighi Jama'at;[8] and the militants have denounced Islamists and Muslim modernists.[9] Another important area of division and difference are the juridical and philosophical schools of Islam, the different *mazahib* (singular: *mazhab*), which are not insignificant. In the case of Pakistan, radicalized sectarian identities, both Shia and Sunni, have received some academic attention (Abou Zahab 2002; Nasr 2002; Zaman 1998, 2002). Within Sunni Islam, further divisions among the Barelvi, Deobandi, and Ahl-e-Hadīs exist, each with further cleavages within the broad *maslak*/mazhab. As Gilles Dorronsoro (2002, 168) has noted, "Under the generic term 'Deobandi' one finds in fact different kinds of discourses and one cannot overestimate the education of their *ulama* and the coherence of their ideology." Similarly, within Shia Islam there are several different schools.[10]

The proliferation of different schools within each sect can be seen in part as a result of the turmoil introduced into the Muslim world by colonialism. In the South Asian context, before colonialism, Muslim scholars had to contend with the role of the ruler and ruled, but the rulers had been, at least nominally, Muslims. The rupture in thought due to colonialism has been greater in the case of Muslim societies than the Western/Christian ones. Accordingly, a large number of schools of thought emerged in Muslim societies, and their relationship changed over time with regard to each other as well as to the state and other political actors. In India, in particular, Muslims faced a complicated situation; not only were they not rulers anymore, but worse, they were in a numerical minority compared to the Hindus in an age when numbers, through electoral politics, were beginning to play an increasingly important role. In addition, the colonial administration, though initially concerned with building on local structures, nevertheless introduced far-reaching changes in everyday life through legal codification, mechanics of disciplinary control, and new technologies. Postindependence, other international factors have also played a role in highlighting the differences between different sects and schools of Islam. In Pakistan, over the last two decades proxy wars between Iran and Saudi Arabia have been fought by the Shias and Sunnis, aided by the local Islamization campaign initiated by Zia. The hardening of sectarian identities due to the violence used by religious groups has gone beyond the Shia/Sunni divide to encompass divisions within Sunnis.

Some insight into the differences amongst the various "fundamentalist" groups is also provided by a look at their annual gatherings, which are increasingly attracting large numbers. The Tablighi Jama'at's annual congregation at Raiwind is considered the second-largest congregation of Muslims after the Haj.[11] It was attended by some two million participants in 2001 (Shafqat 2002, 131). The Tablighi Jama'at's congregation is the most socially diverse one, with participants ranging from high-ranking public officials, merchants, key industrialists, and professionals including university professors and doctors, to manual workers. In terms of ethnic origins, too, it is the most diverse, with visible Punjabi, Pakhtoon, Mohajir, East Asian, African, and Arab presence (Shafqat 2002, 131).[12] In contrast, the Lashkar-i-Tayyiba/Jama'at-ud-Da'wa's annual congregation was attended by one million participants in 2001, and was dominated by lower-middle-class merchants, peasants, and petty government employees, primarily from Punjab and Khyber Pakhtunkhwa (Shafqat 2002, 132).

Ultimately the common thread binding these groups together for Western policy and academia, and at times local administration, is their aggressive use of religion to situate and justify their actions. This commonality was often not recognized by the various groups themselves, for instance, in the case of the Shia and Sunni groups that are bent on annihilating each other, or in the case of Jama'at-e-Islami and JUI, which often took politically opposed stances. Interestingly, the increasing pressure due to changed US policies[13] is forcing many groups to work together. The formation of the MMA, bringing together Barelvis (JUP), Deobandis (JUI), Ahl-e-Hadīs (JAH), Shias (ITP), ulama, militants (ITP and JAH), and Islamists (JI), was a key step in that direction. However, this alliance remained fragile and is now defunct. The ideological divide between the Barelvis and the Wahhabis, the ethnic divide between JUP (significant Pashtoon constituency) and Jama'at-e-Islami (significant Urdu-speaking and Punjabi constituency), and the tactical divide between the militant groups (Lashkar-e-Jhangvi, for instance) and the primarily Da'wa groups (Tablighi Jama'at) has to be understood in a context of shifting priorities and historical path dependencies. The purpose of highlighting these differences is not to imply that the category "Muslim fundamentalist" is obsolete or that it serves no useful analytical purpose. Rather, the intention is to build a nuanced understanding of a dynamic and constantly evolving situation. The importance of acknowledging these differences lies in improving our understanding of the role these differences play in the current situation as different groups compete for access to and control of funds, constituencies, legitimacy, and a role in shaping the future.

One aspect of Islamism that has received very little attention is that of competition among the various Islamist groups. Most of the literature on Islamism either assumes relative homogeneity particularly with regard to shared goals,[14] or does not provide any extensive comment on the existence and impact of competition among the various groups. Some academic work has been concerned with analyzing a particular group in detail,[15] but without engaging with the dynamics of competition with other groups. S. V. R. Nasr, Mohammed Qasim Zaman, and Mariam Abou Zahab have focused on the sectarian dimension of competition among the religious groups in Pakistan, but have not attempted to analyze the impact of this competition on the overall influence of Islamism in Pakistan. In reality the various groups in Pakistan have often viewed each other as competitors rather than as allies. That the outside eye tends to see them as one is a realization that seems to have only recently made its mark among these groups in Pakistan.

While not all Islamists are militants, a significant number are. Militant Islamists, in particular, compete for funds from foreign and local donors that are necessary for their survival and operations. John Cooley (2000) gives some idea of the scale of CIA (Central Intelligence Agency) support for training and recruitment of "jihadis," and Saeed Shafqat (2002) provides some insight into the factionalism and fragmentation of the religious parties as these CIA funds started flowing in. As these groups began to jostle for funds and training, they splintered into various, often personality-centered, factions. Often a leader would break away from a group if he felt confident of his ability to raise funds from international and local sources. The JUI has spawned at least eleven factions, and the JUP splintered into some five factions (Shafqat 2002, 138). However, factionalism is not tied to funding alone; it may result from differences about ends and/or strategies. The Jama'at-e-Islami has spawned various breakaway groups, such as Dr. Israr Ahmed's Tanzim-e-Islami and Dr. Farhat Hashmi's Al-Huda.[16] Moreover, an organization as large as the Jama'at-e-Islami can no longer exert complete control over the different wings and branches. Nasr (2001, 1996) has highlighted the autonomy that IJT was able to wrestle from the Jama'at after the success of its violent tactics in East Pakistan in 1970 and 1971.

A closer look at two groups, the JI and the JD, will, I hope, help construct a more granular picture of the competition and overlap that plays a key role in the social and political imagination of urban Pakistanis. A critical aspect of the fierce competition among Islamists is the very public nature of it. Because of their engagement with politics, there is an interest in carrying out this contentious conversation at a mass scale. It is no accident that Maududi became familiar to many in the early years of Pakistan through his radio sermons. This was part of his commitment to shaping the debate in the newly formed country against an easy assumption of secularism.[17] Critical in this is the desire to reach not a specialized audience, as in the case of many of the traditionalist ulama, but as wide a swath of the population as possible. Publishing pamphlets, books, and magazines, organizing political rallies and study circles, building campaigns and political allies within key institutions, the Jama'at-e-Islami developed a blueprint for mass engagement that has inspired similar activities from other Islamists. In this context, da'wa plays a critical role as a site of and reason for competition among the Islamist parties.

Jama'at-ud-Da'wa; Bringing Together Da'wa and Shahadat

Amir Hamza, one of the founding members of the JD, writes in the introduction to his book *Qafila Da'wat aur Shahadat* (Caravan of Proselytizing and Martyrdom, 2002): "This book that you have in front of you is a historical document of those *Ahl-e-Tawhid*[18] who engaged in *Jihad* in Afghanistan against Russia. As a result of their efforts, and due to Allah's grace, Communism and Atheism died their own death and were buried in Afghanistan. Today there is no one to take their name."

JD official narratives bind the origins of this group with its armed struggle and eventual victory in Afghanistan (Abu Yahya 2002). Markaz Da'wat-ul-Irshad, as it was known then, and Lashkar-e-Tayyiba, its militant wing, were created by Hafiz Mohammed Saeed and Dr. Zafar Iqbal, along with some other like-minded individuals.[19] Journalistic writings and public policy documents generally claim that the Da'wat-ul-Irshad and Lashkar-e-Tayyiba had been financially and technically supported by the Pakistani intelligence service, Saudi Arabia, and the CIA of the United States in their campaign against Soviet presence in Afghanistan.[20]

At the same time, da'wa (or da'wat in the Pakistani context) plays a central role and is inseparable from Jihad for its founders and members. It is a central theme in the work of the organization. The term literally means "to call or invite." Saba Mahmood (2005, 57–59) rightly points out that the term has attracted much less scholarly attention than other terms that Islamists use just as frequently, for example, al-jihad (effort) and al-daula (generally taken to mean the state or system of governance).[21] During the course of my research I realized that it is a critical aspect of their raison d'être as envisioned by the members of these Islamist groups. The practice derives legitimacy from the Qur'anic principle of amr bil ma'ruf wa-nahi'an al munkar (to enjoin others to the doing of good/right and the forbidding of evil/wrong). The principle of amr bil ma'ruf occurs in a number of places in the Qur'an, lending it salience in the eyes of the believers. However, its interpretation over the centuries and in different regions has varied immensely (Cook 2000). While classical Sunni texts have not paid much attention to da'wa, the political and social context of the nineteenth and early twentieth century and the encounter with Christian missionaries supported by a colonial administration prompted a reappraisal of Muslim proselytizing practices (Masud 2000, xii–xxiii). Unlike the Christian missionaries, though, Islamic Da'wa under colonial rule was not aimed primarily at converting non- Muslims. Rather, the aim was, and remains largely so today as well, to bring those who are "Muslim in name only" back into the fold of the believers. In a country like Pakistan, where close to 97 percent of the population is officially Muslim, the various da'wa activities are aimed precisely at bringing about this internal change within a "Muslim" society.

In urban Pakistan, the practice of da'wat varies widely to cover an extensive range of activities including study groups or dars ranging in size from two individuals to hundreds; establishing mosques, schools, and madrasas; social welfare services; printing presses dedicated to dissemination of Islamic ideas, newspapers, and magazines; and public lectures. Dale F. Eickelman and James Piscatori (1996, 35–36) point out that education has been central to all conceptualizations of da'wa historically. In its current and politicized tradition, da'wa has been reformulated to include the idea of social welfare activism that substitutes for ineffective or nonexistent government services.

Moreover, in the current context, as in the past, there is significant debate about whether da'wat is an individual duty or a collective one for Muslims. The Qur'an describes it as both an individual and a collective obligation. A popular *hadīs* (saying of the prophet Mohammed) quoted frequently in Islamist circles conveys the idea that a believer must correct evil by hand or by tongue, depending on individual ability. Failing that, one should at least condemn it in one's heart and be able to distinguish between right and wrong. These three levels provide the basis for the doctrine of *Tartib ud Da'wa* (priority in da'wa), as the three stages of an Islamic awakening, moving from jihad (physical and spiritual struggle, not always synonymous with military struggle) and da'wat (call to the truth) to *hijra* (migration).[22] The difference between Islamist groups like JI and JD, and pietist groups like Tablighi Jama'at that also see da'wa as the defining focus of their efforts, lies in the insistence of the Islamists that the political is as important an aspect of da'wa as the educational and spiritual aspect.

Da'wa forms an important part of its activities, and members of JD would often exhibit a quiet pride at "carrying out the task of prophets." This refers to the fact that historically da'wa has been seen as a function of prophethood. Certainly, one of the reasons given for the lack of institutionalized da'wa activities in precolonial Muslim societies, and prior to their interaction with Christian missionary groups, is that since it was believed that Prophet Mohammed was the last prophet, da'wa was no longer the task of an individual but that of the *umma* as a whole (Masud 2000, xxv). Nevertheless, there was significant variation in practice at all times. In the case of JD, at the time of its inception, the organization's da'wa was geared largely toward recruiting mujahideen for the jihad in Afghanistan. The core of the group's activities was recruitment through da'wa meetings from the lower-middle- and lower-class neighborhoods of urban Punjab and semiurban Khyber Pakhtunkhwa. An initial core of local strong men, or *gundas*, suggests a rather expedient use of the term da'wa to legitimize the group's presence in these neighborhoods. Shahadat, or martyrdom, is another central organizing principle for the members of the group. Shahadat is popularly conceived of as death while engaged in jihad. Social prestige accorded to a *shaheed* (martyr) and by extension to his (it is still a largely male phenomenon in Pakistan) family is grounded in not just religious legitimacy, but also decades of the Pakistani military's policies of romanticizing and rewarding death in battle through land grants, cash payments, medals, and scholarships for the children of soldiers killed in action.

The status-endowing capabilities of shahadat were highlighted for me as I was asked repeatedly by different JD members to meet one of the women leaders in the organization. The editor of JD's monthly magazine for women called *Tayyaybat* (pure/chaste women), she was also the organizer of the twenty-one-day and three-month courses for women that the JD runs in its headquarters in Muridke near Lahore. She is a tireless speaker for JD at dars sessions held all over the Punjab, often traveling hundreds of miles in the same day to fulfill her public speaking commitments.[23] As various people in Lahore JD suggested that I visit her, each would mention respectfully that she had sacrificed two sons to jihad in Kashmir. A cheerful woman, hands and feet died deep red with henna, she did not mention her sons until the end of our first conversation:

> Of course, who wants to send their children under a rain of bullets? The same children that we protect from ills and injuries when they are home? It is hardly a choice one can make easily. By the grace of Allah [*alham du'l illah*, also used to convey thankfulness to God], two of my children are shaheed. I went myself with the first one to drop him at the [Pakistan-India] *border* [in Kashmir]. . . . Have we been left with any other option now [as Muslims]? . . . Shahadat is the only weapon we have to fight American control of our societies.

To her, the connection between Indian control of Kashmir and American control of Pakistani society was the global market. The Indian government gained support from America for continued atrocities in Kashmir because the Americans were interested in Indian markets. America's control of Pakistani markets and thus society was through propping up puppet regimes such as Musharaf's with the help of international agencies like IMF and World Bank. In this context, and notwithstanding the continued use of shahadat as martyrdom, it is interesting to note the shift that is taking place in the JD's discourse regarding Shahadat. If jihad is physical *and* spiritual effort in the path of right, Shahadat also has an additional meaning with a political connotation: it means to bear witness, often to the truth. At the end of the previous Afghan war, the group changed its focus to Indian-held Kashmir. Young men recruited from the lower-middle-class and working-class neighborhoods of the small and large cities of Punjab, Khyber Pakhtunkhwa, and to a very limited extent Sindh were trained and sent into Indian-held Kashmir. After 9/11, with increased American pressure and consequent Pakistani government actions against militant groups, the Lashkar was officially separated from the rest of the group. Hafiz Saeed gave up his position at the head of the Lashkar to become the amir of the renamed Jama'at ud Da'wa. His justification for this organizational split rested on the importance of da'wa work, which he claimed was being jeopardized by US pressure against jihadi groups.

Officially, the group now focused on education and welfare activities, while continuing to provide moral support for jihad in Kashmir and elsewhere. The 137 al-Da'wa model schools started by JD operate in all provinces of the country, although with ninety-five schools, Punjab has clearly been the main beneficiary of JD attentions (Amir Rana 2003, 324). There are also two science colleges and eleven madrasas that are managed by the group. JD has a large network of dispensaries, and free medical camps are held periodically. Doctors and medics associated with the JD donate their time to these camps and treat hundreds of patients within two or three days. In the wake of the highly destructive earthquake in Kashmir and Northern Pakistan in 2005, Jama'at-ud-Da'wa emerged as an organized emergency relief provider and managed to redeem itself somewhat with the local population, who had been increasingly hostile to these ISI-supported (Inter-Services Intelligence, Pakistan's intelligence agency) jihadis. The Jama'at-ud-Da'wa's "humanitarian arm," the *Idara Khidmat-e-Khalq*, maintained a field hospital in Muzaffarabad and Balakot, operated ambulance services and surgical camps, constructed a thousand shelters, and provided electricity through generators.[24] More than the range and organization of its medium-term services, JD was able to impress outside observers and the earthquake-stricken locals by the immediate and dedicated work of its activists right after the calamity. Even as the Pakistan Army and government wasted precious days waiting for NATO-donated Chinook helicopters to arrive to access the remote areas affected by the earthquake, JD activists were among the first to reach these areas on foot. In many instances they were the first to pull victims of the earthquake out of the rubble. These activists then carried wounded persons or their belongings, often on their own backs, across treacherous mountain terrain to the nearest medical camps.[25]

In the changed political context, where the group could no longer focus exclusively on its armed jihad, the leadership was increasingly using Shahadat in its meaning of bearing witness to, and participating in, social and political change within Pakistan. Many of the members and leaders view the organization as a political pressure group and are happy to keep their position as such for the time being. The leadership's vehement denunciation of democracy and electoral politics continues unabated, but many of them in nonpublic conversations suggested to me that they are happy to "influence decisions without having to participate in the 'polluted' political system of Pakistan today." Abdul Rehman Maki, one of founding members of the JD and reportedly second in command to Hafiz Mohammed Saeed,[26] mentioned with some pride during a conversation about the dangers of electoral politics and the merits of the Caliphate system, which JD supports instead, that: "Just last night I went to see Rafique Tarar [previous president of Pakistan], as he is ill. We were given the same timeslot as the Muslim League (Nawaz group) *delegation* [used English term]."[27]

To him this was recognition of the importance of JD; it was accorded the same respect as a leading national political party, albeit one that is currently out of power. It is, of course, and with good reason, a fragile sense of having arrived at the political scene in Pakistan. Maki was escorted to the interview venue by armed guards who carried their weapons in open sight. In this respect he was not very different from other politicians in Pakistan—they all need protection from those they claim to represent. However, during the course of the interview Abdul Rehman Maki seemed to be trying to walk a tightrope between highlighting his party's distance from the existing electoral system within Pakistan at the same time as showing how it had nevertheless achieved recognition within that very system. He also seemed to realize that the kind of recognition that the JD has achieved is unlikely to accord it much strength through elections for now.

Similarly, a prolific JD writer and central organizer, Amir/Abu Hamza, explained that while the organization had started primarily for jihad, it had changed significantly in moving beyond its Ahl-e-Hadīs identity to working with other groups such as the Deobandis and Barelvis on specific issues. He reinforced the issue of bearing witness, shahadat, to the exploitation of Muslim countries carried out through the World Bank and IMF: "They give us loans first. You can ask 'us' who? Our corrupt rulers take the loans and just transfer them directly to their accounts. They spread *anarchy* [he used the word in English] in our homes and through the loans start *interfering* [in English] in our *education system* [in English], our cultural values. . . . It's not just Muslims, many non-Muslims are also against the US."[28]

We had met at his home, a rented upper portion of a small house on the fringe of the poshest locality in Lahore. Notwithstanding the locality, the house itself was modest and simply furnished. His wife, a very friendly woman considerably younger than her husband, sat through the interview partly as a chaperone for me and partly because she seemed to be interested in the discussion. The interview itself was periodically interrupted by men calling out to Amir Hamza from the next room that served as *mardan khana* (men's section), where his bodyguards and driver sat with other visitors. The mardan khana was accessed through a separate set of metal stairs at the back. During these absences, Amir Hamza's wife discussed the difficulty of raising children while having to move house as frequently as his "job" required, although she said, "*Yeh saath saath property* [she used the word in English] *ka bhi kaam kartay hain*" (He also deals in property alongside his other job). There was little time to get to know the neighbors before it was time to move again; sometimes not even enough to unpack seasonal clothes completely. Thankfully, the moving was mostly within the same city for the last few years. Nevertheless, this was particularly hard on the children since they had to make friends all over again in every new locality. Their frustration was compounded by the fact that they were not allowed TV at home and only religious CDs on the computer. Among those, their favorite one was an Egyptian alim reciting (*qira't*) the Holy Qur'an. However, she also allowed them computer games when her husband was not around.

She explained that she did not have much time left for political activities after taking care of her household duties, but appreciated the lack of hierarchy within the organization and its emphasis on pinpointing World Bank–sponsored inequality within Pakistan. One way in which this emphasis on equality, on breaking with *biradari* and *zaat* boundaries of the past, was manifested was through renaming members in the Arabic *kunyat* system. Thus, women and men were often known through their children's names, such as Abu Hamza, Umm Talha. Or they were known as the sons and daughters of their parents, mostly fathers but sometimes mothers too, for instance, with names such as bint-e-fatima or bin-yaqoob. There was no mention of *zaat*, which has been generally translated as "caste" but actually often connotes a relatively flexible notion of occupation and geographical association, as well as a place in social hierarchy. Nobody was known as *sheikh*, or *chaudhry*, or *gujjar* anymore in the JD system. To her this was a big change from the way things were organized in Pakistan currently, and even though she felt herself lucky to have always had a relatively comfortable life, she had a keener appreciation now of how difficult life can be for many. The encounter itself was too brief to allow me to understand both her seemingly placid acceptance of her husband's unexplained absences, the bodyguards, and the secretive house changes, and her critical questioning of the structures of Pakistani society. However, it was useful in providing a glimpse into the everyday ways in which it becomes hard for individuals and organizations to move away from their past. It is difficult to say where this dawning interest in social and political engagement would have led the

JD, given its deeply rooted relationship with militants as well as the dubious world of intelligence agencies, but it is possible to see a strengthening of militant currents within the organization as the war in Afghanistan intensified since this conversation in 2005.[29]

Islamism's Break with Traditionalist Islam

Both JI and JD are grouped under the Islamist banner. I want to emphasize one core aspect of their similarity before focusing on the nature and basis of competition between the two. Despite their differences stemming largely from the context of their origins almost half a century apart, and modus operandi, as Islamists they share a politicized reading of religion that distinguishes them from the traditionalists.[30] The Islamist engagement with politics as the primary means of defining their relationship to Allah and their efforts in the path of His favor is in direct contrast with the dominant trend among the traditionalists. This exclusive focus on the political combined with the emphasis on an unmediated and individualized reading of Qur'an and Hadīs texts is in contrast to the traditionalist emphasis on personal piety through acts of prescribed worship and mediated access through ulama. A leading contemporary Deobandi traditionalist alim, Mufti Taqi Usmani,[31] declares that, contrary to Islamist formulations, considering political engagement as a goal set by Islam would be as ridiculous as to believe that business transactions, about which the shari'a also lays down specific conditions, is an end in Islam. In expanding upon the thinking of Ashraf Ali Thanavi, he suggests that: "In their zeal to refute secularism (English in Urdu transliteration), some writers and thinkers of the present age have gone so far as to characterize politics and government as the true objective of Islam, the reason why the prophets were sent; indeed the very reason for the creation of human beings. They have not only given other Islamic commandments—such as in matters of worship—a secondary position, but have even deemed them to be mere means for political ends, just a way of training people" (Usmani n.d.; 2003, 25–26).

In their zeal to change the depressing state of Muslims after the colonial encounter, the Islamists have "politicized Islam" instead of "Islamizing politics." The traditionalists object to the Islamist reversal of priorities, where divine injunctions regarding acts of worship, means of attaining political power, and previous scholarship on shari'a are often treated as dispensable, or at best alterable. Taqi Usmani is building upon and echoing the thoughts of the influential Deobandi alim, Ashraf Ali Thanavi. As a sufi shaykh as

well as a prolific writer, Ashraf Ali Thanavi had a profound impact on debates within South Asia. In a subtle and nuanced reading of his life and
works, Zaman (2008) brings to the fore the studied ambiguity that was a
hallmark of Thanavi's position toward politics. This ambiguity is studied
precisely in its attempts to support a general principle and concern that
Thanavi articulated consistently: religious norms of worship and belief
ought never to be subordinated to political ends.

On the other hand, as one of the first major writers to articulate the
Islamist perspective in South Asia, Maududi, with his emphasis on the in-
separability of politics and religion, raised the establishment of an Islamic
political order to the ultimate form of worship. He played down the role of
acts of worship in comparison to political engagement by saying: "Society should be so organized that public opinion acts as a means of reinforc-
ing the efforts of the individual and of compensating for any weakness he
might exhibit. This is the reality of that worship which people regard as
merely prayer, fasting and *zikr* (remembrance of God), and which they believe have no relationship with worldly matters, whereas in reality prayer,
fasting, almsgiving, pilgrimage, and the remembrance of God are exercises
to prepare one for the main act of worship" (Maududi 2004, 12).[32]

In 1927 Maududi printed an essay on jihad in the Jami'yat-ulama-i-Hind
paper, *Al-Jami'yat*. In this, Maududi departed sharply from traditionalists
and those he deemed the apologists. The essay was reprinted as a pamphlet later in the year and earned him great notoriety and recognition in
pre-Partition India precisely because of its departure from the dominant
traditionalist understanding of jihad. It is worth noting here that there has
never been a static definition of jihad in the Muslim world but that, in fact,
it has been reconceptualized and redefined in different contexts in vastly
variegated ways.[33] He claimed (1962, 93) that:

It will become clear that all such problems (*fitna* and *fasad*) are born of a
system of government that does not recognize rights, does not take pity
and does not follow rules. . . . It is because of that that truth and justice
are crushed, that oppressors and evil doers gain sustenance for their bad
deeds and that rules that destroy morals and social justice [he used the
term social justice in English in brackets to explain his term *adal ijtama'i*]
are enforced. . . . Thus Islam has given a tried formula for ending this
through effort (*jihad*) and if possible through war (*qatal*), to end all such
governments and instead establish just and equitable governments established on the basis of fear of God.

Further, after critiquing British imperialism (*jihangiryat*) for its ethnocentricity, Maududi (1962, 93) insisted:

Islam does not want this for one nation to dominate the earth and monopolize its sources of wealth, after having taken them away from one or more other nations. No, Islam wants and requires that the human race can enjoy the concept and practical program of human happiness, by means of which God has honoured Islam and put it above the other religions and laws. In order to realize this lofty desire, we need to employ all forces and means that can be employed for bringing about a universal all-embracing revolution. . . . This far reaching struggle that continuously exhausts all efforts and this employment of every possible mean is called *jihad*.

This concept of jihad shared by both JI and JD today is diametrically opposite to the view held by the traditionalists. Traditionalists stress the two kinds of jihad, *jihad kabira* and *jihad saghira*. *Jihad saghira*, the lower level of jihad, is fighting a physical war, but the higher war is the spiritual one. Fighting one's *nafs* is central to this form of jihad. *Nafs* is generally taken to mean two separate but intertwined aspects of personhood. One meaning is the power of anger, hunger, and sexual appetite in human beings; the second relates to the soul, spirit, ego, or identity of a person. Richard Kurin (1993, 81), in his study based in urban Karachi, presents a general understanding of the term that resonates with my experience in urban Lahore: a person (*shakhs*) is thought to have a spirit (*ruh*), intellect (*aql*), life energy (*nafs*), and body (*jism*). Traditionalists argue that Islamists embark upon physical jihad without having made the spiritual journey first, without taming the nafs. As such, they are ill suited to do justice to Islam, even if they are temporarily politically victorious. More importantly, the traditionalists argue, even the chances of political victory are greatly diminished by this inversion of values. This not to say that traditionalists do not recognize the importance of jihad in contemporary life, but it is a slightly differently inflected notion. Thus, Seyyed Hossein Nasr, a leading traditionalist writer, had pointed out in his "Islam and Plight of the Modern Man" (1975, 18): "The contemporary Muslim must and cannot but wage a continuous holy war (*jihad*) not only within himself to keep his mind and soul healthy and intact, but also outwardly to protect what he can of the marvelous spiritual and artistic heritage his forefathers have bequeathed him in the expectation that he too will preserve and transmit it to the next generation."

The inner jihad is given greater importance in traditionalist discourse than the outer jihad, for what would be the point of achieving a victory in the battlefield if there are no good Muslims left to take control of affairs at the end of this process. Barelvi traditionalists often contend that it is the Wahhabi[34] influence in the case of both JD and JI that has led to this inversion of moral values. While the JD is clearly and proudly Wahhabi (or Ahl-e-Hadīs, as they prefer to call themselves), the JI leaders and members do not actually identify themselves with Wahhabism. To the extent that JI policies discourage the visiting of Sufi shrines, extended social rituals of mourning and marriages, and a general skepticism toward traditional spiritual exercises, it can be seen as being influenced by the rise of Wahhabism in the later nineteenth and early twentieth century in India.

However, one of Maududi's central concerns was to make religion accessible and pragmatic for Muslims generally; he did not explicitly support Wahhabism. In his influential writing titled "The Four Basic Terms of the Quran: Allah, God, Worship, and Religious Practice" (*Qur'an ki char bunyadi istilahain: Allah, Rab, Ibadat aur Din*), Maududi does not suggest that there is no role for ulama in a Muslim society but warns against unquestioning acceptance of ulama pronouncements using the Quranic verse in Surah Toba: "They made their *ulama* and *mushaikh* their gods instead of Allah, and similarly Jesus son of Mary, even though they are ordered not to worship anybody but Allah." Maududi (2004, 77) claimed that here the meaning of making ulama and *mashaikh* (elders, religious scholars) the gods is extending unquestioning obedience to them without checking to make sure that their pronouncements "have the seal of approval from Allah and his Prophet" (*khuda o paighambar ki sand kay baghair*).

In downplaying the role of ulama, and in democratizing belief by suggesting that each believer can interpret the Qur'an and Hadis for him/herself and question the reading of established ulama and mashaikh, both the JI and the JD have gone against the very basis of traditionalist practice in *taqlid* (to follow or imitate). The traditionalist practice of *taqlid* has allowed difference of opinion among ulama to coexist with relative sectarian harmony for most of Islamic history. It has been argued that the emergence of four *madhahib* (singular: *madhhab*/schools of jurisprudence) that roughly follow the four great jurists of Islamic thought have been the means whereby Sunni Islam has achieved a remarkable degree of cohesion compared to the divisive history of the other great world religions.[35] The principle of *taqlid* (which is the Shari'a term for "the acceptance by an ordinary person of the judgment of a *mufti*"[36]) frees the majority of the Muslims from the pressures of interpreting the Qur'an and Hadīs from themselves. Such interpretation requires years of learning, including knowledge of Arabic to eradicate problems associated with translation, and knowledge of the life of the Prophet and his companions to be able to evaluate his sayings and Qur'anic injunctions in context. Yet, taqlid is not the same as blind acquiescence to opinions of others. Wael Hallaq (2001, ix) reminds us that "it is the reasoned and highly calculated insistence on abiding by a particular authoritative legal doctrine. In this general sense, taqlid can be said to characterize all the major legal traditions, which are regarded as inherently disposed to accommodating change even as they are deemed by their very nature, to be conservative; it is in fact *taqlid* that makes these seemingly contradictory states of affairs possible."

Any scholar worth taqlid has to have an understanding of contemporary society (*maslahah*) to be able to interpret judicially. Moreover, the term "scholar" portrays only partially the qualifications required for the job. His scholarly achievements must be accompanied by humility and piety. Obviously, not many Muslims can undertake such a responsibility. Therefore, the principle of taqlid allowed the vast majority of Muslims to follow norms established by following one of the four madhahib, even as the imams and scholars themselves continued to diverge in opinion, generally peacefully, borrow from the other madhabs, and/or disagree with aspects of their own madhab. Shaikh Murad[37] reflects the traditionalist point of view when he suggests that the Islamist tendency, which he associates with the work of Syed Qutb, Jamal ud din Afghani, Mohammed Abduh, and Rashid Rida, has had a devastating effect in disrupting this internal harmony of the Muslim world.

> Today in some Arab capitals, especially where the indigenous tradition of orthodox scholarship has been weakened, it is common to see young Arabs filling their homes with every *hadis* collection they can lay their hands upon, and poring over them in the apparent belief that they are less likely to misinterpret this vast and complex literature than Imam al-Shafi'i, Imam Ahmad, and the other great Imams. . . . It is common now to see young activists prowling the mosques, criticizing other worshippers for what they believe to be defects in their worship, even when their victims are following the verdicts of some of the great Imams of Islam. The unpleasant, Pharisaic atmosphere generated by this activity has the effect of discouraging many less committed Muslims from attending the mosque at all. No-one now recalls the view of the early *ulama*, which was

that Muslims should tolerate divergent interpretations of the *Sunnat* as long as these interpretations have been held by reputable scholars.

Even as the traditionalists emphasize the historical continuity of their practice and thereby a certain authenticity, this view needs to be balanced by a recognition of the context in which many of the younger traditionalists, in particular, are discovering texts and adopting practices in their adult lives that are at complete variance with their parents' and grandparents' practices. These dynamics certainly make for an interesting context where, as Zaman (2002, 3) points out, settled notions of tradition are being challenged:

> Not long ago contrasts between tradition and modernity were a convenient shorthand way of explaining what particular societies had to get rid of in order to become part of the modern world. In academic writing at least there is an increasing recognition that tradition is not a monolithic identity any more than modernity is; that appeals to tradition are not necessarily a way of opposing change but can equally facilitate change; that what passes for tradition is not infrequently, of quite recent vintage; and that definitions of what constitutes tradition are often the product of bitter and continuing conflicts with a culture.

The Makings of a Modern Religion: A "Direct" Relationship with Allah

I want to suggest here that while apparently and vociferously "going back to the fundamentals of Islam," the Islamists have posited a break from traditionalist practice. Not only have they focused on the political domain as the key area of worship, they have also subjected religious practice to a certain rationalizing. Many of the first-generation JI activists that I interviewed emphasized that what attracted them to the JI was precisely Maududi's contention that Islam is a "modern" religion.[38] They found his emphasis on providing a logical basis for following Islam and his interest in changing practices to fit with the demands of educated, professionals liberating. As one former JI activist said:[39] "I was in medical college at the time [1950s]. . . . Maududi sahib said, 'You can say your prayers in trousers, you don't have to be wearing a shalwar kameez to do that.' It made life really easy for us. He was concerned with making religious practice compatible with our lifestyles, unlike these *maulvis* who are constantly thinking up ways to make it harder."

Many of my informants saw the Islamists as having opened the possibility of individual Muslims performing *ijtihad*, even as many of the leaders opposed this idea. *Ijtihad* derives from the Arabic root *jehada* (as does *jihad*), which refers to effort. *Ijtihad* then connotes effort applied to the sacred texts. In Islamic law, *ijtihad* refers to analysis of problems not directly answered in the Qur'an, hadīs, or scholarly consensus called *ijma*. Many scholars within the Sunni schools of law had suggested that since most of the issues requiring ijtihad had been addressed by the tenth century, there was no more call to exercise it. Ijtihad has accumulated a largely positive connotation in the modern period as an increasing number of Muslim philosophers, including Mohammed Iqbal in the Pakistani context, have called for its rejuvenation. The more sophisticated informants were often careful to suggest that Islamists like Maududi had not meant that ulama should have no role to play, but rather that they had meant to encourage Muslims to engage with their texts directly. In contrast, traditionalist understanding of ijtihad is very closely tied to the practice of taqlid. Hallaq (2001, 21) reminds us that: "The positive senses of *taqlid* transcend the province of *taqlid* itself as narrowly defined, for if *ijtihad* has a positive image, it is ultimately because of the fact that it is backed up by *taqlid*. To put it more precisely, except for the category (or type) of the *imam*, *ijtihad* would be an undesirable practice if it were not for *taqlid*, for this latter perpetuates *ijtihad* which is quintessentially a creative, independent, and therefore positive activity."

The Jama'at-ud-Da'wa is, in similar vein, actively promoting a direct relationship between the pious Muslim and Allah and emphasizing the importance of a political stance. Some evidence of this emphasis is available from the various JD publications (see *Majala-ud-Da'wa*, in particular 1997–2002). However, the extent and reach of JD-printed literature is limited compared to the JI; here I illustrate this trend through the description of a JD meeting.

A large gathering of close to six hundred women and approximately two thousand men assembled in Masjid Qadsia in Lahore at a protest meeting on June, 5, 2005, organized by the Jama'at-ud-Da'wa against the desecration of the Qur'an in US prison facilities in Guantanamo Bay. The entrance to the women's section was guarded on the outside by two men with guns. Once past the formidable gate and guards, half a dozen women body-searched all entrants, checking bags and layers of clothing very thoroughly. Inside the basement, which was mercifully cool after the sweltering heat outside and which served as the women's section of the mosque, some children sang *na't* (song in the praise of Mohammed) and *hamd* (song in the praise of Allah) while the crowd settled down. Various female leaders of the

Jama'at-ud-Da'wa then took turns speaking into a microphone, and at the end of the meeting, the *khutba* (sermon) by Hafiz Mohammed Saeed in the men's section of the mosque was relayed to the women's section simultaneously. Throughout the meeting, girls weaved through the crowd silently with charts emblazoned with quotes such as "Silence is a form of worship," "One who practices silence confirms personal salvation," and "Do not desecrate the sacredness of a mosque [by talking]." The crowd, though generally disciplined, could not promise silence. At periodic intervals we were told to straighten our rows as we sat on mats on the floor. "*Safain seedhi karain*" (Straighten the rows), the refrain would arise from one end of the room and ripple down to the other end, forcing those of us who had formed little circles to chat to turn around and face the speakers or singers in front.

It was soon clear that large groups had been bussed in from different sections of the city, and the audience consisted of many longtime activists as well as new or infrequent visitors. Next to me sat Razia, who had come in from Shaad Bagh, a lower-middle-class neighborhood of Lahore. As we started talking, she asked me if I was Ahl-e-Hadīs too. I hesitated to answer because I was not sure what the repercussions of suggesting that I was not might be while sitting in an Ahl-e-Hadīs mosque. Noticing my hesitation, she said quickly, "I am not one. We are very different from these people. These people do everything differently from the Ahle-Sunnat [implying but not saying directly that she too might be Ahle-Sunnat]. They do not celebrate any functions after death like the *qul*[40] or the *chaleeswan*.[41] Also, they do not celebrate *'īd Milad-un-Nabi* [the birth and death anniversary of Prophet Mohammed]. [Laughing.] They think they have a *direct phone connection* [she used the words in English] with Allah."

She had decided to come to this function because her daughter comes fairly regularly with her husband and children. Moreover, word had gotten around her neighborhood that there would be a bus to collect them at nine and lunch would be served here around twelve. Now she was waiting to be joined by her daughter, who was traveling in a different bus from her own neighborhood. When Razia's daughter came, she was accompanied by her three children. Moreover, she had managed to convince one of her sisters to join them with her three children. They asked me to join their group, where the discussion soon turned to the potential menu options after the speeches.

Soon we were told to straighten our rows again, as it was time to say the afternoon prayers. Halfway through the prayers, one of Razia's grandsons entered into a swearing competition with another child among the many playing and weaving their way through the praying women. Both children exhibited an impressive vocabulary of swear words in Punjabi and soon had the women around them doubled over in laughter even as they tried to keep up some semblance of serious concentration on their prayers. Noticing the positive response to the competition, each child strove to outdo the other in creativity.

Battling such obstacles to undivided audience attention, at the front of the crowd, one of the JD women leaders had started making a passionate speech:

> We have made the Qura'n into a decoration piece. We expect others to explain it to us. We have taken such good care of the Qura'n, and have kept it with such respect that we have forgotten how to use it. We have put it on the highest shelf in our house and forgotten to include it in our lives. We pick it up, kiss it, touch it to our eyes, and then put it back. How many of you actually read and understand the Qur'an? This is why today, others can walk all over the Qur'an and we are unable to do anything about it.

At the end of her speech and to drive the point home further, she sang:

> *Taqon main sajaya jaata hoon*
> *Pairon talay ronda jaata hoon*
> *Dilon main basta hoon laikin*
> *Dilon main duhraya jaata hoon.*
> [I may be decorated in shelves
> or trodden under feet
> but I live in people's hearts
> and so am repeated constantly in their hearts.]

Most speeches were interspersed with singing, or at least verses, and were delivered in a fiery style, in contrast to the relatively more reasoned style at JI. However, the overall theme remained a constant one: Muslims need to engage with the texts without any mediation and need to take responsibility for determining what constitutes a good Muslim life themselves. Another impassioned speaker challenged the audience: "[General] Musharaf says 'Pakistan First,'[42] and we go along because we have no view of what comes first. . . . We can't even impose Islam in a five-*marla* house, we can't even it impose it on our four-feet-tall bodies, how can Musharaf impose Islam in Pakistan? What kind of Islam will he impose? How can we judge which is the right Islam?"

It is this emphasis on defining the right Islam, in contestation and competition with other versions of Islam, that lies at the very heart of the Islamist's efforts. The conversation ultimately is with other Muslims and other visions of a "good Muslim life." The very similarity of Islamists in rejecting traditionalist claims of authority and in promoting a personal definition of a good Muslim life pits them into competition against each other. I turn to the basis and nature of competition among the Islamists now.

Overlapping Constituencies and Diverging Interests

Rapid urbanization in many Muslim societies, including those in Egypt, Iran, Turkey, and Pakistan,[43] has provided a steady stream of activists and leaders to the Islamist parties in the twentieth and now the twenty-first century. While academic literature notes this trend, there has not been any significant exploration of how this affects the various Islamist groups that are trying to recruit these newly arrived urbanites to their respective groups. In the first four decades of its formation, the JI aimed to attract the *mu'assir tabqa*—the educated and increasingly professional middle class. That it actually attracted mostly lower-middle-class new immigrants to the urban centers of Pakistan began to manifest itself in the leadership of the party during the 1970s. However, the JI remained a largely select group of individuals until some time after Maududi's death. Following a period of upward mobility in Punjab, particularly from the 1960s to the 1980s, many of these JI members have indeed turned into middle-class professionals.[44] At the same time, the populist inclinations of the JI leadership and activists since the 1980s have seen it expanding its base in the lower-middle-class and some working-class constituencies. It is from within these constituencies that the JD is also trying to recruit.

The threat of competition was highlighted for me as I joined JI activists in their campaign in the inner city of Lahore just before union-level elections in 2005.[45] The JI's reach in the inner city has been quite precarious historically, and, much to the dismay of local JI activists, JI top leadership had formed an alliance with its longtime rival, the "left-secular" Pakistan People's Party, for these elections. Many activists spoke of the blow to their credibility due to this move. One said, "If we had known these people (in the constituency) for a long time, we could have salvaged the situation somehow. But we have only just started working in these areas." Similarly, Hafiz Salman Butt, a leading JI politician and longtime resident of the inner city, admitted, "The *androon shehr* [inner/walled/older part of the city] has certainly presented the Jama'at [-e-Islami] with a challenge. Lahoris have a distinctive culture and attitude. There is openness to their attitude (*khula dula pan*). . . . Initially very few local people joined the Jama'at; we had greater success in the newer areas [referring to middle- and lower-middle-class suburbs, often populated by newcomers to Lahore from smaller towns of Punjab]. Now for many years we have worked in certain localities, but we have only made progress when we tried to understand the local culture."[46]

As we inched our way through the rush-hour traffic blocking one of old Lahore's main arteries in a stuffy Suzuki van[47] on our way back from a small rally, one of the JI women, Salma baji (changed name), started describing the robbery of her son's shop. He sold used mobile phones and phone cards from a small shop that had been attacked in broad daylight by gun-wielding men. They had taken all the cash, and as a precaution against a quick reaction on their departure, had tied his hands with the string used to hold his *shalwar* (loose trousers that both men and women wear in Pakistan). After he managed to free himself, he had to first put the string back (which is, at the best of times, a painstaking job without the right implement, called a *naala pani*) and don his shalwar before he could go out and seek help. "What will he do now?" I asked, as she finished recounting his ordeal. The other women fell silent waiting for Salma Baji's response, and there was palpable tension in the air. Salma Baji responded that those who had helped him set it up in the first place would obviously support him now too. Her answer brooked no further discussion.

After she had been dropped off, the other women eagerly returned to the story. Her son had joined the JD much to the dismay of his mother, who had been a longstanding dedicated JI activist in a lower-middle-class area close to the headquarters of the Jama'at-e-Islami in Lahore. In recent years the area had come to be dominated by the JD. Salma baji was dealt a double blow by the strength of the JD in the area. Not only did she have to increasingly justify her positions and strengthen her arguments with more reading and discussions in the face of questioning from friends, neighbors, and others who had heard a different version from JD women activists, she had "lost" her son to the JD. The Jama'at-ud-Da'wa had helped him set up his shop and given him considerable responsibility in the local context. The JD could potentially also be relied upon for some further assistance in either catching the thieves who robbed him or in providing funding to keep the shop going. Doubtless, for Salma baji it was a difficult and embarrassing situation. On a later occasion I heard some women console her by saying that at least he had not become a *goonda* (thug) or a "secularist"—at least he was with those working in the path of God. Nevertheless, several women complained that it was hard for JI activists to compete with such tactics of monetary patronage.

The overlap in their constituencies is also typified by the trajectory of Hafiz Mohammed Saeed's career. The current amir of the JD is of Kashmiri Gujjar[48] origin. Hafiz Mohammed Saeed's family suffered terribly during the partition. Thirty-six members of his extended family were killed in the ensuing violence.[49] As his family emigrated from Shimla in Kashmir where they lived, their houses were burned and their caravan attacked on the way. The family was quite religious, and both men and women had learned to read the Qur'an.[50] After Partition, the family settled in the Sargodha district in village 126 North[51] and started cultivating the land they received in lieu of what they had lost in Kashmir. All seven siblings, including Hafiz Mohammed Saeed, memorized the Qur'an under the tutelage of his mother.[52] The title *hafiz* (literally, one who has memorized the Qur'an) denotes this very act of dedication and discipline. After completing a BA from the Government College, Sargodah, he moved to Punjab University, Lahore. Here he completed an MA in Arabic and another in Islamic studies.

Up to this point, Hafiz Mohammed Saeed typifies the constituency that the JI attracted in Lahore: new to the big city, either the first or one of the first in the family to go on to modern, higher education and from a religious family. It is not surprising then that soon after arriving in Lahore, he joined the Islami Jami'yat Tulaba (IJT), the student wing of the Jama'at-e-Islami. Later on he was also selected as the IJT nazim for the old campus of Punjab University. While still with the IJT, he was very active in the Bangladesh *Na-Manzoor* (not acceptable) movement led by the IJT. The movement aimed to pressurize the Pakistani government to deny official recognition to the newly separated East Pakistan. He was, of course, exposed to the debates and increasingly violent clashes between the secular leftists and the IJT that were a feature of life at Punjab University during this period. He campaigned for the JI in the 1970 elections in which the JI had to face a humiliating defeat. Hafiz Saeed claims that the defeat of the religious parties in the 1970 election convinced him that democracy "is the biggest fraud in the world" and an Islamic revolution can never be supported through democratic means.[53] By 1974, Hafiz Saeed had secured a position as a lecturer in the Islamic Studies Department in the University of Engineering and Technology, Lahore, where he remained until his retirement.

In 1978, Hafiz Mohd. Saeed moved to Saudi Arabia to the King Saud

University, in Riyadh, to further his studies of Arabic and Islamiyat (Islamic studies). During this period he came in close contact with several Saudi religious ulama, including Shaikh Abdul Aziz Ba'az. Shaikh Ba'az was the first Arab alim to declare a fatwa that pronounced the fight against Russians in Afghanistan a jihad and urged Muslims around the world to join in. Soon afterward, Hafiz Saeed returned to Pakistan and participated in the Afghan jihad with a group led by Abdul Rasool Siyaf.[54] It is unclear whether Hafiz Saeed was born into an Ahl-e-Hadīs (Wahhabi) family, or whether he and other close family members changed their orientation after his stay in Saudi Arabia. Indeed, other members of his family also spent time in Saudi Arabia, and his wife suggested to me that the family had long been Ahle-Hadis. The Jama'at-e-Islami ideology does not actively discriminate against many Sunni *maslaks* or against Shiism, and so it was certainly acceptable for Hafiz Saeed to be part of the JI despite his Ahl-e-Hadīs upbringing. Even though some literature classifies the JI as a Deobandi organization, many of the JI middle- and lower-level activists that I interacted with did not think of themselves as Deobandi. In fact, they did not think of Deobandi as an active category of Muslim faith. In any case, the JI includes Shias and Ahl-e-Hadīs even today, although their numbers have dwindled since the 1980s. Increasing Iranian and Saudi Arabian funding for their respective strains of Islamic faith during the 1980s led to the proliferation of sectarian organizations. Some of them increasingly became drawn into a cycle of violence with contention among groups sustained by locally fuelled feuds and rivalries.[55] As a result, even in nonsectarian organizations like the Jama'at-e-Islami, members became bitter about the other sects, and defensive about their own.

Jama'at-ud-Da'wa was in the past bitterly sectarian, often calling for the death and destruction of Shias, Barelvis, and Ahmadis.[56] Over the last three years, the leadership has made a determined effort to tone down its antagonism toward other Muslims. Often during our conversations, the leaders were more careful in their approach to the issue of sectarianism, while out of their hearing, most members would still insist that those Muslims who were not Ahl-e-Hadīs were *murtadid* and *wajib u'l qatl* (acceptable to kill).[57] A telling attempt at presenting the "new and improved" version of the Jama'at Da'wa was made by a new inductee into the middle management of JD, Naveed (not his real name), one of the few Pakhtoon members of the JD I met in Lahore. A graduate in English and double maths,[58] and a self-taught computer designer, he had recently been appointed an editor of one of the JD's magazines. Naveed had a pleasant, open demeanor and seemed younger than his thirty-five years. Dressed in the usual JD style in a baggy shalwar kurta with the shalwar pulled high up his ankles, waistcoat, and cap, he kept his beard trimmed, which was unusual for JD. He had been active with a different Ahl-e-Hadīs group before joining the JD and had found inspiration at a young age from the Jama'at al Muslimin.[59] Speaking about Jama'at-ud-Da'wa's sectarian past, he said: "This label of extremism [used the word in English] is totally unjustified. . . . If you ask me, I was more of an extremist [in English] before joining JD. Of course, outwardly I even wore jeans [English], etc. But I did not even respond to the *salaams* of members of the opposite groups [English]."[60] When I asked which groups those were, he mumbled vaguely, "Oh, you know, Shias and others." This declaration was interesting because of the dissonance at the time of his joining JD between the JD's stances on Shias on record in publications and taped sermons of its leaders, and his presentation of the organization. It seemed like a story he felt would be appropriate for researchers from foreign universities, such as myself, but not one that could be corroborated by records of the JD itself.

My interest here lies not so much in the veracity of Naveed's version of JD history, but in recognizing not only the significant overlap in the constituencies from which the different Islamist groups are trying to recruit their members, but also the fluidity, movement, and antagonism between the groups. Individuals seem to move from one group to the next for a variety of reasons, from better career prospects, political gains in local power structures, doctrinal differences, and family pressures, to mergers and alliances between groups. It is this possibility of movement from one group to the next that makes competition an important aspect of the interaction of these groups. In this respect, an important strategy has been to cast doubt over the strategies of the other group. Asad (not his real name), a lower-middle-class JD activist, had been speaking at length about the importance of changing the leadership and state structure in Pakistan without participating in electoral politics. When I mentioned the JI and its continued involvement in electoral politics, he gave a derisive laugh and said, "So you have seen where that has left them (*un ka anjam dekha hai*)? Every time they face a humiliating defeat . . . and this time it's not they who have won, it is the alliance."[61] Such sentiments typify the response of activists operating at the middle or lower levels of JD. The leaders, often more subtle in their comments, nevertheless insinuated that the JI had been corrupted by its involvement in electoral democracy. For instance, Abdul Rehman Maki claimed that the JI had been weakened by its participation in the electoral process: "It was a big mistake to play on the *pitch of democracy* [democracy *ki pitch par*—mixing English and Urdu]. . . . They have to run after the *vote bank* [in English] and modify their stances constantly."[62]

Competition in Everyday Life: Choice and "Objectification"

JI activists, in contrast, worry about "the bad name" given to Islamist parties by the "Jama'at-ud-Da'was of the world." They talk of the extremism of JD and the problems with their impractical and irrational doctrines for running everyday life. An important method of demarcation in everyday life is modes of dress and bodily comportment. JI women in particular often commented on the impracticality of what women in JD were "forced" to wear. Photographs of bearded men in shalwar kameez, burning the flag of America with raised fists and rage-filled twisted faces, is a common enough representation of Islamists from Pakistan. To the outside eye, the only difference between one picture and the other is the change in the date of publication. Or, as one colleague in Cambridge remarked, "All these crazies look alike to me." While the basic ingredients remain the same—a beard, a shalwar kameez and a cap for men, and a veil of some kind for women—in fact there are subtle differences in each that go toward making a distinctive flavor of Islamism.

Lehmann and Siebzhener (2006, 153–55) detail the distinctive modes of dress and gait that mark the members of different Hasidic groups from each other, even when these nuances remain unnoticed by the outsider. Similar differences exist among the various Islamist groups in Pakistan. JI male members tend to be very neatly dressed with well-trimmed beards. They wear shalwar kameez that are often topped by a long waistcoat particular to North India, and called a *vaaskit* colloquially in Punjab. JD men, in contrast, often do not trim their beards, with the result that their beards give a more unruly and fierce look.[63] They also almost never wear the vaaskit, and often tie their shalwars high enough for the ankles to be exposed, which gives them a less urbane look than the JI men. JI women wear a long overcoat to cover their bodies and a *hijab* (head covering) and a *niqab* (face covering) that are pinned into place. JD women tend to wear a long chador that they use to cover their head, face, and body. The chador is obviously bigger than an average chador (generally 2.5 meters) and requires considerable practice in carrying properly. Even as the requirements for parda are more than fully met by both modes of dressing, the JI dress for women is more practical and one that allows women to carry out most functions at home and work. This difference in dress is also a source of some comment, discussion, and ridicule among the members of the two Islamist groups.

These outward markers of difference from the other groups may not have been developed solely for purposes of distinction, but have become important in this role to the members. The multiplicity of options in pursuance of faith and in fulfilling the demands of piety, like parda, mean that those interested have many choices to make and justify. In the case of competition among religious groups in Pakistan, one effect has been an increased consciousness about the different ways of being Muslim. A comment repeated often, and by a great diversity of people from committed atheists to modernists, pietists, and Islamists was, "Our parents did not have to think about religion. They could just take it as a given, and practice what those around them were practicing." This is an interesting formulation particularly since it was repeated to me by people of different generations. It seemed to me that while it may also be true in the literal sense for each individual making this remark, there was a general understanding that at some unspecified point in the not so distant past, religious practice did not have to be thought through as it does now. Thus, one important implication of the competition among Islamists is what Eickelman and Piscatori (1996, 38) call "objectification." It is the process by which basic questions come to the fore in the consciousness of large numbers of believers: "What is my religion?" "Why is it important to my life?" and "How do my beliefs guide my conduct?" My research shows that members of Islamist groups are constantly making comparisons with *other* Islamist groups and related ways of being. Given the multiple ways of being a good Muslim that are offered to them, there is an increased awareness of, and debate about, what religion means and how it should impact everyday practice.

Salima has been selectively incorporating aspects of belief and practice from different groups for several years now. She is in her late twenties, from a middle-level peasant family whose lands once outside of Lahore are now considered part of the city. A few industrial plants set up nearby have helped change their village over the last twenty years into an urban neighborhood within Lahore. She is the first woman in her family to have received a university education, indeed to have studied beyond the primary classes. Having already finished a masters in Arabic, she is currently studying for an MPhil in Islamic studies at Punjab University. The fact that she is not married yet, "is offset," in the words of her aunt, by her reputation for piousness, kindness, and learnedness among her family and her neighborhood. In addition to the chador that many women in her family wear loosely draped, she has also started wearing a *niqab* (a loose piece of cloth pinned across her face, leaving only the eyes visible) and a *hijab* (a stitched triangular headscarf that is pinned below the chin to cover the hair). Over the last year, she also started attending al-Huda[64] classes and had recently been through their Ramadan "crash course." She supplements these classes with al-Huda cassettes and CDs that she listens to at home. Finally, she also recently started listening to CDs of Dr. Zakir Naik's sermons.[65] One day as we were discussing the ways in which different scholars have used hadis to supplement their contrasting opinions, and how confusing that can be, she started musing about her own experience: "When I was younger we used to listen to the local *maulvain* [woman preacher, may also be the wife of the local maulvi] and believe whatever she told us. Then my brother became involved with Jama'at-ud-Da'wa, and for a while I looked through their literature and found it convincing. Through that literature I found that many of our local practices were un-Islamic. Now I go to Dr. Farhat Hashmi's classes and listen to Dr. Zakir Naik's lectures, and find that their way of explaining Islam makes it so rational."

She had not abandoned her family's Ahl-e-Hadīs belief, but had moved from one group to the other, incorporating aspects of each into her daily practice. For instance, her chador, pinned hijab, and niqab were a mix of Jama'at-ud-Da'wa and Al-Huda practices. She started wearing the niqab only after joining al-Huda, she started wearing the hijab when she joined college, and she had worn a chador since she was in her early teens, when JD became influential in her neighborhood. Each additional layer of clothing generated some discussion in her family and neighborhood. Some close friends and neighbors felt insulted by her choice to wear a niqab because it made them seem less pious or *nayk*. They felt that she was deliberately rubbing her education and piety in their face by this ostentatious layering. Some commented that she was doing this to set herself apart from them, and was showing off in a subtle way. Several stressed that there was no injunction in Islam to cover your face and that this was taking parda to unrealistic extremes, particularly in the summer months. Others felt that it was appropriate because to go to the university she had to move beyond the confines of a neighborhood where people knew each other and could monitor the behavior of young men toward local girls. Still others joked that given the long distance she had to commute in public transport, this was a highly acceptable way to ward off the smoke and pollution that is becoming a big problem in Lahore.

I want to highlight through this brief example and the others cited earlier in this chapter that there is questioning, debate, and contrasting opinions regarding belief and practice that is generated by the presence and activities of the various religious groups operating in urban Lahore. I do not want to underestimate the coercive tactics of many Islamists either at the local or the national level.[66] Nor do I want to suggest that the debate has no defined parameters. Certain questions, such as the existence of Allah or the veracity of the Qur'an, cannot be raised publicly in this context. However, it is also useful to keep in mind that the "secular fundamentalists," as Roxanne Euben (1999, 18–19) calls them, also do not broker much discussion about certain aspects of their "faith." Similarly, Yael Navaro-Yashin (2002, 189) has suggested that "the terms of secularism are not appropriate for the study of secularism." She finds that in studying the "cult" of Ataturk, "belief," "magic," and "mysticism" are appropriate terms. Thus, while there are limits to the debate, the role of religious belief and practice in the public sphere, from modes of dress to means of political engagement, is increasingly dissected from different angles. In bringing these questions to the public sphere, while highlighting the "rationality" and "modernity" of the religion as well as the need for Muslims to engage directly with the texts and bypass the traditionalist mediators, the Islamists are facilitating secularization within Muslims societies through a conscious, critical engagement with what it means to be a "good Muslim" today. This critical engagement proceeds through a framing of religion as a cohesive, coherent whole in which the task of the good Muslim is to weed out internal contradictions and practices. A key move in this direction was initiated by the introduction of mass education that Eickelman (1992) and Eickelman and Piscatori (1996) expand upon. Competition among the Islamists builds upon this wider ability to access the Qur'anic texts, in terms of mass literacy, and adds further impetus for the objectification of religion. Yet, and as I noted earlier, this does not mean an obliteration of transcendence. If anything, varied and new aspects of life are touched by transcendence in some ways as urban Muslims try to grapple with the new technologies, ideas, structures, and routines that shape their lives.

CHAPTER FOUR

Harbingers of Change?

WOMEN IN ISLAMIST PARTIES

*Now that I understand the religious requirements of my belief (iman)
and reasons for parda, I ask myself, how can I not practice it?*

    —JD dars member

*And you, what will you do in the face of this catastrophe? When you die, what
are you going to tell your Allah? That you were too busy cooking? That you spent
your life cleaning and washing clothes? These are our duties, no doubt, but we
have to also answer to God, not just the men. We have our belief (iman) as well.*

    —JI woman leader at an election meeting

In this chapter I question the conflation of secularism with agency by exploring two related questions: Why do women join Islamist parties? And
once they do join, what is the impact of their presence? The first question
has particular significance, since Islamism is widely defined in part through
its misogyny. Why then do women willingly join the very vehicles of their
oppression? There is a wealth of literature assessing the relationship between Islam, Islamism, and women, but very little has been said about this
particular question. The answer provided by secularist feminists is some
version of the "false consciousness" approach (Hale 1996; Zafar 1991; Afshar 1996). In direct opposition to this notion of false consciousness, many
within the Islamist parties cite religious belief as the key motivating factor.
By itself, neither answer may be completely satisfactory, but it is worth noting that the concept of false consciousness has received much more serious
consideration in academic literature than belief. In this chapter I attempt
to give some serious consideration to the second answer, the answer that
these women themselves offer. Religious belief remains underconceptual-
ized. It has been conceptualized primarily in terms of ideology in the social sciences (Althusser 1984; Žižek 1994). Islamists themselves also use

the modernist conflation of belief with ideology, following Enlightenment theorization about belief. Seyyed Hossein Nasr (1987, 21) echoes the traditionalist discomfort with the term when he writes:

> The concept of ideology is very telling as far as the adoption of modern notions in the name of religion is concerned. Nearly every Muslim language now uses this term and many in fact insist that Islam is an ideology. If this be so, then why was there no word to express it in Arabic, Persian and other languages of the Islamic peoples? Is 'aqidah or ususl al-'aqid, by which it is sometimes translated at all related to ideology? If Islam is a complete way of life, then why does it have to adopt a 19th century European concept to express its nature, not only to the West but even to its own adherents?

Linked to the modernist conflation of belief with ideology is the assumption that to be secular is to express one's agency, but to have belief is to somehow give up one's agency, to follow norms and traditions unthinkingly. I discuss the existing trends in the very vast literature on women and Islam[1] below to point out that while the impact of political Islam on women has been looked at in great detail, there is almost no inversion of this question: there is very little research that looks at how women may have impacted political Islam. In attempting to answer this question, I take a critical look at the notion of agency and its close connection with the concept of secularism. My research shows that women are changing Islamist parties from within, opening up new spaces for questions and contestations, even as they continue to give centrality to belief in their lives.

A Disputed Terrain: Women and Islam

The impact of Islamization on women in many Muslim societies has been a significant concern in academic literature, particularly over the last three decades (useful overviews include: Kandiyoti 1991; Haddad and Esposito 1998; Moghissi 1999; Keddie 2007). With the increasing focus on Islamism over this period, particularly since the Iranian revolution and later the fall of the Soviet Union, an immense amount of literature has been produced on women and Islam. Not surprisingly, a large amount of the literature on women and Islam has been produced by and about Iranian women who were not only among the best educated among Muslim women, but who were also involved, willingly or unwillingly, with the first Islamist revolution (Moghissi 1999; Paidar 1995; Poya 1999; Afshar 1998; Mir-Hosseini 2000;

Rostami-Povey 2001). There is also a considerable body of literature focusing on Egypt and Turkey.[2] In fact, until recently, the conflation of Muslim with Middle Eastern was such that most of the literature on women and
Islam focuses primarily on the Middle Eastern context. However, it is useful
to remind ourselves here that today, in terms of population, the real heart-
lands of Islam lie in South and Southeast Asia. Moreover, many of the theological and political innovations of modern Islam have originated in South
Asia. In the Pakistani context in particular, some key writings dealing with
women and Islam include Mumtaz and Shaheed 1987; Asdar Ali 2004; Bhasin, Menon, and Khan 1994; Zafar 1991; Weiss 1986; and Jalal 1991.

It seems to me that academic literature produced primarily in Western
universities and focused on the relationship between women and Islam,
across the disciplines of sociology, politics, history, and anthropology, can
be divided very broadly into four categories. The first category views,
and thus presents, Islam as yet another patriarchal religion, possibly much
worse than other religions in its misogyny. Nikki Keddie (2007, 225–28)
has pointed out a long tradition of scholarship on women in the Middle
Eastern region in particular that has treated Islam as an essentialized entity, and as the primary reason for the oppression of women. This stream
of literature looks into both the revealed sources and the lived tradition of
Islam as a source of gender oppression. This is in line with the tradition of
othering/orientalizing in the Saidian sense through a focus on the women.
Gyatri Chakravarty Spivak (1988), in the context of South Asia, and Leila
Ahmed (1992), in the context of Egypt, have pointed out how a concern
for improving the conditions of "native" women was used as a justification of colonialism. Liberating brown women was the "burden" that white
men and, later, white feminists had to carry as part of their civilizing mission. Leila Ahmed (1992, 167) suggests that such an emphasis on women's
rights privileged the colonist's cultural mores, so that it is no coincidence
that "colonialism's use of feminism to promote the culture of the colonizers and undermine native culture has ever since imparted to feminism in
non-Western societies the stain of having served as an instrument of colonial domination, rendering it suspect in Arab eyes and vulnerable to the
charge of being an ally of colonial interests." Echoes of this burden still
resonate with a Western audience. It is not inconsequential here to remind
ourselves that the invasion of Afghanistan in 2002 was in part justified
through a campaign highlighting the plight of women under the Taliban.
The ubiquitous blue burqa' that women in Afghanistan continue to wear
today, even after their "liberation" by coalition forces, was equated with

the Taliban and their repressive social practices to build public opinion in favor of an invasion of the country.

Taking as a starting point Partha Chatterjee's (1989) early work on the attempts by the British colonial administration to take up women's issues as a way of undermining Indian claims to equality, Jane Collier (1995, 162) speculates that within the colonisist's home country, too, the portrayal of Muslim women as oppressed played an important role in containing the as-pirations of European women:

> Images of veiled Islamic women and walled harems must also have played a role in constructing understandings of Western women's liber-ties. It seems no accident, for example, that consent emerges as a key dif-ference between "oppressed" Islamic women and "free" Western ones during the nineteenth century, when industrialization was transforming adult women from productive members of family enterprises into eco-nomic dependents of wage-earning husbands. . . . Images of oppressed Islamic women, who could neither marry for love nor develop intimate relations with polygamous husbands, must have played a crucial role in constructing images of the Western women as consenting to their dis-empowerment within increasingly privatized and confining homes. And images of "enslaved" Islamic women must have helped reconcile West-ern men to marriages that were difficult to distinguish from prostitution as the devaluation of women's work left women only "love" to offer in return for the money they and their children needed to survive.

The second stream of literature, a relatively recent one and nestled pri-marily in the disciplines of sociology, political economy, and politics, is what I call the secularist stream, and has presented Islam as a willing pawn in the hands of oppressive state, political elite, and societal structures. I say "a willing pawn" deliberately to draw attention to the underlying suspicion among these scholars that Islam, like all religions, is intrinsically patriarchal and oppressive of women. Generally characterized by a teleological grid of progress and regress, the work of Denize Kandiyoti (1991), Haleh Afshar (1998), Khawar Mumtaz and Fareeda Shaheed (1987), and Fareeha Zafar (1991), despite all their differences in other respects, can be thought of as part of this category.

The third stream of scholarship is epitomized by Fatima Mernissi (1985, 1993) and Riffat Hassan, among other writers and activists, many of whom are part of the Women Living under Muslim Laws (WLUML) network.[3] They are Muslim women who believe that their religion has been distorted by patriarchal interpretations. In contrast to the secularist stream, they do not suspect an inherent patriarchal thrust in the Qur'an. Even as they look for answers within the revealed text or practices of the prophet, these scholars differ from traditionalists and Islamists writing about women's status in Islam by taking on board Western notions of gender roles and women's rights and locating them within an Islamic discourse. Thus the rights that they aim to establish within the Islamic tradition are rights of individual liberty or what are broadly identified as "basic human rights,"[4] drawing their lineage from within liberal political thought.

The fourth stream of literature is the most recent one. Housed primarily in anthropology and sociology, its proponents suggest a suspension of predefined categories to understand the relationship between women and Islam. In criticizing certain important assumptions of feminist scholarship in the Middle East, Lila Abu-Lughod has also criticized her own earlier work. She asks if it is possible to recognize women's resistance "without [either] misattributing to them forms of consciousness or politics that are not part of their experience—something like a feminist consciousness or feminist politics" (1990, 47). Abu-Lughod argues for using resistance as a diagnostic of power that allows us to locate the shifts in power among both resisters and those who dominate.[5] Abu-Lughod's argument is similar in some ways to that made by James Scott (1985) and assumes that regardless of the multifaceted forms of power we may have to contend with, it is easy enough to identify resistance. In contrast, Saba Mahmood (2005) in her recent work suggests that in fact it may not be easy to identify resistance, nor particularly useful to imagine resistance simply as the binary opposite of subordination. This stream thus raises questions about what Strathern (1988, 26–28) has identified as the dual thrust within feminism: feminism offers both a diagnosis of women's position and a prescription for change. The contextualized approach brings to the fore a fundamental tension in liberal political theorizing, which is to define the limits and extent of autonomous, agentive action (Buss and Overton 2002; Raz 1986).

While I have attributed a loose chronological order to these categories, they continue to coexist, albeit with the contextualized approach now posing a considerable challenge to the secularist and reductionist modes of reading the relationship between Islam and women. Moreover, there is some movement across categories, and the same scholars sometimes move to a different position. Ziba Mir-Hosseini (2000, 7) has noted how scholars who had made dire prophecies about the status of women in postrevolution Iran in particular, but generally about the impact of state Islamization in many other contexts, and who were previously in what I have called the secularist stream, are increasingly coming to what I have called the more contextualized view, recognizing not just that there have been certain advantages to women under the Islamized regimes, but also that any analysis needs to move away from normative, decontextualized categories to be truly meaningful. Mir-Hosseini (2000, 7) mentions Haleh Afshar as an example of a scholar who took a strong secularist line soon after the Iranian revolution but has now taken a "partisan position on behalf of those in Iran whom she calls 'Islamic feminists.'" Much of Pakistani academic literature falls within the category that I have termed "secularist." It has been produced by secular-liberal feminists and is framed in a teleological grid of progress and regress.[6] Some recent work, however, has challenged this modernization-theory-inspired writing (in particular, Asdar Ali 2004 and Rashid 2006). For instance, in his perceptive critique of liberal feminist readings of women's "pulp fiction" in Pakistan, Kamran Asdar Ali (2004, 140) notes that the "construction of bourgeois individualism may be tempered by other visions of the self that co-exist with it. . . . a self that may accept, contradict and even transgress the imposed construction of mythical but desired 'emancipated' autonomous individual."

In large part this diverse body of literature has been generated as a response to the rising Islamist visibility in Middle Eastern and South Asian societies, and deals explicitly with the impact of the accompanying structural and cultural changes on women in those societies. However, there is little interrogation of the lives and choices of those women who join the various Islamist groups, and their impact in shaping the strategies and operations of these groups.[7] While Mahmood (2005) provides an analytically rich insight into the participation of women in the piety movement in Egypt and brings the role of piety and belief to center stage, she does not engage with the complexity of women in Islamist parties. Engaging critically with the challenge of women's participation in Hindu religiopolitical groups in India, Indian feminists have taken the challenge of understanding women's participation in these groups quite seriously. Susie Tharu and Tejaswini Niranjana (1994) point out that the vigorous participation of women activists and leaders in Hindu fundamentalist groups like the Bharati Janatiya Party (BJP) has led to new dilemmas in theorizing gender, as well as a need for increased self-reflexivity in conducting such research. In a similar vein, I suggest that in order to understand the dynamics of women who are part of the Islamist parties, it is critical that we take their own explanations seriously. To this end, I start with a focus on women activists within the Jama'at-ud-Da'wa.

Parda Inside

"*Baji* [elder sister], there is parda inside," a man with a frighteningly wild beard, turban, rows of bullets across his chest, and a Kalashnikov slung over his shoulder said to me as I drove to the gate of the Jama'at-ud-Da'wa headquarters, or *Markaz*, outside Lahore. Backed by several other men armed in similar fashion, his statement carried a certain weight. I was at this gate to meet with a woman leader of the JD. The markaz, spread over two hundred acres, has a school for boys and one for girls, a college for boys, a library, office buildings, several playing fields, a large mosque, and a small housing colony.[8] The complex has, in fact, outgrown the boundary wall around it and several houses and shops of JD members have now extended into the neighboring village of Nangal Sahdan. In addition to a loose fitting shalwar kameez, I was already wearing a large chador that covered my head and the rest of my body. Nevertheless, my face was uncovered, something I had decided I could not risk while I was driving on the highway teeming with trucks, donkey carts, and European and Asian cars of varying models from the latest to the obsolete. As I took a closer look, this Talibanesque man turned out to be a young boy of seventeen to eighteen years, who seemed to be at least as embarrassed by this situation as I was. A friend's brother who was my contact at JD, and his sister who was our chaperone, helped me put a part of the chador across my face, so that only my eyes were showing. I found inside the markaz that this only met the minimum of requirements for parda. The women walking around inside the markaz had wrapped their chadors around their faces so that their whole face was hidden. A small hole that could barely accommodate one eye, resulting in a severely restricted field of vision, was all the women seemed to be in the habit of relying on.

This encounter at the initial stages of my fieldwork seemed to confirm my worst suspicions about the role of women in the JD, with its militant rhetoric and history of violence. However, as my interaction deepened, I learned to recognize the complexity of the situation. Saima[9] was a young woman in her late twenties whom I met inside the markaz. Saima belonged to a lower-middle-class family that lived in Sheikhupura, a town close to Lahore. She was in charge of the girls' school in the markaz, and was also the assistant editor for the women's magazine that the JD publishes. The magazine, called *Tayyabat* (Chaste/Pure Women), prints political and so-cial analyses with a particular focus on women, recipes, childrearing tips, stories, poems, and articles on matters of religious practice. Saima was very articulate in high Urdu, liberally sprinkling her sentences with Persian and Arabic words. She was extremely deferential toward the editor of the mag-azine. However, it was soon apparent that in fact she was the key person running the magazine, as the editor was very busy with her da'wa activi-ties. During the course of our interaction, she also mentioned that she had initially enrolled in a law college in Rawalpindi (a major city in Punjab). She had to enroll in a private college since her previous grades were not good enough to ensure entry into the cheaper but more competitive public uni-versity. The private law college kept raising its fees every term, and eventu-ally she had to leave the program because it had become too expensive for her parents. The sense of being a burden was highlighted by the fact that there was no guarantee of a paying job upon completing the degree, given the state of unemployment in Pakistan.

On my first meeting with them, Umm-Hammad and Saima invited me to share a lunch with them, spread out on a *dastar khwan* (dining sheet) on the floor. During the course of this lunch I asked how a young, unmarried girl like her could live alone in this markaz, for this was certainly unusual for a woman of her class.[10] Saima answered, "Some people are like the river . . . nothing can stop them. When one path is blocked, the river finds an-other way for itself. But it has to keep moving . . . it has to make its way to the sea." She then elaborated that she had always felt that there must be more to life than raising children and getting married, even though she could see that it brought immense pleasure to some, such as her own sister. She recounted that when Umm-Hammad,[11] the editor of *Tayyabat*, came on a da'wa mission to her neighborhood, Saima spoke to her after the lec-ture. Umm-Hammad suggested that she start writing for *Tayyabat*. Saima became a regular contributor, and soon Umm-Hammad was able to offer her this position at the markaz.

This rather self-consciously poetic rendition of herself as a river was typical of Saima, but as I reflected on her words I realized that the move to Jama'at-ud-da'wa opened up many avenues of independence for her. The "Islamic credentials" of the JD made it relatively easy for her parents to ex-plain her decision to move out of her home within their extended family and neighborhood. Her attempts at a "secular" career had been forestalled by forces of privatization and globalization in the education sector in Pakistan. Interestingly, the more recent moves toward the privatization of higher education in 2003–5 were resisted most stridently by the student wing of Islamist parties like Jama'at-e-Islami, creating a bond of sympathy with many who have been affected by the increasing polarization in the Pakistani education system. Moreover, in her capacity as the principal of a girls' school in the markaz, Saima has gained experience that would be valuable in gaining employment or opening up her own school at some later stage. Finally, JD women like Umm-Hammad are likely to arrange a more suitable marriage for her with someone from within the organization. It may, interestingly, offer her a greater choice in selecting a spouse: Jama'at-ud-Da'wa's network is likely to be much wider than Saima's family's, and she may also feel in a better position to accept or reject proposals of marriage.

This example may suggest a straightforward conclusion that these parties may provide some avenues for independent positions to women not otherwise provided by society. Thus while Islamist parties may be oppressive in some ways, they may actually have liberating effects in others.[12] That conclusion would not be incorrect. But I also want to now introduce some of the complicating factors and highlight the role that belief plays in their decision.

Belief, Agency, and Secularism

The debate between those who see the rise of religious fundamentalisms— Christian, Muslim, Hindu, or Buddhist—as the failure of modernization and development to meet the *material* needs of people and those who see this phenomenon primarily as a response to the inability of modernization to meet the *spiritual* needs of people continues. This research is informed by the ongoing debate, at the same time as it hopes to contribute to our understanding of how the two aspects of the appeal of religion in the modern world are linked and influence each other. In the case of the tribal "Mullah of Waziristan" in Pakistan, Akbar S. Ahmed (1991) provides a perceptive account of the interplay of belief, ambition, and political opportunism, which guided the insurgencies led by the mullah. Similarly, Martin E. Marty and R. Scott Appleby (1993, 624) realized that while the large majority of explanations about why Khomeini issued the fatwa against Salman Rushdie focused on issues of power assertion and export of the Iranian model, an explanation "more scandalous to Western sensibilities but more useful to an understanding of the likely course of events" would have to include the fact that Khomeini was "the genuine article"—that he truly believed himself to be obligated to respond to the *Satanic Verses*.

The skepticism toward religious belief that the quote above hints at is particularly pervasive within academia. Peter Berger (1999, 2) muses about why the MacArthur Foundation may spend vast amounts of financial and intellectual capital on a project to understand religious fundamentalism. He is referring, of course, to the monumental and quite indispensable volumes of the Fundamentalist Project, undertaken by Marty and Appleby. Berger proposes that in part the explanation lies in the fact that it is indeed only academics who are surprised by the continued importance of religion in people's lives, and thus need to spend some concentrated money and effort to understand it now. He suggests that "the difficult to understand phenomenon is not Iranian mullahs, but American university professors—it might be worth a multi-million dollar project to try to explain that!" (1999, 2). On a slightly different note, Susan Harding (1991) points out that groups that are "culturally repugnant" to liberal academics continue to be studied as antimodern, fundamentalist, backward, and irrational. Nevertheless, religious belief is beginning to make a modest appearance in academic writing. In his seminal work on the "public" role of religion in the modern world, sociologist Jose Casanova addresses this very paradox: some time after secularization theory attained paradigmatic status across the social sciences, religion began to play an increasingly public role in countries as diverse as Japan and the US: "But above all, social scientists needs to recognize that, despite all the structural forces, the legitimate pressures, and the many valid reasons pushing religion in the modern secular world into the private sphere, religion continues to have and will likely continue to have a public dimension. Theories of modernity, theories of modern politics and theories of collective action which systematically ignore the public dimension of modern religion are necessarily incomplete theories" (Casanova 1994, 66).

This public role of religion includes the bodily manifestations of belief from the veil to the beard in the case of Muslims. In her book *Politics of Piety* (2005), Mahmood looks at women participants of the mosque movement in urban Egypt. Mahmood's key contribution to liberal feminist theory is to point out that feminist theory has assumed a *substantive* definition of agency that may be fallacious. To quote her:

> Put simply my point is this: if the ability to effect change in the world and in oneself is historically and culturally specific (both in terms of what constitutes "change" and the means by which it is affected), then the meaning and sense of agency cannot be fixed in advance, but must

emerge through an analysis of the particular concepts that enable specific modes of being, responsibility and affectivity. Viewed in this way, what may appear to be a case of deplorable passivity and docility from a progressivist point of view, may actually be a form of agency—but one that can be understood only from within the discourses and structures of subordination that create the conditions of its enactment. In this sense, agentive capacity is entailed not only in those acts that resist norms but also in the multiple ways in which one *inhabits* norms. . . . We cannot treat as natural and imitable only those desires that ensure the emergence of feminist politics. (14–15)

In arguing for a contextualized reading of agency, in shaping the self, Mahmood is arguing against the Kantian tradition that conceives of ethics as an abstract system, which tends "to disregard the precise shape moral actions take" (119). While Mahmood does not explicitly enunciate the relationship between belief and piety, her ethnographic examples illustrate, among other things, that the women in the mosque movement are willing to submit to a certain discipline of body and mind due to their *belief*. I have found Mahmood's articulation of agency beyond the binary of resistance and subordination to be particularly useful. My interest here is to point out not just how agency is mediated by religious belief but also how religious belief itself may undergo substantive changes through the actions of subjects.

I turn now to the example of Rabia to illustrate this process. At the Masjid Qadsia, the Jama'at ud Da'wa's main mosque within the city of Lahore, I attended dars led by the wife of the Jama'at-ud-Da'wa amir and founder, Hafiz Mohammed Saeed, Umm-Talha. Rabia was a regular member of the dars circle.[13] The mosque is situated in the lower-middle-class neighborhood of Chauburji, dominated now by shops, workshops, and stalls. Chauburji refers to a still-imposing structure with four minarets that was the centerpiece of a Mughal garden. The garden has now been replaced by a network of roads and shops, and Chauburji stands in the center of a roundabout at which various arterial roads of this part of Lahore meet. This area was once part of the affluent core of the city of Lahore, but the centers of affluence have now shifted eastward to Gulberg and Defence.

The entrance to the house, annexed to Masjid Qadsia, was guarded by a man in a fierce beard with a gun slung over his shoulders. Sometimes he would sit on a stool with his gun resting on his knees. As the women, shrouded and cloaked in their layers of chador, approached the doorway, he would politely avert his gaze to the floor. The women who came to Masjid Qadsia were from the lower-middle-class urban milieu of Lahore. The dars was held on a weekly basis in the women's section of the house of the mosque custodian and general administrator. The wide variety of pedagogical exercises that are carried out under the banner of dars include lectures to large audiences in their thousands, cassette sermons, mosque addresses following prayers, discussions of exegetical issues in private homes, and prayers before marriage and death ceremonies. The content of the dars may also vary—from personal issues to theological debates and political concerns—as might the teaching methodology, from a Socratic conversation to a lecture. At the Masjid Qadsia, six to eight women sat on the floor around low wooden frames that are meant to support copies of the Holy Qur'an. Each student would read a part of the Qur'an in Arabic first, and then translate each word separately into Urdu or Punjabi. These women were required to spend some time at their homes looking up the meanings of the Arabic words in dictionaries. Umm-Talha would then discuss the context of the particular *ayat* or verses in the prophet's time, as well as their implications for contemporary individual, social, and political life.

Having attended the dars at Masjid Qadsia over some weeks, it was soon clear to me that Rabia put the most effort in looking up the different meanings of the same word. She would also often ask detailed questions regarding the implications of what we had just studied. One day, she asked Umm-Talha, "Should I start practicing parda from my young nephew? He has just turned fifteen and I have been preparing him for sometime to say that I will soon start veiling in front him too. He keeps telling me to delay it a bit. We are very close and I have known him since he was a baby."

In response Umm-Talha recounted her own experience of having to make a decision regarding her brother-in-law, whom she had raised as her own son. She said,

> He was just a child when I got married. I still remember that on the day of my *valima* [second day after marriage that officially celebrates the consummation of marriage], I gave him a bath and changed his clothes myself. However, when his moustache turned dark I started practicing parda from him even though he pleaded with me not to. He kept saying don't start just yet, and I told him if not now, then when? Later on, of course, he resigned himself to my choice and would always make a joke of it when he entered our home. He would enter our house talking loudly

[to announce his arrival], and ask my son Talha, "So on which part of the house have you imposed martial law today?"

Rabia then raised the issue of tensions within her home because of her choice to practice parda. She lived in a joint family system, and all the family members would sit together at the dining table to eat their meals.[14] She said, "It has become very difficult for me to eat while covering my face, so often I take out a deep *ghungath* [a chador-like deep hood] and sit with my face averted from my brother-in-law and other male family members. My brother-in-law gets very angry that I am treating him like an outsider.[15] Sometimes he would even get up from the table in protest when I came in parda."

The other women in the group immediately started asking Rabia how she got the courage to face so much opposition within her own home. One said, "Rabia, you have truly left all of us much behind." Rabia replied, "Now that I understand the requirements of my belief (*iman ka taqaza*) and reasons for *parda*, I ask myself, how can I not practice it?"

Contrary to established accounts of veiling in academic literature (Gole 1996; Haddad and Esposito 1998; Weiss 1986, etc.) and popular media, Rabia did not face any pressure from her immediate family or from demands of earning a livelihood outside her home. Nilufer Gole (1996) and others have suggested that veiling can be seen as a response to sociological changes that include increased female participation in the labor market. I agree with Gole that this is indeed an important trend, but point out that we may also need to probe contradictory situations for a fuller understanding of the phenomenon. If anything, Rabia's choice to practice veiling is resisted by the men in her family. Several other women too, in the course of this research, explained that their decision to practice parda made these men, who were their close relatives, feel as if they were not trusted as family members anymore. In another meeting a woman recounted how she used to sit on the motorbike, a common mode of transport for the lower middle class, with her sister's husband. Ever since she has refused to do so, he has not spoken to her. This process undoubtedly generated anger, but also sadness within the families. The women themselves often spoke with much regret and sadness about the lost relationships with their brothers-in-law,[16] cousins, nephews, and uncles.

Nevertheless, Rabia and the vast majority of the women I met in both the JI and the JD during the course of my fieldwork did not see it as a gender issue. By this I mean that the issue was not framed in terms of a woman's choice. This was in spite of the fact that sometimes the fiercest opposition to their decision to observe parda was by the men in their family. These women invariably framed their decision in the context of their personal belief and a relatively private relationship with God. Using mostly the term *iman* and only rarely *aqeeda* for belief,[17] the women always placed it at the center of their decision. Practicing agency in this context includes an aspect of subordination, of their will to God's, as well as of resistance, in this case to the men in their family. Agency is then a mix of subordination and resistance at the same time. Moreover, while the reasons and impact of veiling at a public level have received much attention, I want to use this ethnographic vignette to also highlight the oft-forgotten sociological aspect of public veiling. Erving Goffman (1972), in his seminal work in intersubjective presentation, has shown how the public persona extends to the domestic sphere. What is private in political conceptualization is still public in this sociological context.

Jama'at-e-Islami Women: Slowing Down to Let the Men Catch Up

I want to turn now toward the impact that women are having within Islamist groups. It is easier to see the impact that women have had in the context of JI because not only is JI a much older organization but also because women have been quite actively involved in its political and social activities for at least the last four decades. The impact that women have had within the organization is relatively limited within the Jama'at ud-Da'wa, which has only recently turned its attention toward recruiting women.[18] The changes that women have instigated within the two groups are not the direct result of a "feminist" consciousness nor are they driven by a clear plan of increasing diversity within these organizations. Nevertheless, due to the different sets of concerns and dilemmas that they must negotiate on a daily basis, women in JI have introduced a plurality of perspectives and answers to questions regarding the role of religion in their lives. At the same time, women do not operate as a bloc within the party and many women have changed their lives significantly to meet the demands of political activism and personal piety that have been placed upon them as members of the Jama'at-e-Islami.

The Jama'at-e-Islami began organizing its women section most actively during the 1970s. The encounter with left women's groups, many of which were later transformed into NGOs, and their subsequent strength as a lobby group led the JI leadership to support initiatives for action by women within the party. A senior JI women's leader reminisced:

> We were just young girls then, and we would be sent to attend meetings of Aurat Foundation or Shirkat Gah [two of the largest left/liberal feminist NGOs in Pakistan]. At first we understood nothing at all. The whole discussion would whiz past our heads (*sar kay upar say guzar jati thi*). Partly because of the things they talked about and partly because of the language barrier [referring to the upper- and upper-middle-class English-speaking bias in these NGOs]. . . . We would come back and report to the *shura* [consultative meeting] everything we had managed to understand. We received so much encouragement and the shura took our reports so seriously that we would go back with a renewed sense of enthusiasm. Slowly we also began to understand the issues being raised. . . . So now we have decided that we have to stop reacting to the international agenda for Pakistani women and have to be able to define our own agenda.

In a bid to define its own agenda, the JI women's wing has extended the reach of the organization into very different fields. In addition to the various unions, particularly the College and University Lecturers' Association, to which both male and female Jama'at members belong, the women's wing has been instrumental in extending the range of services offered under the JI's charitable wing, al-Khidmat.[19] Al-Khidmat operates as an umbrella for a collection of smaller groups, many of which work in complete isolation from each other. Since Qazi Hussain Ahmed became the amir of the Jama'at and started supporting the activities of the trust that were in line with the more populist thrust of his own policies, al-Khidmat has grown into a large network supporting schools and training institutes of vocation skills for women, facilitating dowry chests, and contributing to widows and orphan funds, among other activities. In the course of my fieldwork I accompanied JI women to various schools and training institutes in the larger Lahore area. The training institutes are structured to help women generate income from activities they can perform within their homes: sewing, embroidery, and craftwork. Some JI women have also undertaken a significant project called *baithak* schools. These are primary schools run in the poorer neighborhoods, with subsidized education provided to children who would otherwise not go to school. Moreover, there are hospitals and dispensaries, either run directly by JI activists or bequeathed by their founders to the JI.

JI women play an active role in the management and running of many of these entities.

At the same time, the JI is keen to extend its reach within the wealthier segments of society. The daughter of Qazi Hussain Ahmed[20] runs a series of dars that are aimed at precisely the upper-class woman. Attired in expensive clothes with subtle diamond jewelry, and an even more subtle layer of makeup, Samia Raheel Qazi sprinkles her dars with English and with comparisons to other parts of the world. This series of dars is held in a palatial house in an expensive locality of Lahore called Defense Housing Colony. In the same house, some younger women started an Islamic "Sunday school" for their children. Interestingly, despite the association with the church's weekly calendar, Sunday was the most convenient day for these families. Friday, the Muslim day set aside for collective prayers, is a half day for almost all schools, but not a holiday. A core group of the women behind the Sunday school for rich Jama'at children had spent time in America before coming back to Pakistan. Some were, in fact, recent returnees, since after 9/11 they found America "a hostile place for Muslims." Thus, while the typical JI woman may be a middle-class, low-salaried professional, the JI is making a determined effort at inroads into both the strata above and below its core constituency. Women within the JI are both the vehicles and targets of this expansion.

Honor Killings and Individual Belief

Within the political sphere, JI women have built an increasingly visible position, participating in protests and demonstrations, campaigning for political candidates, and mobilizing on specific issues.[21] In addition to their political wing, which supports JI's electoral campaigns, some JI women activists had started a research-based think tank in Lahore. The coordinator of that organization explained to me that "For years, we have responded to the agenda handed down by Western governments and Western feminists. We have to stop reacting now and develop our own understanding." I had gone to her office to interview her, but at the end of the interview she asked me if I would run a series of workshops for her staff on how to conduct research. I ran three workshops for her staff, which comprised eight girls just out of college and university and four long-term, mid-level JI activists.

The girls in the staff belonged primarily to the newly educated middle class. By "newly educated," I mean a class that has had a stable and comfortable life for close to two generations, but whose female members did not receive college education until recently.[22] Most of the girls in this group were from Jama'at families. This meant that their close family members or parents had been Jama'at members for at least one generation before them. Some had been members of Islami Jam'iyat Talibat (JI's women's student wing in schools, colleges, and universities), and one girl there had been a national-level organizer. Two girls were there because of a general "Islami" trend in their lives, and were not linked directly with the Jama'at.

I suggested to these young women that we could choose a particular issue on which to focus our research exercises. After some discussion they chose honor killings as the issue that they would like to grapple with first. International media coverage of honor killings, particularly in the Pakistani context, has been relatively continuous over the last decade.[23] In 2005, General Musharaf's government stepped up a media campaign against honor killings as part of his agenda of fostering Enlightened Moderation in Pakistan. The women at JI felt torn by this issue. On the one hand, they did not condone honor killings, on the other they did not wish to be seen as falling in line with a "Western" and "military dictatorship"–driven agenda (Qazi n.d.). They felt that the issue had been given disproportionate attention by Western governments to pressurize Muslims. At the same time, they were unanimous in declaring that honor killings were un-Islamic, a product of illiteracy and general cultural licentiousness, and, most critically, a result of the contamination of Islamic ideals by what they perceived to be Hindu practices.

During the second workshop, when the women had come back with press cuttings I had asked them to collect, I asked Uzma to read aloud the cutting she had brought. The article she had chosen included a statement given by a long-term JI affiliate that honor killings had not been condemned in Islam. After she read this statement, there was a deep silence in the room. The JI women in the room were genuinely surprised and shocked to hear a JI leader provide what they thought of as religious sanction to a prac- tice to which they had an instinctive repulsion. It seemed to me that even Uzma had not read beyond the headline and was reading the cutting for the first time. Afia Baji, the organizer of the think tank, spoke first, saying that perhaps he was quoted out of context, perhaps he did not mean what it is made to look like. Shama' (not her real name), who had completed a mas- ters degree in communications from the University of Punjab, said, after a pause, "Well, even if he did say it, it does not mean that this is really how it is (*yeh waqe'i aisay hai*). I don't think Islam supports honor killings and I have not seen any evidence to make me suspect that it does." Another longtime, midranking activist remarked thoughtfully, "Yes, if Maulana Maududi's writings teach us anything, then it is that we need to communicate with the Qur'an ourselves. I don't believe there is anything in the Qur'an specifically condoning honor killings." In the discussion that followed many other women echoed this sentiment, pointing out that perhaps what he meant was that honor killings were not mentioned in Qur'an, and so there could be no question of either support or condemnation. Then Shama' suggested that they could invite the particular JI scholar attributed in the news with this support for honor killings to a conversation with the group. Others readily agreed that a discussion with him would be useful in clearing up this confusion and allowing the women to think through their own position.

The emphasis that these women laid upon an individual relationship with Allah and Qur'an should not suggest a complete disregard for taqlid or the ulama. Taqlid is a very important principle in traditional Islam, which recognizes the difficulty of having a deep knowledge of the hadīs, fiqh, and Qur'anic material to be able to make informed decisions about the various Qur'anic injunctions. Traditionalist Islam's reliance on ulama, who were expected to build a detailed knowledge of all the source material, played an important role also in regulating conflict within the Muslim society. Different ulama could disagree with each other and followers could make the decision about which one to follow based on the arguments raised by each alim. Islamists challenge what they believe to be individual passivity due to a reliance on ulama. This belief manifested itself in a resistance to establishing *madaris* (singular: *madrasa*), and for the first five decades of its existence, the JI did not establish any of its own. However, over the last three decades, the JI has been building a network of madaris in addition to its initial presence in institutions of higher and professional education. Nevertheless, we can discern a difference in emphasis from the traditionalists when the JI women are willing to give their own reading of the Qur'an an almost equal weight compared to that of the ulama and other religious experts. Their involvement in and exposure to Islamism has supported competing thrusts within their own life: a new vision of individual belief linked closely to collective responsibility.

From Elections to Sex Manuals: The Modalities of Religious Obligation

JI women leaders were almost all college educated, albeit often not at the elite colleges in major cities. Nevertheless, there is greater practice and appreciation of "knowledge" and "analysis." This is reflected in the high esteem accorded to one longtime JI woman activist whom I did not, in fact, manage to meet. However, she was held as an example and was a source of inspiration to many others that I did spend much time with. Not only has she authored several books, but she also has nine children. Activists spoke about how she woke up at four in the morning to write, say her prayers, and cook food for the day even before her children woke up. She also managed to fit lectures and political mobilization into her busy routine. Many women I met in the inner city of Lahore claimed that their daughters had studied the Qur'an with her. She was held up as a model of the ideal Muslim woman, fulfilling her primary role of a homemaker but not neglecting her political obligations either. This commitment to political obligations was a recurring theme among the JI women. They often spoke of the JI interchangeably as a party and as a movement, and claimed that the "quality" of the JI vote was much better than others, by which they meant that its voters tended to be more consistent and educated. This need for political involvement was also a recurring theme in the lectures by many JI leaders during the campaign for local body elections in Lahore.

On the campaign trail for local elections in Lahore in August 2005, the accepted format seemed to be that a JI activist or leader would read from the Qur'an and give a short dars about the general political situation, finishing off by admonishing listeners to "vote for Islam, vote for pious people who would be sure to serve you." He/she would then be followed by local political activists talking about the candidates of that area. If the candidate was present, he or she would then introduce himself/herself and talk about specific plans and/or past contributions to the locality. The pattern was quite similar in the campaign meetings held separately for men and women. Sometimes there were joint rallies at which women sat in separate tents and the address of the JI male candidate was broadcast from outside the tent to the women inside. Pamphlets about the "Islamic duty" to vote were distributed in both sections.[24]

At a typical women-only meeting, held on the local school grounds in the inner city of Lahore, women from the neighborhood were seated on chairs arranged in rows facing a raised veranda from which a senior JI activist gave her lecture. Many of the women in the audience were part of the extended family of one of the candidates that the JI was supporting in these elections. But many others had been attracted by the possibility of earning some spiritual *sawab* (reward) by listening to the dars. The JI leader started by reciting part of a *surah* (*Surah an-Nisa*) of the Qur'an in Arabic, and then the translation in Urdu.[25] After that, she moved on to explaining the *surah* with reference to the current situation. Soon she had worked to a highly charged list of all the problems that Muslims were facing in the world today. Foremost on her list was the cultural imposition of an alien, non-Muslim way of being. Other problems, such as wars and international persecution, were seen to be tied to this particular impulse to subjugate Muslims. Now, softening her voice, she asked her audience: "And you, what will you do in the face of this catastrophe? When you die, what are you going to tell your Allah? That you were too busy cooking? That you spent your life cleaning and washing clothes? [Moving from a confrontational "you" to a more inclusive "we."] These are our duties, no doubt, but we have to also answer to God, not just the men. We have our belief (iman) as well."

During the course of this research I heard various other JI women exhort either the men in the organization or those in their families to support women's da'wa and political work by taking on more duties at home, particularly those related to childcare.[26] One JI leader whom I got to know very well during the course of my fieldwork was often quite vocal in asking for greater support from the men in the organization. In addition, she was a vocal critic of those who had joined the tehreek out of political expediency and career interests. She and her husband are both professionals working in the service sector. I had actually been introduced to her through her husband. We had now spent considerable time with each other not just during the election campaign but also during my meetings with her at her home. Cognizant of the fact that I knew her husband in his professional capacity, she began to very subtly distance herself from him. She mentioned how some men, including her husband, had used their affiliation with the JI to further their own careers. She would often remind me that religious belief was a great leveler of social and gender distinctions, and that her political commitment was purer because it emanated from her belief. She had not sought any particular office either within the Jama'at or through Jama'at connections in her place of work, as others had done. I do not want here to set up a simple binary between the "political" man and the "religious" woman. Rather I want to highlight the intertwining of belief and practice in defining agency, and to suggest that the focus of agency among women is not always resistance to male domination. Resistance may be an incidental outcome rather than the primary focus.

In their pursuit of a life organized by Islamic principles, urban JI women have to contend with the demands of modern technologies, international migration, and the relatively wide range of cultural heterogeneity that permeates all parts of urban life in Pakistan. One such aspect has been in-creased awareness about and discussion of sexual practices for pious Mus-lims. As a JI women's wing leader said to me,

> We, in the women's wing, have to remind ourselves to stop and wait for the men to catch up. Only recently there was a debate about writing sex manuals for young Muslims. Obviously, our children see so many dif-ferent things through international media now, and they want to know what is permissible and what is not. So we prepared a manual. However, the men's section said it was too explicit and that we should censor cer-tain parts to make it acceptable as a JI-sponsored publication. After they refused to budge from their position, we said ok. The official document is the censored one. But we also had the full manual printed through an-other publisher. . . . As I said, sometimes we [women] laugh amongst our-selves and remind each other that we have to slow down, we are at least ten years ahead of the men, so we have to pace ourselves.

The need for sex education had to be dealt with in a logical, scientific, *and* religious method; this much the men and women agreed upon. In this context it is useful to keep in mind what Mervat Hatem (1998, 97) has shown in the context of Egypt, that contrary to the rhetoric employed from both sides, there is significant overlap in the positions of the Islamists and the secularists regarding the importance of science, "reason," professional education and technology in the building of the new society, and the basis of a modern marriage. Moreover, Islamists do not challenge the founda-tions of a nuclear family, nor the notions of a marriage based on privacy with a focus on the couple's compatibility.[27] There is also a significant over-lap in views about female chastity and model behavior between Islamists and secularists. Shared cultural norms that define gender expectations are most frequently not challenged by the secularists either. Many secular feminists themselves are vociferous supporters of some aspects of such cul-tural norms. As Nadje Al-Ali (2000) has shown, there is significant variation among the secularist women activists in Egypt regarding their relationship with religion and its implications for feminism: "there is also nothing inher-ently progressive or democratic about secularism. It is only through careful historical and political contextualization that any meaningful association can be made. . . . Egyptian women far from being passive victims, are en-gaged in the difficult task of subverting hegemonic discourses related to the state, Islamists and conservative male intellectuals" (148).

From exhorting women to move beyond "cooking and cleaning their homes" and become more politically engaged to championing the cause of "proper" sex education, molding subjectivities in direct relationship with a text despite opposition from within their homes, and defining their own position on "women's issues" such as honor killings, the JI and JD women's stances are distinctly modernist. The fundamental difference that these women believe separates them from "secular" feminists is the notion of religious belief and how it impacts their actions. However, as I have attempted to show here and elsewhere in this book, the domain of religious belief is constantly shifting and evolving. The process of negotiation with traditionalist Islam, the appropriation of modernist methods and perspectives, and the questioning of religious practices and beliefs that accompany such a negotiation is a hallmark of Islamist activity. Not only is it analytically productive to move beyond the idea of a religion as a fixed entity, but it would be dangerous not to do so. In attempting to bring all aspects of modern life under religious scrutiny but from a modernist perspective, Islamist women and men are engaging in a refashioning of belief in Muslim societies. This refashioning is best looked at not in terms of an increase or decrease in the *quantity* of belief, but a change in the texture, substantive elements, and *quality* of belief. Secularization debate has been for far too long mired in measuring the quantity of belief in terms of church attendance and visible markers of religious identity. It may be useful now to think about the more subtle but decidedly significant changes in belief itself.

In this context, it is also pertinent to note that religious belief remains associated with the burden of tradition and unthinking, blind following, while secularization has agentive connotations. There is, however, an inherent contradiction here—almost all theorists of secularization saw it as a structural process linked to modernization and larger than any one individual's choice, yet there was a sense that to be secular was to somehow assert individual choices and to resist mindless subjugation to religious laws. This particularly agentive quality attributed to secularism is the product of a specific history of association between patriarchal forces and religious institutions, both of which have changed significantly since feminist theory first associated progress with secularism. To know and understand that allows us to begin to subject the various constitutive elements of liberal political conceptualization to greater scrutiny in the light of contemporary developments. Agentive action needs to be understood as historically and culturally grounded, including belief as a potential substantive element.

Belief and Authority

The changes in structures of authority with which Islamism is linked contain the paradox of rationalized and individualized religious practice within a hierarchical organizational structure. Even as individuals are encouraged in forming a direct and individual relationship with God, their worldly contribution is mediated through a political organization that is structured and hierarchical. However, this contradiction is not ultimately irreconcilable for the members of these Islamist organizations. These contradictory pulls toward individualization and collective action, toward a notion of freedom at the same time as submission to authority are fundamental features of modernity. While they are most pronounced in radical movements that were avowedly modernist—from the Bolsheviks to the fascists—liberal polities have not been free of these contradictions either.

Among Islamists, authority is constructed through a melding together of political ability with piety. Activists would speak of their respect for leaders based not just on their personal piety and religious learning but also on their ability to bring people together or to mobilize and organize certain sections of society. Even as Hafiz Mohammed Syed continuously emphasized his religious learning, his years in Saudi Arabia and his facility with Arabic language, his association with ulema and the religious leanings of his family, many activists emphasized to me his ability to bring different factions of the organization together, whether by force or by persuasion was left open to discussion. The case of Jama'at-e-Islami is more illuminating. While the Jama'at e Islami is hierarchical, it is not without a system of representation within the organization. The amir is ultimately an elected leader and, unlike the Jama'at-ud-D'awa, there are several equally likely candidates contesting senior positions. Syed Munawar Hussain, the current amir, faced serious competition from other JI leaders during his election in 2009. The other contenders were Liaqut Baloch, a national-level politician who has served as a member of the National Assembly as well as the Provincial Assembly in Punjab, and Siraj ul Haq, who has served as a minister at the provincial level in Khyber Pakhtunkhwa. At least ostensibly, the candidates do not campaign for themselves and, in fact, in public contexts can be seen enumerating the positive points of competing candidates. A key ingredient in their claim to authority within the organization is personal piety. As much as any historical figure or prophetic life, these leaders provide a living example to many within these organizations as they try to strike a balance between personal piety and worldliness, public obligations and personal ambitions, knowledge and habit. Time and again activists in both organizations emphasized the central role of belief in not just motivating but supporting this balancing act in their life.

That over the last two centuries there have been significant changes in the *structures* of Islamic religious authority is increasingly gaining recognition within academic literature (Eickelman and Piscatori 1996; Masud, Messick, and Powers 1996; Zaman 2002; Hefner 2000). Some of same scholars have also alerted us to the changes in the *content* of Islamic authority in terms of the issues and subjects that are considered within the purview of authoritative rulings. The role of new media, mass literacy, international migration, new legal regimes, and global communication have all been highlighted as leading to a fragmentation of Islamic authority (Mandaville 2001, 2007; Anderson and Eickelman 2003; Eickelman 1992; Turner and Volpi 2007; Salvatore 2007; Modood and Ahmad 2007). This notion of fragmentation of Islamic authority needs to be nuanced by the recognition that there may never have been a seamless, consistent, unanimous discourse of authority (Hallaq 2001; Weiss 1991). Indeed, in a rather schematic approach to the formation of authority within Islam, Hamid Dabashi (1989) has used and critiqued the Weberian scheme of charismatic, legal/bureaucratic, and traditional authority to suggest that from the very early years of Muslim history, competing notions of authority—what it is and who may exercise it—as well as arrangements of religious and political authority—whether they are to be separated out or not–came about. Even as we acknowledge the heterogeneity of notions and practices of authority in Islam over the last fourteen centuries, we can recognize that the modern period has seen a significant change in the pace and scale of fragmentation of both political and religious authority, particularly when compared to the period immediately preceding it. The Islamists are both a product of this fractured authority and contributors to its further splintering.

But what precisely are the implications of this fragmentation? The ready equation of this fragmentation in authority with a decrease in belief may be satisfying in its simplicity, but does not really hold up in the light of historical and contemporary experience. There can be little doubt that the imperatives within the European context were different from the context in South Asia and the Middle East. Given the fact that the Catholic Church inherited the state from the Roman Empire, it had a hold over political structures that was not replicated in the Muslim world. Despite the fact that its particular blend of political and religious authority was uniquely its own, the European experience has nevertheless framed contemporary discourse in all parts of the world about the relationship between authority and belief. But even within Europe, whether or not the fragmentation resulted in a less believing populace remains open to question, not only because we haven't necessarily measured closely what happened *after* Enlightenment, but also because we may be incorrect in what we presume happened *before* it. When the church controlled various aspects of human life, there was less emphasis on individual belief. Casanova (1994, 16) alerts us to the difference between personal devotion and structural religiosity: "Even when historians are able to determine with relative certainty the proportion of priests and religious people within society, this statistic tells us little about their actual religiosity. We have sufficient information about widespread corruption in the papal court, about rampant hedonism in the monasteries, and about simoniacal priests. If the religious virtuosi led such lives, there is no reason to believe that the ordinary Christian led more virtuous lives. Indeed, precisely because the official Christian structure of society guaranteed that everybody was leading Christian lives, it was not so necessary to stress personal devotion."

Thus, while we cannot be sure of the extent of religiosity among individual members of European Christiandom prior to the eighteenth and nineteenth centuries, we can be quite certain that writers and scholars of the later period were convinced that religion was inextricably linked to dogma and irrationality (Chadwick 1975; Aron 1968; Gauchet 1997; Thompson 2010). It was a relationship they were determined to put behind them.

Despite several reversals and geographical variations, the view of the preceding centuries as more religious—certainly not without empirical evidence at least at the structural level if not at the individual level—emerged as a framework within which progress was measured. Weber's influential work on *The Protestant Ethic and the Spirit of Capitalism* (1950 [1904]) emerged in a context where intellectuals were grappling with a relatively rapid pace of change in everyday life (Aron 1968). However, Weber's work, while sharing the assumption of some change in religious belief and practice, contains a sophisticated appraisal of the long-term implications of changes in and through religious belief. In *The Protestant Ethic* Weber is concerned to emphasize that the narrative that he presents is not the only explanation, but one plausible and possible one for the emergence of capitalism. In that sense it remains a tentative exploration into the changes within belief and their relationship with economic and political structures. Paradoxically, given his concern for keeping center stage the human motivations and agency, Weber also derails the link between agency and outcome.

What comes out of a particular set of actions may be very different than what the actors themselves expected. In this context he highlights first the subtle distinctions among Protestants and then emphasizes the increase in religious surveillance and personal piety that went hand in hand with their break from the authority of the Catholic Church: "[T]he God of Calvinism demanded of his believers not single good works, but a life of good works combined into a unified system. There was no place for the very human Catholic cycle of sin, repentance, atonement, release, followed by renewed sin. Nor was there any balance of merit for a life as a whole, which could be adjusted by temporal punishments or the Churches' means of grace" (1950, 117). The increase in personal piety is linked closely in his narrative with the rationalization of belief. Indeed the sentences quoted above are preceded by his observation that "the rationalization of the world, . . . the Catholics had not carried nearly so far as the Puritans (and before them the Jews) had done" (1950, 117). He then goes on to elaborate that "the moral conduct of the average man was thus deprived of its planless and unsystematic character and subjected to a consistent method for conduct as a whole. It is no accident that the name of Methodists stuck to the participants in the last great revival of Puritan ideas in the eighteenth century just as the term Precisians, which has the same meaning, was applied to their spiritual ancestors in the seventeenth century."

Weber's reading of the Protestant challenge to Catholicism and of the rise of capitalism has never been without contestation both on empirical grounds and on its theoretical shortcomings. My purpose here in highlighting his work is not to attempt to prove or disprove his contentions. More critically, I do not propose to read into this the lateness of Muslim societies when compared to the European context. It is not a reiteration of a stageist view that Muslims are going through the reformation that Christians in Europe experienced many centuries ago. At the same time, while keeping the differences in mind, I do not want to underestimate the similarities: it is a similar, but not the same, process, and will certainly not lead to the same kind of subjectivities and norms. A key difference that needs to be kept in mind is the vastly different notions of the "public" and the place of religion in it. The Protestant reformers were not clamoring, at least initially, for greater state control, unlike the Islamists. Indeed, the notion and reality of the "state" that the Islamists contend with is very different from the one that the early Protestant reformers had to deal with.[28] Our focus on difference, on "provincializing Europe," has to go hand in hand with an acknowledgment and clear understanding of the similarities in experiences of modernity around the globe: there is no clear mapping of the South Asian, or Muslim, or Latin American experience onto the history of the European one, and yet, not only does the European experience inform and thus shape experiences elsewhere, but there are certain features common to economic and political structures shared by the disparate populations of the world today. Contemporary capitalism weaves together divergent local historical trajectories within a global context, even as the local trajectories strain to shape the global context. Thus, and as I discuss in more detail in the next chapter, acknowledging the parallels with a Weberian reading of the changes in and through belief within Christian Europe does not mean that we expect the South Asian experience to produce exactly the same subjectivities and normativities.

Here, my primary purpose in underscoring Weber's influential work is to point out a strand of secularization theory that has remained subsumed within debates about private/public, less/more religion. Weber is indeed one of the key influences in the sociology of religion and theories of secularization. Yet the focus on the public/private divide and the interest in measuring the changes in quantity of belief was such that many of the dots that Weber hesitated to connect were, using his work, perhaps too hastily joined to form a theory of secularization. The jump from rationalized religious belief to no belief, from privatized observance to reduced religious belief, from disenchantment to a state of Fauerbachian return to full possession of humanity was one that packaged quite a few assumptions and missed several steps in the logic. In drawing attention to this less developed strand of secularization theory, my purpose is to begin to disentangle these complicated knots of assumptions regarding the relationship between belief, its quantity, and its quality, structures of authority, state projects, and social dynamics.

Islamists

SECULARIZING *AND* LIBERAL?

The importance of Pakistan in understanding emerging trends in Muslim politics cannot be overstated. Pakistan, a relatively young state and a fragile nation, is shouldering a heavy burden in the "war on terror." Indeed, much of the war is being carried out within Pakistan, be it the bombing of villages in Waziristan or the wide-ranging access granted to US and UK intelligence services in apprehending and detaining Pakistani citizens as well as others.[1] The implications of this central role in the "war on terror" remain unclear but certainly do not seem to be very promising for local politics and society. Quite apart from this recent and dubious rise in importance, Pakistan, along with the larger region of North India, is home to many of the organizational, philosophical, and political innovations in Muslim thought and practice in the last two centuries. While popular Western imagination conflates "Muslim" with "Arab," in fact today Arabs represent less than a fifth of the world's one billion Muslims. The demographic centers of the Muslim world lie in South and Southeast Asia. A better understanding of the changing role of Muslim "fundamentalists," and in particular the Islamists, in Pakistan has immense implications for an understanding of emerging trends in Muslim politics.

In the case of Pakistan, the increasing role of religious groups since Zia's Islamization campaigns, and in particular of the Islamists, has been analyzed in some detail primarily in terms of their relationship with state structures.[2] Many of these researchers have highlighted the link between Islam and national identity. The general consensus among them seems to be that Pakistan's formation on the basis of religious communalism and official adherence to vague notions of an affiliation with Islam has led to unresolved "political, cultural and ideological confusion" (Sayeed 1997, 27). Particular religious organizations like the Jama'at-e-Islami (Nasr 1994, 2001), the Tablighi Jama'at (Metcalf 1994, 2002), and the Jam'iyat-i-ulama

Pakistan (Pirzada 2000) have been studied in some detail. Ethnic identity and its link with Islam have also received some attention.[3] Mehdi (1993) and Anita Weiss (1986) have focused on the changes in laws due to Islamization. The impact of Zia's Islamization campaign on women, in particular, has received much attention.[4] Yet most of these studies provide a relatively static view of the role of Islamists in Pakistani politics as the large majority was conducted in response to the Zia years. They are framed in a teleological grid of progress and regress, inevitably seeing the religious as the backward. Moreover, these studies do not assess the changes in the role of the Islamists in the last two decades. Critically, the studies mentioned above do not interrogate the larger societal impact of Islamist mobilizations in any depth, nor do they question the categories used to assess the role of the Islamists, and normative associations with those categories.

Here, I have used a detailed account of the role of Islamists in contemporary Pakistan to facilitate our understanding of two important and linked concepts, secularism and secularization. I have argued that the Islamists are facilitating secularization at a societal level even as they continue to oppose secularism as an official policy. This secularization is not premised on a strict demarcation of the public realm from the private, but rather proceeds through a critical interrogation of what the role of religion is to be in these realms. The Islamist insistence on the internal coherence of religious practice, its appropriateness to tackle the challenges of modern life, as well as the competition among Islamist groups have led to a broad and deep conscious thinking-through of the role of religion in contemporary Muslim life. This "objectification" does not imply a loss of transcendence but a shift in emphasis. Religious practice can no longer be a matter of communal following of norms; it has been changed into a largely individualized decision that must be justified internally, that is, within a subject, and externally, to others around the subject

In this, the difference between the Islamists and the Muslim modernists, like Sir Sayeed Ahmed, is most pronounced. While the modernists took various Muslim practices seriously as part of their cultural identity, they did not interrogate Eurocentric categories and binaries of analysis: religious/secular, public/private, modern/traditional. The Islamists in contrast refuse to take these categories seriously. They refuse to accept that the private and the public can be separated as clearly as it has been suggested to them; they refuse to believe that the religious cannot be modern. This fundamental questioning and repositioning of the debate about the public-private divide and the role of religion therein has certainly generated a host of paradoxes. On the one hand, the salience of Islam in political discourse has meant that so-called secular parties have relied heavily on Islam for legitimacy, and on the other, I show how the Islamists have facilitated a deeper questioning of different aspects of religious practice and belief.

My attempt here is not meant to provide a schematic and definitive answer to the dynamics of Islamism within Pakistan. Rather, I want to suggest precisely that political and social entanglements cannot proceed along strictly linear formations. In a perceptive critique of postcolonial theory, David Scott (1996) is concerned to go beyond the claims of Eurocentrism in social science concepts. In this and a more recent paper (2003) he makes a persuasive case for understanding the political context in which particular concepts find resonance and sustenance. He points out that:

> The contrast-effects produced by the epistemological critique to which postcolonial criticism . . . has been committed for the last fifteen years or so have lost much of their critical force. In part this is because our present, so marked by the collapse of those modernist hopes that animated our political pre-occupations in the aftermaths of sovereignty, provokes another demand than the one this criticism was designed to meet. This new demand is to rethink the claims and the categories of that very political modernity in which these hopes found the voice—that of a morally neutral citizen-subject—in which to speak. Finally, meeting this demand entails folding the critique of the Enlightenment project into a practice in which our target is defined in terms of challenging the story of our political present (and thus of our prospects for alternative political futures) according to which there is a single horizon towards which it is desirable *for us all* to head. (Scott 1996, 22; emphasis in original)

Put another way, Scott raises the possibility that not only do various polities and societies not start from the same departure point, they may not all be moving in the same direction. Postcolonial critique has been particularly useful in highlighting the first part of this proposition. But lurking behind the nuanced arguments has been an assumption that greater understanding of different vantage points toward history and the present would allow us eventually to move toward similar goals. And Scott rightly, I think, raises the question whether this can really be so. I will pick up on this discussion in the next section by focusing on tolerance, the idea that underpins much of the debate about secularism.

Secularism and Tolerance

In a much-quoted paper, Charles Taylor claimed that "The end of hier-archy is not of itself the dawn of liberalism. Rather it ups the ante: either the civilized coexistence of diverse groups, or new forms of savagery. It is in this sense that secularism is not an option in the modern age" (1998, 47). Taylor is worried specifically about the immense potential for oppres-sion and violence that he sees as inherent within the structures of modern states. He is not alone in imagining a descent into savagery if the principle of secularism is not defended and reinforced. The manifestation of violent communalism in India and of religiously inspired violence in different parts of the world has led to a strong belief among the liberal and left segments that secularism is to be defended at all costs. In Pakistan, the government of General Musharaf had imposed a version of secularism under the ban-ner of Enlightened Moderation as a pivotal policy that helped legitimize his regime, if not to the majority of Pakistanis, then at least to an interna-tional audience. Secularism's rationality and modernity was once again contrasted with the irrationality and backwardness of religion, and put to service by a dictatorial regime. Yet again this vision of secularism is devoid of any substantive engagement with the structures of the society in which it operates, but buoyed by its supposed inevitability as well as desirability.

In analyzing the continued use of Christian imagery and discourse within the working class in England, Alasdair MacIntyre (1964) observed that as the processes of industrialization and urbanization came together, more distinct and divergent classes and class interests emerged that could no longer be contained within a particular class's absolutist view of religion. Different classes proceeded with a loss of religious framework at differ-ent speeds. For MacIntyre, the questions answered by secularism are the same ones answered by religion. However, the loss of a framework and vocabulary inhibited the range of questions that could be asked. Thus for him (1964, 30–31), "a consistent and systematic secularism, if it is the doc-trine of a social group, depends upon the possession of a vocabulary by that group in which these questions can be asked and answered. Hence the loss of a framework and vocabulary by the English working class is itself perhaps the major inhibiting force, which prevented secular views dominat-ing them. It is not surprising that instead there remains with them a strong vestigial Christianity, manifested wherever at times of birth, marriage and death questions about meaning, purpose and survival become inescapable." MacIntyre's view assumes a relative inevitability to the triumph of secularism. Yet he recognizes the tortuous process that may precede its triumph. The variation in the path to secularism among the different classes of England is embedded in the history of their interaction with each other as well as the contours of the religious framework available to them.

Setting aside the question of historical inevitability, even when recognizing the variations in paths and normative value ascribed to secularism, we may ask precisely what is of value in the concept. Going back to Taylor's argument about the inherent potential for mass-scale, intensive savagery within modern structures and technologies, it appears that secularism is to be valued for its promotion of tolerance among different kinds of people who are now thrown into closer interaction than ever before. Taylor (1998, 52) suggests a "secularism of overlapping consensus," which he posits will *have* to work in spite of the many challenges that are likely to come its way. Precisely how this secularism of overlapping consensus is to be built is left open. Within the liberal deliberative framework an alternate conception has been suggested by Bruce Ackerman with the notion of conversational restraint. He suggests:

> When you and I learn that we disagree about one or another dimension of the moral truth, we should not search for some common value that will trump this disagreement: nor should we try to translate it into some putatively neutral framework; nor should we seek to transcend our disagreement by talking about how some unearthly creature might resolve it. We should simply say nothing at all about this disagreement and put the moral ideas that divide us off the conversational agenda of the liberal state. In restraining ourselves in this way, we need not lose the chance to talk to one another about our deepest moral disagreements in countless other, more private, contexts. . . . Having constrained the conversation in this way, we may instead use dialogue for pragmatically productive purposes: to identify normative premises all political participants find reasonable (or at least not unreasonable). (Ackerman 1989, 16–17)[5]

Despite their differences in other aspects, both Taylor and Ackerman seem to leave aside matters of imbalance in power in their formulations aimed at promoting a kind of tolerance of the other. Indeed they leave aside matters of how the other came to be the other. Tolerance itself is not free of power relations (Brown 2006). The depoliticization of the discourse of tolerance in recent years has led to a triumphalist discourse that presents tolerance as the unqualified achievement of Western liberalism. Yet, as Wendy Brown shows, tolerance may well be a mode of continued abjectifiction and marginalization. Brown's approach helps us contextualize the use of the term "tolerance" and the political situation in which this use is embedded and understood. Further, her analysis allows us to question the implicit and seemingly timeless association between secularism and tolerance.

Islamist Secularization: Imagining a Liberal Polity?

Having brought into question an automatic association of secularism with tolerance, and linking back to my larger argument about the relationship between secularizing and secularism, I want to suggest that not only may peaceful coexistence be made difficult precisely due to state management of religion (i.e., secularism), but also that secularization may not lead unconditionally to the liberal subject. For what does it mean to say that Islamists are secularizing? Does it mean that they will produce a "liberal" subject? What kind of polity will be organized by such religious rationalists? The answers to these questions are not readily available, and I raise them to suggest avenues for future research. It is in this context that I find Scott's warnings about the possibility that we may not all be moving toward the same political horizon particularly pertinent. There is unlikely to be a linear association between the kind of secularization that I see the Islamists promoting in urban Pakistan and a liberal political subject and polity. The contemporary association of secularism and secularization with liberalism is then open to question as the Islamist notions of justice, freedom, and the individual differ significantly from those dominant in contemporary liberal discourse.

This is something that requires much more careful research and analysis, and here I can only offer a suspicion about what is *not* the biggest difference between the liberals and the Islamists. Often the most fundamental difference between the Islamists and the liberals is taken to be their relationship with violence. However, I am not sure if that is indeed the most critical divergence, and it seems to me at this stage that we will need to dig deeper to think about substantive differences. The Islamists believe themselves to be fighting a defensive war insofar as they see themselves as responding to attacks made by others, be they the secularists within the country, aggressors across the border, or the invading armies of the US. Many among them are engaging in a civilizational war that is couched in a language similar to that prevalent within many liberal polities, including the

US and the UK. Interestingly, of course, there are important differences within this larger category "Islamist." Islamists such as the JD have tended to privilege the role of militancy in their activism. The contrast with JI, which has engaged opportunistically in violence through its student wing or through its support for a group of mujahideen within Afghanistan, is quite marked. There can be no easy and direct association of Islamism with violence, and certainly it seems naïve and ahistorical to suggest a preordained compulsion to violence within Islamism. What this does alert us to is the fact that just as there are different strands within Islamism that may be more or less inclined toward violence, so there are variations within the larger umbrella of liberalism that we need to parse out as much as possible within the current political context.

Why is this even important to think about? Why is it useful to think through the variations as well as the cracks and fissures in liberal conceptions of the world? Here again, I find that Scott (1996) synthesizes succinctly what many others have alluded to in the last decade. Scott (1996, 10–16) suggests, while criticizing the more vulgar triumphalism of Francis Fukuyama's *End of History and the Last Man*, that we are today operating in a changed "cognitive-political context." The existence of an alternative in Marxism-socialism allowed a certain horizon to postcolonial critics, even if many did not actually subscribe to the alternative. However, given the contemporary reconfigured context of communist collapse and liberal self-congratulations, avenues for productive critical engagement require "the need to rethink the story of liberalism and democracy, which has for more than a generation informed our vision of political sovereignty" (Scott 1996, 16).

If liberalism is the dominant ideology informing contemporary politics, then we need to probe, investigate, and thus understand it better. My attempt here is not aimed at valorizing Islamism and Islamists. Rather, I hope on the one hand to humanize, contextualize, and understand better the aspirations, ideas, groups, and ultimately individuals who are an important part of the modern political landscape; and on the other to explore and interrogate concepts that inform our understanding of this landscape, as well as our attempts at reshaping it. If we are to spend our political energies, it may be worthwhile pausing to evaluate what we are hoping to defend before we draw the battlelines.

Notes

Introduction

1. The Islamist unions were, and continue to be, strongest in state-owned service sectors, e.g., public universities and colleges, banks, water supply and hydel energy, telephone service, and airline industry. Some of these services have been fully or partially privatized in recent years.

2. Roy (1994) suggests that Islamism has failed. Kepel (2002) and Ahmad (2009) support the view that Islamism has now morphed into post-Islamism with a decentring of the focus on state and greater acceptance of plurality within and outside the movement. While there are important currents of increased plurality in the context of Islamist groups in Pakistan, I find that the situation in Pakistan is not easily categorized as "post-Islamist" given the continued political engagement of the JI and JD with the state. I sympathize with Ahmed's contention (2009) that Islamism is a process, dynamic and ever evolving but am not convinced that it has morphed into a different type altogether in the case of Pakistan. The difference between the JI India that Ahmed has studied and the JI Pakistan that I have researched highlights the impact of the context in which Islamism operates. Bayat (2005, 5), in responding to the widespread use of the term "post-Islamism" that he coined to speak about changes in Iran points out that he understands the term to represent "both a condition and a project." As a condition, it refers to the draining of energy from the initial sources of legitimacy of Islamism. As a project, post-Islamism refers to a more explicit negotiation with democracy and liberalism. His own use of the term is thus much better suited to understanding the situation in Pakistan that those it has been put to by the other scholars mentioned above.

3. The current conflation of "terrorist," "militant," and "Islamist" is particularly misleading. While some Islamist groups have in the past used violence and/or continue to do so today, they are not primarily militant groups. See Iqtidar (2008) for the importance of removing the automatic association of terrorism with Islamism.

4. Transliterated, "Jama'at-ud-Da'wa" means a proselytising group. I discuss the meanings and roots of the term "da'wa" in more detail in chapter 3.

5. In April 2010, the province called the North West Frontier since colonial times was officially renamed Khyber Pakhtunkhwa.

6. See Iqtidar (2009) for some more detail on the emergence of Lashkar-e-Tayyaba as an alleged "militancy consultant" in the wake of the ongoing war in Afghanistan.

7. Roy (1994) may suggest that JD can no longer be seen as Islamist but as neofundamentalist. Neofundamentalists, according to him, are less state centric and

tend to focus on changing the society, which would lead toward a transformation at the state level. However, Roy (1994, 75) himself recognizes there is no complete transition from Islamist to neofundamentalist, and so he "speak[s] of a drift because there is no break between Islamism and neofundamentalism." I remain unconvinced of the usefulness of coining new terms and categories without exploring fully the meanings of existing ones. Moreover, Roy's notion of a chronological shift from Islamism to Neofundamentalism underplays the fact that both exist at the same time. I find it more useful to recognize the diversity within Islamism as a necessary part of it rather than as signalling a fundamental shift in its focus.

8. With enough seats to form governments in two out of four provinces and 62 out of the 342 seats in the National Assembly, MMA (Joint Religious Alliance) emerged in a kingmaker's position in the 2002 elections. There are significant questions about whether this electoral victory of the MMA really demonstrated popular support. There are allegations of military support for the MMA to enable General Musharaf to play the role of the US ally in keeping a "fundamentalist revolution" at bay. These allegations are based primarily on the fact that the army allowed MMA to hold election rallies in areas where other parties, particularly the Pakistan People's Party, were not given official permission. However, three key issues demand some consideration. First, the army, like any large institution, is not a monolith. So while individuals with strong Islamist or militant Islamic tendencies may have provided support to certain groups within the MMA, at the policy level the military is very much operating against the religious groups in Pakistan. Suicide attacks on General Musharaf give some glimpse into his standing with some of the religious groups. More critically, it is not clear whether the holding of political rallies alone could have persuaded voters to change preferences. Finally, it is hard to discredit MMA claims that they had enough mobilization momentum to hold the rallies anyway, and the army was forced to give them official permission to forestall any showdown just before the elections that the general needed to establish his democratic credentials.

9. I provide some information regarding US support for JI during the late 1960s onward in chapter 2. Much has been written about the US support for Islamism in Pakistan. See, for instance, Ali 2003; Rashid 2000; Cooley 2000; Shafqat 2002. Nasr (1993, 1994) provides a relatively sympathetic view of the relationship between JI and the army during Zia's regime. However, he is right to identify that the JI was an organization in crisis during the Zia regime precisely due to the change this involvement in Afghan Jihad brought into JI and due to the opportunism exhibited by many members of the organization.

10. *Maslak* refers to the school of jurisprudence being followed, for example, Hanafi or Hannabali (Hallaq 2001). The majority of Pakistanis are Hanafi Sunnis. However, in colloquial Pakistani use, *malask* is often employed to also distinguish between the different kinds of more recent groupings within Sunnis, for example, Ahl-e-Hadīs, Barelvi, and Deobandi.

11. This is a particularly Islamist reading of the term. Maududi defined secularism as *Ilhad* (atheism). However, many other Islamic scholars disagree.

12. Holyoake, widely credited with coining the term "secularism," used it in his

1854 lecture "Principles of Secularism" to express a positive and ethical element precisely to distinguish the secularist from the infidel and the atheist. He wrote, "Secularists consider free thinking as a double protest—as a protest against speculative error and in favour of specific moral truth. The term 'secularism' has not been chosen as a concealment or disguise or as an apology for free inquiry, but as expressing a certain positive, ethical element which the terms infidel, atheist, sceptic do not express" (1896, 3).

13. See Khurshid Ahmed n.d. for a recent critique. Ahmed is a profile JI writer and commentator. He was elected senator in 1985, 1997, and 2002 and headed the JI's policy think tank Islamic Research council.

14. See Bruce 1999 for an overview. However, Martin (2005, 124–25) suggests that this might be a conclusion particularly popular with the English and European scholars. Scholars based in America, like Bellah, Berger, Luckmann, and others, had to contend with the reality of continued religiosity, manifested among other things by the relatively stable levels of continued church attendance in the wake of a constitution explicitly separating religion and politics in America. At a time when European church attendance declined sharply, American church attendance remained stable at 40–43 percent over the period 1939–81 (Bruce 1996, 129). Bruce (1996, 169), however, suggests that while the attendance has remained mostly steady, the churches have changed: the more radical sects have become denominations and the mainstream denominations have become ecumenical and tolerant.

15. Various contributions to Katznelson and Jones (2010) highlight the contrasting and contradictory thrusts, periodic reversals, and improbable gains in secularization within different parts of Europe. Connolly (2006) emphasizes the importance of disaggregating the European experience to think about the various "minority" traditions in European Enlightenment that do not fit neatly into dominant narratives of the secularization in Europe.

16. In the context of the Middle East, see Tamimi (2000, 13–29) and other contributions in the same volume for an overview of the relationship between states and secularism. Closer to Pakistan, the increased political presence of "communal" and religious groups in India has led to vast amounts of literature that exhort the Indian state to remain true to the Nehruvian policy of secularism. See, for instance, Engineer 1999, 2003, and particularly Vanaik 1997. A more critical look is presented by Bhargava et al. 1998.

17. In the case of Pakistan, see Papaneck 1967 for advocacy of the trickle-down effect of economic "modernization."

18. In the case of South Asia, Bayly's earlier (1987) and more recent (2004) work has been particularly prominent in underscoring this mutual influence.

19. For another less known but interesting work on Orientalism, see Kabbani 1994 [1986]. Said's argument is not predicated on the assumption of incommensurable differences between Muslims and the "'West." In other works Said (1995) has been concerned to expressly demolish the case for such incommesurability.

20. A rather banal example that nevertheless proves critical once its implications are recognized is the ordering of spatial imaginary. While European imagination buttressed by imperial might conceived of India as a "subcontinent" and Europe as a "continent," the definitions could easily be reversed. The Indian "subcontinent," consisting of the states of Pakistan, India, Bangladesh, Nepal, and Sri Lanka, was then, as now, larger in terms of the physical space covered, total population, ethnic diversity, and numbers of cultures and languages, than the "continent" of Europe. Frank (1998, 2), building on Marshall Hodgson's observation, points out that the Mercator projection allows "little" Britain to appear the same size as India on modern maps. Also see Lewis and Wigen (1997).

21. In the Islamist context this includes a conflation of Europe and the US as one monolithic Christian "West," home to material development and modernity, but also to social breakdown, particularly the disintegration of the family.

22. I use the term in the same spirit as Asad in *Anthropology and the Colonial Encounter* (1973).

23. Sadik Al-Azam, *Is* Islam Secularizable?: http://www.secularislam.org/separation/isisislam.htm, last accessed August 1, 2005. Sadik Al-Azam is a prominent Arab intellectual.

24. An interesting example of indirect but far-reaching Muslim influence in Europe is provided by Salvatore (2005, 419–22) when he points out that while Spinoza's writings provided an elegant and cogent justification of secular republicanism found in the Netherlands during the century of radical Enlightenment, it is mostly neglected that Spinoza's thought was heir to the vibrant cultural world of Al-Andalus. Spinoza was the son of a Sephardi Jewish family that had resettled in Amsterdam due to the persecutions carried out in Al-Andalus after the *reconquista*. Spinoza's thought is heavily indebted to Islamic philosophy and in particular to al-Farabi, Ibn Sina, and the Andalusian Ibn-Rushd. However, his decision to remain detached from any specific cultural and religious tradition has resulted in the fact that these influences go unacknowledged in his work. *Acquiescentia*, a key word in Spinoza's formulation, cannot be translated properly into any modern European language, but can be seen as a translation of *Islam*, in the sense of trustful surrender to God. (In this analysis Salvatore builds on the work of Eric Voeglin, *The New Order and Last Orientation*, vol. 7 of *The History of Political Ideas*, vol. 25 of *The Collected Works of Eric Voeglin*, ed. Jurgen Gebhardt and Thomas A. Hollweck [Columbia, MO: University of Missouri Press]).

25. In contrast to these liberal thinkers, Mehta finds that the conservative thinker and politician Edmund Burke, with his emphasis on the local and sentimental as opposed to the universal and rational, came closer to understanding the folly and arrogance of hoping to govern a people with their own history and culture. Therefore, he suggests that once one recognizes as Burke did "that human experience derives its density from the passionate commitment that a life form produces, then the challenge of cosmopolitanism is to understand these forms as contemporaneous ways of being in the world" (1999, 41–42).

26. For a generally accepted description of the characteristics of a secular state, see Audi 1989; Wiethman's (1991) discussion of Audi's paper; and Audi's (1991) response.

27. A nascent stream of scholarship within political science and international relations is beginning to recognize the importance of historical context and local

trajectories in shaping secularism as it is practiced in different parts of the world (Kuru 2007; Hurd 2008). Masud (2005, 368) suggests that the very difference between the English term "secularism" and the French term "laicism" alerts us to the differences in the actual manifestations of the project. The English term "secular" means age in a temporal sense. The French "laicite" derives from laic, i.e., lay people as opposed to clergy. Both reflect the difference in actual playing out of "secularism" in the local context. Quite apart from the variations historically in secularism across different regions of Europe, it is also useful to keep in mind that it is by no means a settled notion in contemporary times either. See, for instance, Lehmann (2006) for the relationship between conversion-based religious movements and secularism in contemporary Europe.

28. The titles of many of these works reflect the anxiety surrounding Islam, secularism and secularization: "Can Islam Be Secularised?" (Boroujerdi 1994); "Is Islam Secularisable?" (al-Azam 1994); "Islam and Liberal Democracy: The Challenge of Secularization," (Filali-Ansary 1996); *Islamism, Secularism and Human Rights in the Middle East* (Monshipouri 1998).

29. Van der Veer (2004, 33) highlights that the Muslims and Hindus in the context of the British colonial administration were not totally misguided in this understanding given the role that Christian beliefs, terminology, and values played in influencing colonial policy.

30. See, in particular, Salvatore 2005, 412. Also Shamsul 2005, 449–72.

31. Other Muslim scholars have of course made precisely the opposite point, often conflating secularism with atheism. Thus Rahman (1982, 15) wrote: "secularism is necessarily atheistic" and thus un-Islamic.

32. Flores's (1993) overview of the debate in Egypt can be seen to revolve around precisely this question. His overview can be easily applied to the debate in many other Muslim countries. Other notable contributions to the debate about Islam, Islamism, and secularism include those contained in Tamimi and Esposito 2000 and Monshipouri 1998. In the case of Pakistan in particular, see Tarik et al. 1998.

33. Anthropological research has been important in highlighting the fragility of the concept of secularism. However, Asad (1993, 2003), Starrett (1998), and Mahmood (2005) are not concerned directly with Islamism and its relationship to secularism.

34. Taylor's (2004, 23) distinction between social imaginary and social theory is useful here. Social imaginary focuses on the way people imagine their social surroundings, which is distinct from theoretical frrameworks and is carried in stories, images, and legends. It is also more widespread and thus makes possible common practices and a shared sense of legitimacy.

35. Manuel (1983) provides an interesting glimpse into this through a focus on Galileo, Kepler, and Newton.

36. Other contributors in the same volume (Calhoun 1992) have raised similar concerns about the exclusion of groups from the public sphere due to property ownership, race, and sexual orientation, pointing again to the need for a more nuanced reading of the public sphere, keeping the play of power in mind.

37. Masud (2005, 381) warns against ideologizing secularism by reminding us that these processes work in a dialectical manner: "These discourses on secularism also suggest that the more secularism and Islam are ideologized, the more it is difficult to speak of change and reform."

38. Masud (1993, 195) highlights the limitations of studies of Muslim politics that focus on the writings of leaders and ideologues of Muslim politics by calling them "studies of scholars by scholars for scholars."

39. Piscatori's (1983, 1–2) observation that "to date there have been only a few empirical studies that try to go beyond the impressionistic and general and take the measure of Islam's current political activity. . . . Islamic politics is an elusive and contentious subject to study" remains a relevant one today too.

40. That interdisciplinarity has almost become an end in itself regardless of any disadvantages or advantages it may bring with it has provoked some concern. Strathern (2006, 196) asks: "Why must interdisciplinarity be *seen* to be on everyone's agenda these days? Why its new visibility? . . . Why does it seem like a new rationale for re-grouping departments and re-conceptualising teaching?" Strathern proposes that disciplines provide "a community of critics" that allow for concepts to be questioned in detail through informed criticism. I find that it is useful to think about the limits of interdisciplinarity and not just its advantages when approaching a research project.

41. See for instance, Roy 2002, 1994; Fuller 2003; Ayubi 1991; Esposito 1997.

42. Masjid Qadsia complex includes a mosque for men with a capacity of two thousand and a women's section, which could accommodate one thousand. The complex also includes the various offices of JD bureaucracy, its publications offices, including those of its printing press Al-Andulus, its weekly magazine *Ghazva*, its monthly *Al-Da'wa*, and a library/bookshop. Finally, a three- or four-bedroom house for the Lahore organizer and mosque custodian is also part of the complex. The land for the complex was reportedly bought at Rs. 750,000,000,000 and construction cost an additional Rs. 200,000,000,000 (Amir Rana 2003).

43. Ahmad 2009, 26. Also see Burke 1988.

44. See, for instance, Quentin Skinner in Tully 1988 and Asad 1993, 171–99.

45. Mr. Ahmed Salim is a longtime activist, prolific writer, and political commentator based in Lahore. He has built a large private archive that is accessible on a fee-paying system. His archive, called the South Asia Research Resource Centre, is particularly rich in newspapers, magazines, pamphlets, and reports related to progressive movements in South Asia.

46. The "Easy Urdu" option was introduced to allow children who had lived abroad or were taking these exams in countries other than Pakistan to take Urdu as an optional language course. This option, therefore, assumes a certain lack of long-term association with the language.

47. A similar trend in advertising can be discerned in the Indian context.

48. Transliterated, the term means "tell me more." It connotes a joy in conversation and is often used to turn conversation toward a new topic or to start a conversation. In this case, *aur sunnao* was used by a cell-phone company as the tag line to its print and multimedia advertisements.

49. According to the 1998 census, the population was nearly seven million, but government estimates in mid-2006 suggest it is closer to ten million now. More information is available at the government of Punjab website: http://pportal.punjab .gov.pk/portal/.

50. Through a focus on his own family, Aziz (2006) gives a detailed insight into some of these developments.

51. The province has also been caricatured by its own residents, and others, as being too closely tied to a feudal mentality. Thus, an oft-cited joke suggests that there is only one culture in Punjab, and that is "agri-culture."

52. Established in 1882, Punjab University is the oldest "modern" university in Pakistan. King Edward Medical College, Government College, Kinnaird College for Women, Forman Christian College, Islamia College, Lahore College for Women, Aitchison College, and Oriental College are some of the better-known modern educational institutions that operated as regional centers of excellence in the pre-Partition era up to the mid-1970s.

53. See Allegra Donn, "A Historic Foundation for the Future," *Financial Times,* May 5–6, 2007, for an evaluation of shifts in property prices in Lahore.

54. See, for instance, Amin 1988; Samad 1996; Talbot 2002.

55. Indeed, often when many Western analysts like Roy (2002), Esposito (2002), and Kepel (2002) refer to Pakistan, it is in primarily in the context of the two provinces of Khyber Pakhtunkhwa and Baluchistan.

56. Gilmartin (1979, 1998) provides a good base for understanding the emergence of religious groups in Punjab politics. Weiss (1986) has focused on Lahore and Punjab in a more recent context: the Islamization campaign carried out by General Zia. Most of the work on religious groups in the context of urban Punjab has focused on sectarian clashes and violence, for instance, Abou Zahab 2002; Nasr 2000; and Zaman 1998.

57. Chandavarkar (1998) highlighted a similar dynamic in the case of early twentieth-century Bombay working class.

58. My use of the term "grounded" here should not be seen to imply the use of grounded theory methodology (Corbin and Strauss 1998). Rather, I use it to imply an analysis that is firmly situated in a particular context and takes a detailed look at the local dynamics, in contrast to a broad and general view of trends.

Chapter One

1. Certainly, movements of renewal have been a continuous feature of Islamic "tradition." In the centuries preceding European colonialism, several revivalism movements (Wahhabi, Mahdi, Fulani, Padri, and others) were initiated in Muslim societies as diverse as those in Africa and Southeast Asia (Esposito 1999, 645). My argument here is that Islamism draws upon this "tradition" of revivalism, but is, of course, shaped by the context in which it arose. See also Brown 1996.

2. Bilgrami (1999, 380–88) contends that it is precisely the vagueness of the notion of "modern" and "premodern" that allows scholars to indulge in ahistorical generalizations. Here his criticism is particularly targeted toward the intellectual support that Nandy (1998) and Madan (1999) extend toward a neo-Gandhian secularism. Arkoun (2003, 20) suggests a periodization that is based not on political events but on the changes in history of thought, specifically in the context of Islam. In the particular context of the similarities between Islamists and some "Western" critics of modernity, see Euben 1997.

3. Eisenstadt (1999, 197) suggests that the first "original" modernity as it developed in Western Europe had three important, closely connected dimensions: (1) structural/organizational ones, such as growing structural differentiation, urbanization, industrialization, communications, etc., which had been identified and analyzed in the first studies of modernization after WWII; (2) institutional ones, including modern nation-states, national collectivities, and above all capitalist-political economies; (3) distinct cultural programs and closely related specific modes of structuration of the major arenas of social life.

4. Guha, (2003), among others, has objected that Kaviraj's view depends on the assumption of increased enumeration and categorization of populations undertaken by the colonial state, but does not take into account the extensive enumeration strategies that the Mughal Empire undertook to extract revenues. However, this does not significantly alter the crux of Kaviraj's argument. His main concern is to show that the intensity of state intrusion and its impact on cognitive structures was much more pronounced within the modern colonial state. Moreover, he correctly emphasizes the colonial administration's interest in shaping cognitive processes that I discuss here.

5. Scott (1998, 80) has suggested that information collection and manipulation for effective, subtle control is a key activity carried out by the modern state. The information collected needs to be simplified for effective use, and these simplifications have: "at least five characteristics that deserve emphasis. Most obviously, state simplifications are observations of only those aspects of social life that are of official interest. They are *interested*, utilitarian facts. Second, they are also nearly always written (verbal or numeric) *documentary* facts. Third, they are typically *static* facts. Fourth, most stylized state facts are also *aggregate facts*. . . . Finally, for most purposes, state officials need to group citizens in ways that permit them to make a collective assessment. Facts that can be aggregated and presented as averages or distributions must therefore be *standardized* facts."

6. See, for instance, Jalal 2001 and Devji 2007.

7. Devji (2007, 65) proposes that "Islam" as a unified category could emerge in modernist debates as "a historical agent and authority in its own right, as a constitution of the totality of Muslim beliefs" only when localized, contradictory, and embedded forms of prior identification were made to disappear during the colonial period.

8. Alavi (1988) provides a broad overview of some class- and occupation-based trends in relation to support for different religious groups among North Indian Muslims.

9. Metcalf (2004a) provides a view of the gradual impoverishment and despair among Delhi Muslims who had previously been affiliated with the Mughal court.

10. While her research is focused primarily on education policies during colonial rule, Chatterjee (2007, 6–10) identifies four stages of what she calls the "British religious policy." The first started at the beginning of nineteenth century with increasing pressure from Rationalist Utilitarians and Christian Evangelicals and led to the dissociation of the government from non-Christian religions as well as more active support to missionary activities and institutions. After the 1857 mutiny, the administration became more sensitive to non-Christian Indian demands, although specific modalities varied regionally. By the 1880s, the state policy of avowed neutrality was increasingly strained by local demands for representation and by the early twentieth century was rendered largely meaningless. See also van der Veer 2001, 21–25, for some discussion of regional and temporal variations.

11. Incidentally, Maududi had rejected the demand for Pakistan as a means of dividing Muslims. It was only after Pakistan became a reality that Maududi decided to acknowledge it. He moved to Pakistan after Partition because he calculated that the chances of setting up an Islamic state would be higher there.

12. In part this is a result of trajectories of Western scholarship. "Islam" has been studied primarily in the context of the Middle East and not South Asia, while India/South Asia was conceived of as home primarily to the Hindus. The very presence of Islamism, and indeed Islam beyond India, has led many to study it without embedding it into the South Asian context. Tribal boundaries around disciplinary specializations may also have some role to play in this context.

13. Robinson 1998, 277.

14. The term "communal" has a particular history in South Asia. Its use by colonial administration and later application to present-day tensions between Hindu and Muslim groups in India has led to a largely negative association with it. For an overview and critique of the term, see Menon 2007. Jalal (2002, 236) points out that the use of communalism with its negative associations was important as a foil for the "lauded sentiment" of nationalism.

15. The similarities and continuities of this position with the current US regime are made all the more striking for the century and a half that separates them. See Mamdani 2004 for an analysis that speaks of similar arguments in the current context. In particular, it is interesting to note the gullibility associated with the "ignorant" average Muslim at the hands of the "fanatics."

16. Mohammed Iqbal, a leading Muslim philosopher and poet based in Lahore at the turn of the century, articulated a similar critique of the quantitative focus in the philosophy and structure of elections when he wrote: *Iss raz ko ik mard-e farangi nay kiya fāsh / harchand ki dānā issay khola nahin kartay / jamhūriyat ik tarz e hakumat hai kay jiss main / bandon ko ginā kartay hain tolā nāhīn kartay.*

(This secret was revealed by an Englishman / although the wise know not to reveal it / Democracy is a form of government in which / men are counted for their quantity, but weighed not for their quality. [This rather literal translation is mine.])

17. For instance, Masud (2000, xxxiv) documents the combination of Hindu and Muslim practices, ideas, and celebrations among the Meos of Delhi right up to the twentieth century. He contends (2000, xxxv) that use of both Hindu and Muslim names for individuals was quite common among North Indian communities in Awadh, Balgaram, Kashmir, Sind, and Bengal.

18. The contemporaneous impact of non-European influences such as Wahhabism on the revitalizing and rethinking of many Islamic practices was also significant and led to considerable rethinking among the Muslims of North India. The Wahhabi movement was a movement of puritanical revivalism that originated in present-day Saudi Arabia. In India, a significant response was mounted by Barelvi ulama to the Wahhabi challenge. Barelvis are associated with more "traditional" practices of saint worship, religious festivals, and rituals. As a result of their resistance, the term *Wahhabi* continues to carry substantial negative connotations and in contemporary Pakistan, Wahhabis tend to refer to themselves as Ahl-e-Hadīs. See Metcalf 1982 for a detailed analysis of the Ahle-e-Hadīs reformism in North India.

19. See also Freitag 1991 for a nuanced understanding of the shifting and contingent nature of the public sphere under later colonial rule.

20. Kugle (2001, 258n3) is worth quoting here in detail: "The shariah is a notoriously difficult concept to define. In broadest terms, the shariah is the accepted custom of the Muslim community in doctrinal belief, ritual action, commercial transaction and criminal punishment. More technically, the shariah consists of a network of decisions by jurists on whether a specific action is obligatory, recommended, permissible, discouraged or forbidden when compared against the known sources of revelation. As such, the shariah is a wide umbrella of moral sanctions, covering other theoretical possibilities as well as practical exigencies. The shariah embraces contradictory juridical decisions and a multiplicity of juridical methods, insisting only that they be based on certain authentic sources and reasoned deduction. This crucial element of flexivility and multiplicity is often lost when the term shariah is translated as 'the law of Islam' or even 'Islamic law.' Rather, shariah is a broad set of customs authenticated and sanctified by legal decisions. The principles and institutions of legal specialists who make such decisions generally know as *fiqh*, should be understood as 'Islamic law.'"

21. I am grateful to Justin Jones and Eleanor Newbigin for suggesting these works by Kugle and Skuy.

22. An exception is Rahman's "Muslim Modernism in Indo-Pakistan Sub-Continent" (1958, 82–99), in which he identifies three key stages in the development of "Muslim modernity" typified by Syed Ahmed Khan, Sayyid Amir Ali, and finally Mohammed Iqbal.

23. Maududi initially opposed the formation of Pakistan on the grounds that nationalism was a Western concept and it would break the Muslim ummah of India into competing groups. However, after the formation of Pakistan, JI did not officially acknowledge these earlier comments. Instead, the organization highlighted the allegedly close relationship between Maududi and Iqbal, the national poet of Pakistan and the first Muslim leader to publicly propose the idea of a separate Muslim homeland. Contrary to this JI propaganda about the close relationship between Iqbal and Maududi, they met only once and then too on the suggestion of a friend. While Iqbal did appoint Maududi to head the model Muslim community he had envisioned and funded at Pathankot, he was soon dissatisfied and had wanted to remove Maududi (Nasr 1996, 26).

24. Jalal 2001 highlights the controversies surrounding Ahmedi Muslims to bring out precisely this lack of internal cohesion that is often glossed over in discussions about Muslims.

25. The particular context of India has generated a huge amount of literature that engages with secularism from different aspects. Mufti's contribution falls within that context. The most widely cited of these is the volume edited by Bhargava (1998), *Secularism and Its Critics*. However, the particular context of India means that the binary of secularism in India is communalism. See Menon 2007 for an attempt at a fundamental repositioning of the secularism debate in India.

26. Also see Piscatori 1986.

27. While my focus here is on South Asian Islamism, it is pertinent to note that similar developments mark Middle Eastern Islamism. Al-Azmeh (1993, 52) claims that "the Islam that Afghani [another key Islamist ideologue] attacked was the traditional Islam of the ecclesiastics. Like Luther, whom he greatly admired, Afghani can be said to have 'overcome the bondage of piety by replacing it by the bondage of conviction . . . [and] shattered faith in authority because he restored the authority of faith.'"

28. Despite the opposition Maududi received from traditionalist ulama, Maududi continued to exhibit a certain pride in his association through family ties with sufi pirs and scholars. See Maududi 1971.

29. The *chador* is a piece of loose cloth draped over the head and the body. The *burqa'* is a tailored dress worn over other clothes. In its various permutations, the *burqa'* covers the face, allowing limited visibility either through holes pierced into thicker material or a layer of thin material drawn over the whole face. I look at the traditionalist critique of Islamism and at the difference between JI and JD women's veiling practices in chapter 4.

Chapter Two

1. Qayyum Nazar was a well-known Urdu writer.

2. See in particular the contributions by Benin, Goldberg, and Lubeck in Burke and Lapidus 1988.

3. "Awamification" derives from the word *awam*, meaning the people or masses. It was a term used frequently by Bhutto and the PPP in the 1970s to refer to an increase in the rights of the masses.

4. Ahmed's remarks indicate the increased social mobility of the 1960s to the 1980s. Ethnic linkages, not commented upon by Ahmed here, play a role in this upward mobility, and Punjabis benefitted the most in this period. In any case, overall upward mobility was seriously challenged from the 1990s onward. Over the last decade, Pakistani society has undergone increased polarization, and the percentage of population living at or below the poverty line has risen from 17 percent in the mid-1980s to 38 percent in the late 1990s (World Bank 2002). This rapid change, economic stagnation, and increased social polarization are features shared by the "progressive" mobilizations of the 1960s and the "fundamentalist" mobilizations of today.

5. Pervaiz Inayat Malik, interview, April, 26, 2005, Law Chambers, Fane Road, Lahore.

6. This couplet mocks the value of fatwas and fatwa issuing. The first verse implies that a fatwa is a lightweight object, like husk, that can be scattered while winnowing. In the second verse the singer suggests that he will sell this lightweight object in street after street to con people out of their money (*watan ga*)—suggesting that this is what all those dealing with fatwas do.

7. It would, of course, be fallacious to assume a unified, homogenous left. In Pakistan, apart from a local manifestation of the international division between the Russian and the Chinese camps, there were various personality-based factions as well as different types of organizations, political and cultural, broadly espousing socialism and communism as their ideologies.

8. I am mindful of the danger of generalized use of categories of class grounded in a particular historical context, as highlighted by Jones 1983 and Chandavarkar 1998. Typically those identifying themselves as "leftists" in Pakistan, including the educated elite, focused on issues of broader representation and access for the middle and lower classes, premised on a class-based analysis.

9. Maududi too was involved in the earlier stages of the Hijrat movement, but moved away from it after disputes with its leaders, apparently because of his insistence that the strategies and goals be planned and realistic (Ahmed and Ansari 1979, 361).

10. See Leghari 1979, 24–25; also see Malik 1985a for more details.

11. The more prominent among these included Danyal Latifi, Ataullah Jahania, Abdulla Malik, Chaudhry Rahmatullah, Anis Hashmi, and Ghulam Nabi Bhullar.

12. According to the reporter from CPI's journal *People's War*, the communists organized meetings for ML leaders with approximately two hundred thousand people over a tour lasting one and half months: "The League's leaders lashed the Unionist party for its black rule and its adherence with imperialism and demanded release of Congress detainees. They put forward the demands of kissans and workers as enunciated in the manifesto recently brought out by the Punjab League and received tremendous response from the peasants who gathered at the meetings in thousands, despite threats of Unionist minded officers in the districts" (quoted in Leghari 1979, 28).

13. Zaigham (2005, 15) claims that Danyal Latifi was so disgusted by the changes that Mumtaz Daultana made to the manifesto after the formation of Pakistan that he decided to move to India and remained associated with the Communist Party of India Marxist (CPI[M]) until his death. Mumtaz Daultana was known as the "Red" Muslim Leaguer in his early days.

14. Even prior to the Communist Party's 1943 resolution to support Pakistan, nationalist communists had started working more closely with the nationalist parties. It has been argued that CPI's blind following of the Stalinist two-stage theory that supported British rule in India alienated the nationalist freedom fighters. This stance resulted in a gain for the nationalist parties like the Congress and the Muslim League. (In the case of Punjab, see Sulehria n.d.)

15. Nasr (1996, 41) suggests that Maududi was drawn into politics by Jinnah's example: "Mawdudi believed that Jinnah's popularity emanated from his appeal to Islamic symbols. If a secular Muslim could sway the masses in the name of Islam, surely Mawdudi could, and ought to, do better."

16. C. R Aslam, interview in *Awami Jamhoori Forum* 20 (March 2005): 22.

17. The opposition needed a strong consensus candidate to oppose Ayub Khan in these elections. The only candidate acceptable to all was the well-respected sister of Mohammed Ali Jinnah, the leader of the Muslim League that had led the call for a separate nation-state.

18. Interview conducted November 22, 2005, at his residence in Mansoora, Lahore.

19. During the agitation against Bhutto in 1977, Jama'at also made an alliance with ANP (Awami National Party/Wali Khan), but by then the ANP had undergone several changes and was operating largely as a nationalist party.

20. Other key ML Leaders who interacted with Punjab MSF regularly included Ch. Khaliquz Zaman from UP, Hamid Nizami, Maulana Jamal Mian Farangi Mahal, M. H. Isphahani, and Qazi Mohammed Isa.

21. Hanif Ramay, assistant coordinator at the Pakistan Institute for Labor Education and Research, Lahore office. Union organizer at Rustum Sohrab, Tetra/Packages, RGA, Ittefaq foundry. Labor councillor for Kot Lakhpat industrial area. Interview conducted April 3, 2004, at PILER office, Kot Lakhpat.

22. When, in 1966, the Chinese foreign minister visited Lahore, the road from the old airport to the governor's house (close to fifteen miles long) was lined by an unbroken, several-person-deep chain of people who had come to welcome him (Ahmed, Aziz ud din, interview 2005).

23. From their respective points of view, *Zindagi* (pro-Jama'at) and *Lail-o-Nahar* (pro-Russia left) both talk about the easy access to Chinese literature in Pakistan during the 1960s. Those within the Pakistani left who were aligned with Russia also complained of the relative official leniency allowing Chinese literature to dominate the local market.

24. This point was made by many JI informants in addition to the left activists that I interviewed.

25. A joke from the era illustrates this well: Why is the comrade sweating in a fur coat in Lahore? Because it is snowing in Leningrad.

26. There were several other parties, of course. Mian Iftikhar ud din and some other left elements in the Muslim League created the Azad Pakistan Party in Punjab. A Hari Party was created in Sind. Surakh Posh Jama'at, Awami League, and Ganatantari Dal, the East Pakistan equivalent of the Azad Pakistan Party, were also created during these years. The NAP was formed by an alliance of a breakaway faction of the Awami League led by Maulana Bhashani and the Azad National Party led by Abdul Ghaffar Khan from West Pakistan.

27. Prof. Aziz ud din Ahmed, interview, April 11, 2005, at his residence in Lahore.

28. P. Inayat Malik, interview at his law chambers, April 26, 2005.

29. The perception of the left as being anti-Pakistani gained popularity in part because of the fact that the leadership of the Communist Party of Pakistan had been "imported" from India. Sajjad Zaheer, the first general secretary, and Sibte

Hassan, another key member, were both Communist Party of India members who had been instructed to work in Pakistan in the Calcutta CPI meeting of 1948. More critically, soon after the formation of Pakistan, CPI reversed its earlier policy of active support for Muslim nationalism, and by the 1960s the dominant trend within the Communist Party was to view the formation of Pakistan as a mistake.

30. Dr. Mubashir Hassan claims that Bhutto never made half the promises that were attributed to him. Some amount of active political deception was nevertheless undertaken. The PPP 1971 manifesto in Urdu for instance, makes certain promises regarding worker and peasant rights that the English manifesto does not mention (interviews with Hassan, Inayat, Manto, and Ahmed Salim).

31. Qasim Anwar, interview, May 1, 2005, at his residence in Lahore.

32. Dr. Mubashir Hassan, interview, April 20, 2005, at his residence in Lahore.

33. Interview, April 20, 2005.

34. Salim Ahmed Salimi, interview, November 29, 2005, Idara Ma'arft-i-Islami, Lahore. Mr. Salimi is a member of the JI shura and has been a rukn since 1963.

35. A few JI women mentioned to me that they had participated in door-to-door canvassing for local and provincial elections, as well as for da'wa campaigns, as students before 1970 even though the "leftists," in this case the PPP activists of 1970, claimed this tactic as their own innovation in the Pakistani context.

36. In Islamia College, for instance, where MSF had been strong and IJT was formed, many students moved from MSF to IJT. The role that Islamia College, Lahore, played in nationalist, religious, and leftist student mobilizations, often as the place of founding for several different groups, in united Punjab before Partition, and in Pakistani Punjab after Partition is one worthy of detailed further research.

37. Reading the biography of one of JI's key ideologues of the period, Khurram Ja Murad, one gets the sense that it was a network of extended family and friends largely from certain parts of North India that formed the core of Jama'at leadership, at least in Karachi in the first two decades after Pakistan's formation (Murad 1994).

38. Al-Huda, "Samina Aapa," second in command to Dr. Farhat Hashmi, interview, April 2005, Gormani House, Lahore. Al-Huda is a pietist group focused on women only. Started by Dr. Farhat Hashmi, a PhD in Islamic studies from Glasgow University and a onetime associate of the JI, the group focused initially on upper- and upper-middle-class women, but has over the last few years expanded its services to lower-middle-class women as well.

39. This is highlighted more starkly when one compares the Jama'at I Islami with the Tablighi Jama'at (TJ), for instance. The TJ does not publish any literature, does not aim to use science and technology in its methods, and actively looks down upon "worldly education." The JI in contrast publishes various magazines, pamphlets, and books, conducts regular study circles, and engages, albeit in a particular way, with debates on science and modernity.

40. Anas n.d., 1.

41. Gilani, 1969a, 36.

42. Just one writer, albeit a particularly prolific one, Dr. Asad Gilani, authored at least twenty-five such pamphlets, with multiple editions of each (Mrs. Zobeida

Asad Gilani, interview, November 22, 2005, at her residence in Mansoora, JI head-quarters).

43. It is possible that further editions were issued later. This information is stated in the copy of the pamphlet I was able to access.

44. Rana Abdul Rehman, prominent union worker in Lahore and a major orga-nizer in the Kot Lakhpat area, interview, April 29, 2005, at Book Home, Lahore.

45. *Zindagi* is an important resource because of its relatively indirect link with the JI. It operated as a mouthpiece for a wider audience than the Tarjuman ul Qur'an, which served a more specialized audience, and *Asia*, which was too closely associated with the JI. Nevertheless, there can be little doubt about its leanings. Many JI members remarked to me during the course of my fieldwork that it was also one of "our own," and similarly the left activists would group it with other JI publications. At its peak, *Zindagi* was a fairly good magazine that, in spite of its ideological bent, provided space for a range of views to be published and debated.

46. The Jama'at's tactics have also included equating PPP with socialism; the failings of PPP then come to represent the failings of socialism for all times.

47. See, for instance, *Zindagi*, September 1, 1969, 26–28; October 13, 1969, 27–32; etc.

48. Liaqut Baloch, well-known Lahore-based IJT leader and now an important Jama'at leader, interview, November 5, 2005, Falah-e-Khandan office, Lahore. Also Waqas Anjum Jaafari, interview, November 29, 2005, Idara-Marafat I Islam office, Mansoorah.

49. This strategy is similar to the one he used with labor unions. Asdar Ali, in a sensitive history of the 1972 workers riots in Karachi (Ali 2005), shows how Bhutto, once in power, moved to meet "the strength of the street" with the "strength of the state."

50. Interview, November 29, 2005.

51. A recent incident has made international headlines. See "At Top University, a Fight for Pakistan's Future," *New York Times*, April 20, 2010.

52. Prominent Jama'at student and labor organizer, member of JI shura, inter-view, December 2, 2005, at the Jama'at-e-Islami Ichra office.

53. Interview, July 10, 2005, Falah-e-Khandan office, Lahore.

54. Hafiz Salman Butt, then Nazim IJT, interview.

55. There are efforts to build unofficial IJT presence in the private colleges where unions are generally banned, but they have been largely unsuccessful so far.

56. Kepel (1995, 24) hints at a similar process in Arab Muslim states by suggest-ing that the universities were symptomatic of the floundering welfare utopias in postcolonial nation-states and that as a free service they could not meet all the de-mands placed on them except through corruption. Once the Islamists were able to gain access through government support for suppressing leftist influences, they provided certain tailored services like cheap lecture notes and free revision classes that strengthened their relations with this constituency.

57. The Okara district in Central Punjab lies between River Ravi on the west and the now dry River Biyas on the east.

58. Farooq Tariq, general secretary, Labor Party Pakistan, union organizer in the carpet-weaving industry, Anjuman Muzarain Punjab, Pakistan Printing Worker's Union, etc., interview, April 4, 2004, at LPP office, Lahore. Conversations with leaders of the Communist Mazdoor Kissan Party (Communist Laborer and Worker Party) and Awami Tehreek.

59. The left groups supporting the Okara movement, like Labor Party Pakistan, National Workers Party, and Communist Party of Pakistan, often operate as or through NGOs, even when they claim to be political parties. Most operate on foreign and local aid, have very limited spheres of influences, and have an almost negligible presence in national or regional electoral politics.

60. It is useful to note the strength of JI's national reach compared to regional parties that may have been more resolutely and explicitly antifeudalism. For instance, the Mohajir Qaumi movement (MQM) certainly has espoused an explicit antifeudal stance since its very inception. However, the MQM is a regional party limited to urban Sindh. The success of its recent moves at building a national presence remains to be seen.

61. Zaidi (1999, 12–22) provides a good overview of these debates in the Pakistani context, while building a case for the view that Pakistan is not a feudal country. See the chapter titled "Is Pakistan Feudal?"

62. Chakrabarty 2000, 28.

63. Qasbahs, larger than villages, smaller than towns, combine interesting dynamics of urban and rural mobilization.

64. The story is a commentary on the madness of Partition. Set in a lunatic asylum, it juxtaposes the "rationality" of the political leaders with the "irrationality" of those in the asylum. To me, the most memorable lines of the play remain the protagonist's oft-repeated question, "Is Toba Tek Singh in Pakistan or Hindustan?" bringing into sharp focus the difficulty, as well as absurdity, of allocating a shared history and way of life to either one or the other state.

65. Ahmed Bashir, "Toba Tek Singh Kissan Conference," *Lail-o-Nahar* (Lahore), April 5, 1971, 25. Sohan Singh Josh was one of the founders of the Kirti Kissan Communist Party in Punjab.

66. See, for instance, *Zindagi*, *Nidai-Millat*, and *A'ain*, January–April 1970.

67. Another well-known member of the Progressive Writer's Association.

68. Abid Hassan Manto, member of the Kissan Committee 1969–70, interview, May 7, 2005.

69. Shafqat Tanvir Mirza (in "Kissan conference aur humaray akhbar" [Kissan Conference and Our Newspapers], in *Nusrat* [Lahore], April 5, 1970, 13–16) provides an interesting comparison of the various aspects of the conference reported by Jama'at or Jama'at-sympathetic magazines like *A'ain*, *Zindagi*, *Asia*, and *Nida-I-Millat*, and left-leaning newspapers and magazines.

70. See *Dawn*, March 22–25, 1970, and *Pakistan Times*, March 22–25, 1970, front page.

71. *Pakistan Times*, March 23, 1970, 9.

72. *Dawn*, March 23, 1970, 1.

73. *Pakistan Times*, March 25, 1970, 1, 10.

74. Interviews with Manto, Aziz ud din Ahmed, Tahira Mazhar Ali, and Pervaiz

Inayat Malik, all organizers and participants in the Kissan Conference 1970. Details of the various speeches made were included in the back pages of some newspaper reports, including *Dawn* and *Pakistan Times* of March 25, 1970, with *Pakistan Times* providing more coverage, in keeping with its "left" leanings. In addition, magazines like *Asia*, *Zindagi* , *Nusrat*, *Al-Fatah*, and *Lail-o-Nahar* printed quotes from some speeches.

75. *Pakistan Times*, March 25, 1970, 10.

76. Prof. Aziz ud din Ahmed, interview, Lahore, April 2005. Nazeer and Basheer are common Muslim names. In Persian they mean: One without parallel (Nazeer) and One who carries good news (Basheer). Faiz's verse is suitable enough to the conference's theme in its content, if not in its choice of language. The couplet being referred to is: "*Suno kay hum baizaban au baikas, Bashir bi hain, aur nazir bhi*" (And hear, we who are voiceless and powerless / are also the bearers of both good news and warnings).

77. Bahadur (1977, 121) notes that it is pointless to try to determine whether Bhashani or Bhutto coined the term, but it is relevant to assert that "both Bhutto and Bhashani had hardly ever subscribed to the philosophy of scientific socialism."

78. Maulana Hazarwi (JUI), Maulana Mufti (JUP), and Maulana Kausar Niayzi (formerly of JI) were among the prominent ulama who lent their support to left causes and later to the PPP government. Nasr (1996, 120) argues that the politicization of Islam by JI had politicized ulama parties, which, once in the political arena, became its competitors. This view is quite sympathetic to JI's version. JUI and JUP both had inherited traditions of political involvement from the JUH (Jam'iyat ulama Hind), and it is possible to argue that rather than the JI's political activity, it was the heightened politicization through leftist mobilizations that provided the impetus for these ulama organizations to get involved in electoral campaigns.

79. JI sources were generally vague about numbers, claiming often that it was "an immense outpouring of support for Islam." Newspapers of the time have also not given any numbers, although close to one hundred thousand in Lahore is the highest estimate.

80. Salim Ahmed Salimi, interview.

81. Salim Ahmed Salimi, interview.

82. It is useful to note, following Bayly 2000, that literature from China built on a specific conception of revolution that differed in important ways from the Russian literature. The Chinese Communist Party was also more supportive of local decisions and directions in other countries, whereas the Russian party had tended to keep very tight control on communist parties in other countries, including Pakistan.

83. Ch. Rehmat Ilahi, interview, Mansoorah, Lahore, November 22, 2005.

84. A number of senior JI members discussed this during our interviews. Moreover, the shock of losing is evident also from the various self-critical articles and letters in *Zindagi*, *Asia*, and *Tarjuman ul Qur'an* in the months following the elections.

85. See also Binder 1961, 211.

86. I am grateful to Irfan Ahmad for sharing his conversations with some JI India elders who claimed that the move to organize around professions was un-Islamic, arguing that the Prophet (PBUH) could have, but did not, use this tactic.

87. While the Jama'at is the strongest among the Islamist groups in terms of union organizing, others are also active in this area. The JUI is believed to be active in some Karachi unions. Some groups have a localized presence in a particular plant (e.g., Jama'at ud Da'wa in some Lahore factories). The JI seems to be the most systematic in its approach. The Jama'at also has another initiative known as the *Tehrik-e-Mehnat* (Movement of Labor), under which they work within other unions. Under *Tehrik-e-Mehnat*, they start inviting union members to their events, *ijtemah* (gathering), and *seh-roze* (six-day-study circles). This allows them to build a presence in unions not directly affiliated with the National Labor Federation.

88. Once he was in power, Bhutto's version of "Islamic socialism" entailed a betrayal of the very activists who had supported his rise to power. Bhutto had encouraged workers and students in their stand against the Ayub government. For this, many were put in prison. After coming to power, Bhutto released some activists, but most were not reinstated into their jobs. More significantly, as worker unrest continued, Bhutto warned them that "strength of the street will be met by the strength of the state." See Asdar Ali 2005 for a sensitive account of Bhutto's policy, taking into consideration the various ethnic and organizational divisions within the labor unions in Karachi.

89. The Zia regime is significant for its repression of left elements, including union activists, in Pakistani society. Political activists, union leaders, and students were jailed, tortured, and "disappeared." Political parties were banned for some years, and a campaign of Islamization as a tool of state control began in earnest.

Year	Number of punishments for political activity
1978	1,327
1979	1,831
1980	612
1981	1,197
1982	4,212
1983	6,012
1984	2,100
1985	2,513

In compiling this table, Noman (1988) has used newspaper reports, official statements, and reports by Amnesty International. The figures in the table are thus likely to be significantly underestimating the actual incidence.

The repression of political activists, including many union leaders and activists, and the banning of labor unions was compounded by the migration of many urban workers to the Middle East during this era. This led to a rise in real wages of the workers in organized sectors of the industry as well as relative indifference to oppositional movements against the government (Noman 1988, 131). An ILO study noted that "with such large scale migration of workers, people feel that with a little bit of luck, it is possible to be among the next batch of emigrants. . . . The working class has come to believe that it is upwardly mobile" (Noman 1988, 161).

90. Interview with Nabi Ahmed, Convenor Pakistan Worker's Federation and the most prominent labor leader from Karachi, along with Usman Baloch. He is well known for his work in the formation of unions in large multinationals like Siemens and UniLever. Interview conducted April 5, 2004, at Shobra Hotel, Lahore.

91. NLF won the referendum at WAPDA (Water and Power Development Authority, the national electricity generation and supply company) three days after I interviewed S. D. Saqib in April 2004. Saqib led the NLF-affiliated Payam union to victory against the Hydro union, which had officially represented WAPDA for almost thirty years. Khurshid Ahmed, the leader of Hydro, had been the ILO (International Labor Organization) representative from Pakistan for these thirty years.

92. The policies of privatization and liberalization actively followed during the regimes of both Benazir Bhutto and Nawaz Sharif have resulted in the so-called welfare legislations taking a back seat. The immediate impact of the "structural adjustment" and accompanying policy of abandonment of welfare and protective measures and minimal labor legislation has been massive downsizing, almost total retrenchment of the old work force manning nationalized industries on their privatization and their substitution by casual labor. In Pakistan, resistance to these policies has been neutralized by reducing the role of the labor courts significantly and making the grievance procedure increasingly time and resource consuming. In addition, by using a clause in the Federal Services Tribunal Act, the industrial workers of the state-owned or state-controlled industries were transformed into "civil servants" whose terms and conditions of service became the exclusive jurisdiction of the Civil Services Tribunal by virtue of section 2-A in the Federal Services Tribunal Act (Amjad 2001, 170). The Musharaf regime has continued such policies with renewed focus on creating export processing zones that would be exempted from labor legislation. The Removal from Service Ordinance 2000 allows management in publicly owned enterprises to terminate the services of any worker without presenting a reason. However, the most significant impact has been made by a new ordinance called Industrial Relations Ordinance (IRO) 2002. According to the previous IRO (1969), Collective Bargaining Agent (CBA) and non-CBA unions could both exist in an enterprise. Now unions need a minimum of 15 percent of the vote in a plant or enterprise to be registered. This makes it difficult for non-CBA unions to build a presence. In addition, it has become difficult to form a federation. Under IRO 2002, a federation can only exist if it operates at the national level with registration in all four provinces, and at least one CBA union in each province. Labor courts, which provided some avenue for compensation and relief during a dispute, can no longer do so. In fact, labor tribunals at the provincial level have been abolished, and such cases can only be heard at the federal courts.

93. Iqtidar, *Dawn*, May 12 and June 12, 2002.

94. Interviews with Hafiz Salman Butt, Liaquat Baloch, and Salim Ahmed Salimi.

95. Interview with S. D. Saqib, Wapda Paigham (Message) Union, National Labor Federation. Key organizer in Payam union in Punjab Urban Transport Corporation. Led the Paigham union to victory in a referendum for CBA status three days after the interview, defeating the Hydro union that had been representing WAPDA for thirty years. Interview conducted April 13, 2004, at the NLF office, Lahore.

96. Other key federations in Pakistan are: All Pakistan Federation of Trade Unions, Muttahida Labor Federation, Pakistan Trade Union Federation, All Pakistan Federation of Labor, and All Pakistan Trade Union Organization.

97. Interview with Nazim Husnain, president of All Pakistan Lecturers Association, Lecturer Railway College, general secretary of the Joint Action Committee (doctors, teachers, and lawyers), key figure in the protests against privatization of healthcare and education during the 2000s. Interview conducted April 7, 2004, at the residence of Mr. Husnain, Lahore.

98. Interview, April 13, 2004.

99. Interview with Farooq Tariq, Labor Party Pakistan.

100. Tarrow defines movements as "collective challenges, based on common purposes and social solidarities, in sustained interaction with elites, opponents, and authorities" (1998, 4).

101. Joel Benin and Hossam el-Hamalawy, "Strikes in Egypt Spread from Centre of Gravity," May 9, 2007, http://www.merip.org/mero/mero050907.html, last accessed May 18, 2007.

102. Singular: *rukn*; literally: member. The hierarchy of JI membership is *hami/mutafiq* (supporter), *umeed war rukn* (candidate member), and *rukn* (member).

103. This is not to suggest that Maududi was not familiar with Marxist writings before this period. Maududi was familiar with not just Marxist writings (Nasr 1996, 146), but had also come in contact with Muslim socialists in Delhi in his youth, most notably the Khairi brothers (Aziz 1987, 88–92).

104. US Embassy Karachi, dispatch no. 660, December 11, 1951, 790D.00/11-2851, quoted in Nasr 1996, 172n142.

105. Details of the Machchi Goth affair are succinctly covered by Nasr (1994, 31–41), but others, like Niazi (1973), have also written about it.

106. See, for instance, *Tarjuman ul Qur'an* 4, no. 6 (1971).

107. Nasr 1996, 45.

108. He took over again as amir in 1977, during the anti-Bhutto *Nizam-I-Mustafa* campaign. Mian Tufayl served as amir from 1972 to 1977 and then again from 1978 to 1987.

109. Interviews and conversations, April–December 2005.

110. Interviews with various Shura members, particularly Salim Ahmed Saleemi, Ch. Rehmat Ilahi, Liaqut Baloch, and Hafiz Salman Butt.

111. Ibid.

112. Many of these constraining factors did not exist for front organizations like the IJT, which turned to violent tactics to assert their will in campuses, most notably in Punjab University.

113. See, for instance, Murad 1994 and 1999. Murad argues for a more transparent and quick process.

114. Benin and Stork (1997, 15) point out the vacuum created by the collapse of the Soviet Union for "policy intellectuals" as well as for the military budgets in the United States, and the threat posed by Iran, as the context in which Islamic fundamentalism emerged as a "serviceable contender" for the role of a policy touchstone.

115. See, for instance, the *Dawn* interview quoted in "MMA Vows to Carry out

Land Reforms," http://www.mma.org.pk/news/2002/10/mma.ows.carry.out.land
.reforms.shtml. One of the motivations highlighted by MMA for its million-man
march against the American war on Iraq was to "pack up secularism and feudalism
from Pakistan" (*Pakistan Tribune*, March 29, 2002).

116. In the training sessions and preelection (Local Bodies, Lahore) meetings
I attended from July to August 2005, slogans against feudalism and in favour of
democracy were raised in almost all the events, but were often not accompanied
by detailed analysis.

117. "2006 Shura Resolution on Political Situation," http://www.jamaat.org/
news/2006/jan/03/1001.html.

118. Close to 38 percent of Pakistan's population is believed to be living at or
below the poverty line (World Bank 2002).

119. Interviews and observations, 2005. Nasr (1994, 71) believes that Maududi
used the word to harness its positive connotations at the time.

120. See, for instance, Murad 1988 and also the *Tarjuman-ul-Qur'an* editorial,
January 1996. Murad, an engineer by training, was a key JI writer and ideologue.

Chapter Three

1. This was a slogan popularised by the general in his attempt to curb enthusiasm
for pan-Islamism.

2. A *marla* is equal to approximately thirty square yards.

3. I should specify that Metcalf in her work does not promote such a view. Indeed, certain uses of the term "fundamentalist" could cover whole populations, as
pointed out by Mahmood (1994, 29) in her critique of the Fundamentalism Project
volumes 1–3, edited by Marty and Appleby. She quotes John Voll, one of the project
contributors, who points out that in the case of Egypt, "if one looks at those who are
actively involved in some way in the Islamic resurgence, then the number of people
is in the millions, and in some respects, represents the majority of the society."

4. Lashkar-e-Jhangvi is a Sunni militant group and Sipah-e-Mohammed is a Shi-
ite militant group in Pakistan. Some details of the sectarian violence between Shia
and Sunni groups are discussed later in this section.

5. See, for instance, Euben 1999, 174–75.

6. See, in particular, Roy 1994; Esposito 1997, 2002; Benin and Stork 1997; and
Eickelman and Piscatori 1996.

7. This scepticism, in his view, stands them in good stead in the current situation,
where this distance tends to enhance their legitimacy in the eyes of the unrepre-
sented or those excluded from a say in the state's operations.

8. For a contrasting view on the apolitical stance of the Tablighis, see Sikand
2003. Sikand argues that the process of identity formation as a "Tablighi Muslim"
is ultimately a political action; the apolitical positioning of the Tablighis has allowed
them unprecedented access in the relatively hostile milieu of not just India but of
various Western countries as well.

9. For more details, see Abou Zahab 2002, Zaman 1998, in the Pakistani context.
For similar differences in the Middle Eastern context, see Benin and Stork 1997.

10. In Pakistan the largest group (15–25 percent of the population) is Twelver or *Ithna A'sharia* Shias (Zaman 2000, 139). Other Shia groups include the Bohris, Islmailis, and Khojas.

11. One of the five pillars of the religion, Haj, a pilgrimage to Mecca in Saudi Arabia, is compulsory for every Muslim who can afford it.

12. See also Sikand 2003.

13. This pressure manifests itself not just in the "war on terror," which is focused primarily on Muslim groups—the reportedly vast network of unspecified numbers of affiliates called al-Qaida—but within Pakistan it translated into US support for a military dictator who has allowed US bodies like the FBI unprecedented access to Pakistani citizens. Benin and Stork (1997, 15) point out the vacuum created by the collapse of the Soviet Union for "policy intellectuals" as well as for the military budgets, and the threat posed by Iran as the context in which Islamic fundamentalism emerged as a "serviceable contender" for the role of a policy touchstone. It is perhaps not coincidental that the polemical work of Huntington (1993), *Clash of Civilizations*, was first published in the US journal *Foreign Affairs*.

14. Roy 1994 is a typical example. Roy recognizes some of the differences between what he calls the neofundamentalists and the Islamists, but assumes that since the differences are of strategy and focus, of means and not ends, they are of little consequence.

15. In the context of Pakistan, see Nasr 1994, 1996 for the Jama'at-I-Islami and Pirzada 2000 for Jam'iyat-Ulama Islam.

16. Dr. Israr Ahmed, a onetime JI associate and member, disagreed with Maududi's decision to engage in electoral politics, arguing that a sufficient number of "good Muslims" were not yet ready to take over the running of the state. A medical doctor by training, he continued to engage in the study and teaching of Qur'an, even after his break with the Jama'at-e-Islami, and he was, until his death in 2010, a regular on various TV channels, particularly Peace TV, an Islamic channel in Pakistan. The Tanzim was formed in 1975, even though Dr. Israr Ahmed's break with Jama'at-e-Islami came in the late 1950s, when the Jama'at first entered electoral politics. Dr. Farhat Hashmi's father was a long-time JI activist in Sargodha, a medium-sized town in Punjab. She too was active within the IJT during her student years at Punjab University. After obtaining a PhD in Islamic studies from Glasgow University, and after her marriage to a fellow student at Punjab University who had Wahhabi tendencies, she started her own group that focuses only on women. Al-Huda is now a multinational network employing different pedagogical tools and methods from study circles to CDs, pamphlets, and Internet sermons.

17. In her writings on the life of her parents, Maududi's daughter Humaira Maududi (2005, 26–32) reminisces that early in 1948 her father said to the politician and later prime minister of Pakistan, Chaudhry Mohammed Ali: "Only a few days earlier a train from Shimla (in Kashmir) has reached Lahore in which there is not a single person living. At this stage, we have not even recovered the daughters of Muslims from the homes of the Sikhs. We have not even buried all the dead bodies of the martyrs. But talk of making Pakistan a secular state has already started!" She suggests that it was as a result of this political engagement that Maududi took on emergency relief work at the same time as a national tour and radio speeches to pressurize the government to adopt the Objectives Resolution, which would declare Pakistan an Islamic country.

18. Believers in the Oneness of Allah.

19. Hafiz Mohammed Saeed and Dr. Zafar Iqbal were both teachers of Islamic studies in the University of Engineering and Technology in Lahore. During General Zia's rule (1977–88), Islamic studies and Pakistan studies were made mandatory subjects in professional colleges and universities. This provided employment opportunities and inroads for many Islamists into the educational system.

20. See, for instance, the BBC's profile of the JD leader at http://news.bbc .co.uk/1/hi/world/south_asia/3181925.stm, last accessed January 20, 2009.

21. Mahmood (2005, 58–59) provides a brief overview of the evolution of the term "da'wa" in the Egyptian context. Mahmood's account resonates with my understanding of the Pakistani experience.

22. Compare Masud 2000, xxiii.

23. Interestingly, while there seems to be a specific term, *da'iya*, in use for women who perform da'wa through public lectures in Egypt (see Mahmood 2005, 57–58, for the evolution of the term in that context), I did not come across one particular term in common usage in Pakistan. If anything, the English words "leader" or "speaker" were often used for these public speakers.

24. See the report "Earthquake Jihad: The Role of Jihadis and Islamist Groups after the October 2005 Earthquake" by the International Crisis Group for more details. Report accessed at http://www.crisisgroup.org/home/index.cfm?id=4270 on October 27, 2006.

25. See, for instance, the much-quoted article in the *Washington Post*, "Extremists Fill Aid Chasm after Earthquake," at http://www.washingtonpost.com/wp -dyn/content/article/2005/10/15/AR2005101501392.html, accessed October 27, 2006.

26. Maki is also the brother of Hafiz Saeed's wife, Um-e-Talha.

27. Interview, Abdul Rehman Maki, July 18, 2005, Mian Mir, Lahore.

28. Interview, Amir Hamza, July 11, 2005, Cantonment, Lahore. He was also concerned with highlighting how, under his stewardship, the circulation of the JD magazine had risen from seventy thousand to about two hundred thousand, precisely because he was able to highlight populist issues (*awamiyat ka zaur barha hai*).

29. See Iqtidar 2009 for a discussion of the impact of the ongoing Afghan war on JD.

30. The typology developed by Shepard (1987) provides some useful indications toward understanding the differences between Muslim modernists, Islamists, and traditionalists. Sheppard (1987, 318–19) defines the traditionalist as someone whose allegiance lies with the particular mix of shari'a and non-shari'a in his region before Western influence. Shepard then distinguishes between the traditionalist— someone who has not internalised the Western challenge, being neither forcefully attracted nor immensely challenged by it—and the neotraditionalist—a the traditionalist who begins to appreciate the depth and scale of Western influence and is more nuanced in his relationship with both the "Western" and elements of its local

(Muslim or non-Muslim) influences. I have not followed this distinction within traditionalists here.

31. Mufti Taqi Uthmani runs the Dar ul Ulum Karachi that was founded by his father, Mohammed Shafi, an eminent and prolific Deobandi alim and sufi shaykh. Mohammed Shafi was in turn a student and disciple of Ashraf Ali Thanavi, a leading critic of Islamism within South Asia.

32. See also Maududi 2000, n.d. *Islam Kiya Hai!*

33. See Jalal 2008 for some of the different ways in which jihad has been conceptualized over the centuries within South Asia.

34. Wahhabism derives its name from its founder, Mohammed ibn Abdul Wahab (1703–92), who had preached a puritanical, scriptural version of Islam, largely stripped of rituals and mysticism. It is supported as the state religion in Saudi Arabia and was widely promoted by the House of Saud in other parts of the world, particularly after the Iranian revolution. Given the backlash against Wahhabism after its initial success, the term carried significant negative connotations in North India in the late colonial period. The Wahhabis preferred to refer to themselves as the Ahl-e-Hadīs. See Metcalf 1982, 268–70, for an overview.

35. Shaikh Abdul Hakim Murad, "Understanding the Four Madhabs," www.masud.co.uk/Islam/ahm/madhab.html, accessed October 30, 2006. Murad, a British Muslim and a well-known traditionalist, teaches Islamic studies at the University of Cambridge. Murad's succinct paper provides a good understanding of the traditionalist perspective on the practice of taqlid and its importance in promoting harmony among Muslims. Murad's writings are available primarily as popular tracts on the Internet. This is in part due to the international audience that he caters to. See also Usmani 2000.

36. Hallaq (2001, 1–23) provides a good overview of the different levels of proficiency in Islamic jurisprudence while at the same time emphasizing the fluidity of the arrangement and its difference in this with the Christian church. In simplest terms, a *mufti* is somebody who is authorized to issue a *fatwa*, a rule based on his understanding and knowledge of at least one *madhab*, or school of Islamic jurisprudence. It is useful to remind ourselves again that no mufti has ever enjoyed the kind of unitary authority that was the norm for the pope of the Christian church in premodern times and that continues to be the case in the Roman Catholic Church. Moreover, fatwas are not backed by enforcement mechanisms and have no binding capacity even on the person or persons who sought the fatwa.

37. Winter 2004.

38. This is reinforced through publications with titles such as *Islam Daur-e-Jadid ka Mazhab* (*Islam: A Religion for Modern Times*).

39. Clifton, Karachi, April 2007.

40. The third day after a death, when family and neighbors traditionally get together and read the Qur'an in memory of the deceased and then share a meal.

41. The fortieth day after a death, which is celebrated in a similar manner.

42. This was a slogan popularized by the general in his attempt to curb enthusiasm for pan-Islamism.

43. See Davis 1984 for Iran; Bayat 2007 for Algeria; White 2002 for Turkey; and Nasr 1994 for Pakistan.

44. I emphasize the particularly Punjabi context of this upward mobility because Punjabis benefited immensely from their dominance in the armed services during the Zia years in particular. See also Samad 1996 and Talbot 2002.

45. In a move that echoes that of Pakistani's first military dictator, Ayub Khan's "Basic Democracy Scheme," General Musharaf has introduced a system of local governance in which some of the powers held by magistrates and local civil bureaucracy has been devolved to locally elected union councillors, who then elect a nazim for a specified area. Lahore, being a large metropolitan area, has nine town nazims and one city nazim, who performs many of the duties that previously a mayor would have.

It is important to point out that the situation in urban Sindh, in Karachi, and in Hyderabad is significantly different from Lahore in this respect. In Karachi, the JI has a stronger relationship with the lower-middle-class and working-class Mohajirs (i.e., Muslims who migrated from India after the partition).

46. See also the detailed study by Wilder (1999) of some of the same constituencies that Hafiz Salman Butt is talking about. Wilder's analysis of voter behavior shows that contrary to popular and academic assertions, *biradari* (patrilineal kinship group/clan) and familial ties play a less significant role than political platforms in this part of Punjab. Interview, Hafiz Salman Butt, Jama'at-e-Islami office, Ichra, August 31, 2005.

47. The JI operates a well-managed transport service for activists on campaign trails or da'wa activities. Each vehicle has a log that has to be signed at the end of the day by the activists responsible for that vehicle.

48. The term "Gujjar" refers to previously nomadic tribes that were associated with cattle herding. Gujjars traditionally spent the summer months in Kashmir and the winter months in the plains of Punjab.

49. Interview, Hafiz Mohammed Saeed, weekly *Nida-e-Millat* (*Voice of the Nation*), Lahore, March 22–28, 2001. Corroboration of narrative by Um-Talha, his wife, after a dars session in Masjid Qadsia, June 20, 2005. This may go some way in explaining his radically anti-Hindu and anti-India rhetoric. Nevertheless, people affected by the horrors of Partition violence have reacted in a variety of ways, including supporting peaceful initiatives to ensure that it does not happen again (see, for instance, Butalia 2000).

50. Interview, Umm-e-Talha (literally, mother of Talha, wife of Hafiz Mohammed Saeed), July 4, 2005, Masjid Qadsia, Lahore. She is also his cousin, and her father, a religious scholar, was partially responsible for the education of Hafiz Mohd. Saeed. Her brother, Abdul Rehman Maki, is generally considered to be second in command to Hafiz Mohd. Saeed.

51. Large tracts of western Punjab were made arable after a network of canals was laid down during the British rule. The resulting Canal Colonies were demarcated in a strictly "rational and scientific manner," with coordinates of the village substituting for its name. For an absorbing account of the history and political economy of the Canal Colonies, see Ali 1988.

52. Amir Rana 2003, 20. Amir Rana provides a very useful biographical sketch of Hafiz Saeed, which I have used here.

53. Interview, weekly *Nida-e-Millat*, March 22–28, 2001.

54. Hafiz Mohd. Saeed claimed to have met Osama bin Laden while with the Sayaf group. However, in recent years, he has started downplaying this claim.

55. Abou Zahab 2002; Nasr 2002; Zaman 1998.

56. See, for instance, *Majjula al Da'wa*, the JD's monthly magazine, issues for 1998, 1997, and 2000.

57. *Wajib u'l Qatl* is often taken to mean "necessary to kill," but the division of the commandments in fiqh into *farz, wajib, sunnah, mandoob, makrooh tanzihi, makrooh tahrimi, haraam* indicates that there is a range within which wajib is different from farz, the absolutely necessary commandments. The term *wajib* covers a range of meanings from obligatory/binding to reasonable/just. Platts's (1994, 1172) translation of the term *wajib u'l qatl* is "deserving death." It is also instructive to remind ourselves that it has been a matter of not inconsiderable debate to establish when, who, and why someone may be wajib-ul-qatl.

58. Double maths is a peculiarly Pakistani mode of describing a combination of subjects that include mathematics and statistics courses.

59. Another South Asian revivalist movement similar in its puritanical message to the JD, but without its emphasis on political and military action.

60. Interview, July 16, 2005, Punjab University, Geology Department.

61. He is referring to the alliance of religious parties, the MMA.

62. Interview, Abdul Rehman Maki, July 18, 2005.

63. Compared to these two, members of the Tablighi Jama'at, with whom I also spent some time during the early stages of my research, offer a further variation. Tablighi men generally do not trim their beards, but shave their moustaches.

64. Al-Huda is a pietist group for women only. Started by Dr. Farhat Hashmi, a PhD in Islamic studies from Glasgow University and a onetime associate of the JI, the group focused initially on upper-class and upper-middle-class women, but has over the last few years expanded its services to lower-middle-class women as well.

65. Dr. Zakir Naik is an Indian Muslim who heads a da'wa foundation in Mumbai. He uses TV appearances, videos, CDs, and DVDs to promote his message.

66. See chapter 2 for details of IJT's violent tactics at Punjab University in combating the influence of the left-secular elements.

Chapter Four

1. Interestingly when one looks for literature on "women and religion" within the Cambridge University Library search engine, roughly more than 50 percent of the entries refer to literature on "women and Islam." This gives some indication of the disproportionate attention that Islam has received in recent years regarding its relationship with women.

2. In the case of Egypt, the more recent and interesting work has been Ahmed 1992; Abu-Lughod 1998; Mahmood 2005. For Turkey, see Kandiyoti 1991, 1996; Gole 1996.

3. In Pakistan, Shaheed and Mumtaz are perhaps the most prominent secularist feminists who have moved closer to the Islamic feminist framing. Their organization Shirkat Gah acts as the Asia coordination office for the WLUML network.

4. See Nussbaum 2000 for the difficulty of establishing what may constitute "basic." While acknowledging the difficulties, Nussbaum attempts an answer in her book.

5. See also Abu Lughod 2002.

6. The most well-known texts are Mumtaz and Shaheed 1987; Khan 1993; Zafar 1991.

7. A useful exception is Shahabuddin (2008). She argues through her study of the women activists of the Jama'at-e-Islami in Bangladesh that functioning as a political party, Jama'at-e-Islami Bangladesh has been forced to become more sensitive to their demands.

8. See also Amir Rana 2003, 321. I have also used the Jama'at ud Da'wa Urdu website at http://www.jamatuddawa.org/data1/pages/muridke.htm (last accessed June 17, 2007) for more details on the markaz. However, the website has been taken offline since the 2008 Mumbai attacks.

9. I have changed her name in accordance with anthropological conventions. While the name of the editor of the magazine, Umm-Hammad, is well known, Saima uses a nom de plume in the magazine.

10. It is relatively common to find peasant or working-class girls living away from their families in the capacity of domestic servants. However, Saima belonged to a lower-middle-class family, and such a move is relatively unusual in that milieu.

11. In a conscious move to Arabicize their names, members of the JD follow the system of *kunyat*. The kunyat system is gendered, but allows greater flexibility in choosing which relative one wants to be linked to publicly. The prefix *umm* means "mother of," *bint* means "daughter of," *abu* means "father of," and *bin* means "son of." Therefore, Umm-Talha means "the mother of Talha." At the same time it is arguably a more egalitarian system of naming, as it disavows the larger links of caste, *biradari*, and paternal lineage—an innovation of sorts in the South Asian context.

12. See Sarkar 2001, 1993, for some discussion of similar dynamics in the case of women who participate in the Hindu fundamentalist movement.

13. Again, Rabia is a pseudonym in accordance with anthropological conventions, while Umm-Talha's name remains unchanged, as she is a key leader in the women's section of the Jama'at-ud Da'wa.

14. Rabia was socially a rung above the other participants of this particular dars circle at Masjid Qadsia. Rabia drove to the dars in a small Suzuki car, and the fact that she ate at a dining table raised some comment after she had left. One of the other women said, "Rabia is really courageous. They are people who have their meals on a dining table! To belong to such a family and turn to parda is really quite a big thing."

15. Rural and urban Punjabi contexts involve significantly close interaction between members of the extended family across gender barriers.

16. The term "brother-in-law" is too generic to portray the range of relationships it involves in the Pakistani context, including: *jeth* (older brother of the husband), *dewar* (younger brother of the husband), *nandoi* (husband to the sister of a woman's husband), and *behnoi* (husband to the sister).

17. *Iman* may be translated as "faith" or "belief," while *aqeeda* is generally held to be closer to the idea of creed or sectarian belief system.

18. Interviews with various women leaders and organizers within the JD, in particular Umm-Soban, a key organizer for women's activities in Lahore and the surrounding areas. All mentioned how they had started structured outreach activities for women only in the past six to seven years.

19. Al-Khidmat charity was started by a member of the wealthy Chinioti trading community in Karachi soon after the 1965 war with India. At that time, she had started a fund to provide support to the soldiers, their families, and others directly affected by the war. At a later stage, she became quite close to the Jama'at, and offered to Maulana Mawdudi to affiliate al-Khidmat with the JI. Maududi had, however, not supported an institutional affiliation at that time in keeping with his notion of a vanguard party.

20. Qazi Hussain Ahmed's daughter, Mrs. Samia Raheel Qazi, was elected a member of the Pakistani National Assembly in 2002. She combined da'wa activities with her political work.

21. See Jamal 2005 for some insight into the manner in which left/liberal women activists, generally from elite backgrounds, were originally dismissive of JI women activists and then over the last two decades began to view them as a serious challenge.

22. In fact, it is possible to argue that women's educational qualifications are a very useful way of navigating the murky waters of Pakistani class mobility. In particular, the recent boom and bust cycles since the 1980s, the proliferation of consumer items across a wide spectrum of classes, and the vast differences across ethnic divides and provincial standards mean that it has become difficult to distinguish between the lower-middle, middle, and upper-middle classes on a national level. I find that one useful indicator of a family's status and changes in it over the last few decades is the level of women's education going back several generations.

23. See, in particular, the various reports publicized by Amnesty International at http://www.amnesty.org.

24. A popular pamphlet was based on Khurram Ja Murad's essay "Elections and the Nation's Responsibility" [Intikhabat aur qaum ki zimadari].

25. Surah an-Nisa is a particular set of verses in the Qur'an that deals with the rights and duties of women.

26. The more politically active among the JI women also had a support network of other JI women. During election campaigns and times of high stress, the women who did not actively campaign would send home cooked meals to the homes of the more politically engaged women.

27. Indeed, as Tjomsland (1993: 4–9) has discussed in the case of Islamists in Tunisia, the Islamists are more likely to insist on a nuclear family arrangement that posits a break from the traditional extended family.

28. On the changes in the Islamists reading of the state, see Iqtidar 2011.

Conclusion

1. At a symposium titled "Business, Security and Terrorism" held in February 2007 at the University of Cambridge, I was struck by the comment made by a former head of the MI6. When asked about his worst-case scenarios regarding terrorism, he placed the death of General Musharaf, "who has allowed us unprecedented intelligence access in Pakistan," at the top of his list. A biological bomb strike in London came further down on this list.

2. Alavi 1988); Ali 2003; Ahmed 1997; Gardezi 1991; Gardezi and Rashid 1983; Malik 1999; Nasr 1994, 1996, 2001; Shafqat 2002; Waseem 1987.

3. Ahmed 1986; Amin 1988; Malik 1997.

4. Mumtaz and Shaheed 1987; Weiss 2002; Zafar 1991.

5. Ackerman's recent work (2006) is a good demonstration of how a pragmative "conversational restraint" may be important in sustaining the liberal state, in this case through the provision of an emergency constitution.

References

Abid, Abdul Karim. 2004. *Siyasi Samaji Tajziyay* [Political and Social Analysis]. Lahore: Manshoorat.

Abou Zahab, Mariam. 2002. "The Regional Dimension of Sectarian Conflicts in Pakistan," in Christophe Jaffrelot, ed., *Pakistan: Nationalism without a Nation*. London: Zed.

Abu-Lughod, Lila. 1990. "The Romance of Resistance: Tracing Transformations of Power through Bedouin Women," *American Ethnologist* 17(1): 41–55.

———. 1998. "Introduction," in Lila Abu-Lughod, ed., *Remaking Women: Feminism and Modernity in the Middle East*. Princeton: Princeton University Press.

———. 2002. "Do Muslim Women Really Need Saving? Anthropological Reflections in Cultural Relativism and Its Others," *American Anthropologist* 104(3): 783–90.

Abu Yahya, Mohammed Zariya Mohammed. 2002 [2001]. *Da'wati Nisab Tarbiyat* [Training Course for Proselytizing]. Lahore: Al-Andulus.

Ackerman, Bruce. 1989. "Why Dialogue?" *Journal of Philosophy* 86(1): 5–22.

———. 2006. *Before the Next Attack: Preserving Civil Liberties in the Age of Terrorism*. New Haven: Yale University Press.

Afshar, Haleh, ed. 1996. *Women in Third World Politics*. London: Routledge.

———. 1998. *Islam and Feminisms: An Iranian Case-Study*. Basingstoke: Macmillan Press.

Ahmad, Irfan. 2009. *Islamism and Democracy in India: The Transformation of Jamaat-e-Islami*. Princeton: Princeton University Press.

Ahmed, Akbar S. 1986. *Pakistani Society: Islam, Ethnicity and Leadership in South Asia*. Oxford: Oxford University Press.

———. 1991. *Resistance and Control in Pakistan*. London: Routledge.

———. 1997. *Jinnah, Pakistan and Islamic Identity: The Search for Saladin*. London: Routledge.

Ahmed, Aziz-ud-Din. 2000. *Pakistan Main Tulba Tehreek* [Student Movement in Pakistan]. Lahore: Mashal.

Ahmed, Feroze. 1972. "Has the People's Rule Arrived? I," *Pakistan Forum* 2(5).

Ahmed, Irfan. 2006. "The State in Islamist Thought," *ISIM Review* 18:12–13.

Ahmed, Khurshid. N.d. *Raushan Khiyali Aitadal Pasandi ya Amreeki Deen-e-Ilahi* [Enlightened Thinking and Moderation or American Religion]. Lahore: Manshoorat.

Ahmed, Khurshid, and Zafar Ishaq Ansari, eds. 1979. *Islamic Perspectives: Studies in the Honour of Maulana Sayyid Abul A'la Mawdudi*. Leicester: {AU: publisher?}.

Ahmed, Leila. 1992. *Women and Gender in Islam*. New Haven: Yale University Press.

Ahmed, Rafiuddin. 1994. "Redefining Muslim Identity in South Asia: The Transformation of the Jama'at-I-Islami," in M. Marty and R. S. Appleby, eds., *Accounting for Fundamentalisms: The Dynamic Character of Movements*. Chicago: University of Chicago Press.

Ahmed, Rashid. 2000. *Taliban: Islam, Oil and the New Great Game in Central Asia*. I. B. Tauris: London.

Al-Ali, Nadje. 2000. *Secularism, Gender and the State in the Middle East: The Egyptian Women's Movement*. Cambridge: Cambridge University Press.

Alavi, Hamza. 1998. "Pakistan and Islam: Ethnicity and Ideology," in Fred Halliday, Hamza Alavi, and F. Halliday, F., eds., *State and Ideology in the Middle East and Pakistan*. Basingstoke: Macmillan.

Al-Azam, Sadik. 1994. "Islamic Fundamentalism Reconsidered; A Critical Outline of Problems, Ideas and Approaches," *South Asia Bulletin* 14(1): 73–98.

Al-Azmeh, Aziz. 1993. *Islam and Modernities*. London: Verso.

Ali, Imran. 1988. *The Punjab under Imperialism, 1885–1947*. Princeton: Princeton University Press.

Ali, Tariq. 1983. *Can Pakistan Survive? The Death of a State*. London: Penguin.

———. 2003. *Clash of Fundamentalisms*. London: Verso.

Ali, Tariq, and Susan Watkins. 1998. *1968: Marching in the Streets*. Washington DC: Free Press.

Al-Rehman, Syed Mutaqin, and Salim Mansur Khalid. 1981. *Jab wauh Nazim-e-A'ala Thay*. Lahore: Idara Matboo'at Talba.

Althusser, Louis. 1984. *Essays on Ideology*. London: Verso.

Amin, Tahir. 1988. *Ethno-National Movements of Pakistan: Domestic and International Factors*. Lahore: Vanguard.

Amir Rana, Mohammed. 2003. *Jihad aur Jihadi*. Lahore: Mashal Publications.

Amjad, Ali. 2001. *Labour Legislation and Trade Unions in India and Pakistan*. Karachi: Oxford University Press.

Amjad, Rashid. 1978. *Pakistan's Growth Experience: Objectives, Achievement, and Impact on Poverty, 1947–1977*. Lahore: Progressive Publishers.

Anas, Ahmed. 1989. "*Jamiat ka Tasisi Pasmanzar*," in Salim Mansoor Khalid, *Tulba Tehreekin*. Lahore: Al-Badar Publications.

———. N.d. *Mohammed, Qur'an aur Islam; Roosi Mushriqeen ki nazar main*. No publisher.

Anderson, Benedict. 1991. *Imagined Communities: Reflections on the Origin and Spread of Nationalism*. London: Verso.

Anderson, Jon, and Dale Eickelman. 2003. *New Media in the Muslim World: The Emerging Public Sphere*. Bloomington: Indiana University Press.

An-Na'im, Abdullahi. 1999. "Political Islam in National and International Politics," in Peter Berger, ed., *The Desecularization of the World: Resurgent Religions and World Politics*. Washington DC: Ethics and Public Policy Centre.

Arkoun, Mohammed. 2003. "Rethinking Islam Today," *Annals of the American Academy of Political Science* 588: 18–39.

Aron, Raymond. 1968. *Main Currents in Sociological Thought*. Vol. 2, *Durkheim, Pareto, Weber*. London: Weidenfeld & Nicholson.

Asad, Talal. 1973. *Anthropology and the Colonial Encounter*. London: Ithaca Press.

———. 1991. "From the History of Colonial Anthropology to the Anthropology of Western Hegemony," in G. Stocking, ed., *Colonial Situations*. Madison: University of Wisconsin Press.

———. 1993. *Genealogies of Religion: Discipline and Reasons of Power in Christianity and Islam*. London: Johns Hopkins University Press.

———. 2003. *Formation of the Secular: Christianity, Islam and Modernity*. Stanford: Stanford University Press.

Asdar Ali, Kamran. 2004. "Pulp Fictions: Reading Pakistani Domesticity," *Social Text* 78:123–45.

———. 2005. "Strength of the Street Meets the Strength of the State: The 1972 Labour Struggle in Karachi," *Journal of Middle Eastern Studies* 37(1): 83–107.

Asher, Catherine B. 2000. "Mapping Hindu-Muslim Identities through the Architecture of Shahjahanabad and Jaipur," in David Gilmartin and Bruce Lawrence, *Beyond Turk and Hindu: Rethinking Religious Identities in Islamicate South Asia*. Gainesville: University Press of Florida.

Asian Development Bank, Pakistan Report. 2005. http://www.adb.org/documents/books/ADO/2005/pak.asp.

Audi, Robert. 1989. "Separation of Church and State and the Obligation of Citizenship," *Philosophy and Public Affairs* 18(3): 259–96.

———. 1991. "Commitment and Secular Reason: Response to Professor Weithman," *Philosophy and Public Affairs* 20(1): 66–76.

Ayubi, Nazih. 1991. *Political Islam: Religion and Politics in the Arab World*. London: Routledge.

Aziz, K. K. 1987. *The Idea of Pakistan*. Lahore: Vanguard Books.

———. 2006. *A Journey into the Past: Portrait of a Punjabi Family, 1800–1970*. Lahore: Vanguard Books.

Bahadur, Kalim. 1977. *The Jama'at-I-Islami of Pakistan: Political Thought and Political Action*. Delhi: Chetana Publications.

Barkey, Karen. 2008. *Empire of Difference: The Ottomans in Comparative Perspective*. Cambridge: Cambridge University Press.

Barlas, Asma. 1995. *Democracy, Nationalism, and Communalism: The Colonial Legacy in South Asia*. Boulder: Westview Press.

Bayat, Asef. 2005. "What Is Post-Islamism?" *ISIM Review* 16: 5.

———. 2007. *Making Islam Democratic: Social Movements and the Post-Islamist Turn*. Stanford: Stanford University Press.

Bayly, Christopher. 1987. *Indian Society and the Making of the British Empire*. Cambridge: Cambridge University Press.

———. 1996. *Empire and Information: Intelligence Gathering and Social Communication in India, 1780–1870*. Cambridge: Cambridge University Press.

———. 2004. *The Birth of the Modern World, 1780–1914: Global Connections and Comparisons*. Malden: Blackwell Publishers.

Bayly, Christopher, and Leila Tarazai Fawaz, eds. 2002. *Modernity and Culture: From the Mediterranean to the Indian Ocean*. New York: Columbia University Press.

Bayly, Susan. 2000. "French Anthropology and the Durkheimians in Colonial Indochina," *Modern Asian Studies* 34(3): 581–622.

Bellin, Eva. 2008. "Faith in Politics: New Trends in the Study of Religion and Politics," *World Politics* 60: 315–47.

Benhabib, Seyla. 1992. "Models of Public Space: Hannah Arendt, the Liberal Tradition and Jurgen Habermas," in Craig Calhoun, *Habermas and the Public Sphere*. Cambridge, MA: MIT Press.

Benin, Joel, and Joe Stork. 1997. *Political Islam: Essays from Middle East Report*. Berkeley: University of California Press.

Berger, Peter, ed. 1999. *The Desecularization of the World: Resurgent Religions and World Politics*. Washington DC: Ethics and Public Policy Centre.

Bernholz, Peter, Manfred Streit, and Roland Vaubel, eds. 1998. *Political Competition, Innovation, and Growth: A Historical Analysis*. Berlin: Springer.

Bhargava, Rajeev, ed. 1998. *Secularism and Its Critics*. Delhi: Oxford University Press.

Bhasin, Kamla, Ritu Menon, and Nighat Said Khan. 1994. *Against All Odds: Essays on Women, Religion and Developments from India and Pakistan*. New Delhi: Kali for Women.

Bilgrami, Akeel. 1998. "Secularism, Nationalism and Modernity," in Rajeev Bhargava, *Secularism and Its Critics*. Delhi: Oxford University Press.

Binder, Leonard. 1961. *Religion and Politics in Pakistan*. Berkeley: University of California Press.

Bloom, Allan. 1987. *The Closing of the American Mind*. New York: Simon and Schuster.

Boroujerdi, Mehrzad. 1994. "Can Islam Be Secularised?" in M. R. Ghanoonparvar and F. Farrokh, eds., *In Transition: Essays on Culture and Identity in the Middle East*. Austin: Texas A&M University Press.

Brown, D. 1996. *Rethinking Tradition in Modern Islamic Thought*. Cambridge: Cambridge University Press.

Brown, L. Carl. 2000. *Religion and State: The Muslim Approach to Politics*. New York: Columbia University Press.

Brown, Wendy. 2006. *Regulating Aversion: Tolerance and Identity in the Age of Empire*. Princeton: Princeton University Press.

Bruce, Steve. 1992. *Religion and Modernization: Sociologists and Historians Debate the Secularisation Thesis*. Oxford: Clarendon Press.

———. 1996. *Religion in the Modern World: From Cathedrals to Cults*. Oxford: Oxford University Press.

———. 1999. *Choice and Religion: A Critique of Rational Choice Theory*. Oxford: Oxford University Press.

Burke, Edmund. 1988. "Islam and Social Movements: Methodological Reflections," in Edmund Burke and Ira Lapidus, eds., *Islam, Politics and Social Movements*. London: I. B. Tauris.

Burke, Edmund, and Ira Lapidus, eds. 1988. *Islam, Politics and Social Movements*. London: I. B. Tauris.

Buss, Sarah, and Lee Overton. 2002. *Contours of Agency: Essays on Themes from Harry Frankfurt*. Cambridge, MA: MIT Press.

Butalia, Urvashi. 2000. *The Other Side of Silence: Voices from the Partition of India*. Durham: Duke University Press.

Calhoun, Craig. 1992. *Habermas and the Public Sphere*. Cambridge, MA: MIT Press.

Casanova, Jose. 1994. *Public Religion in Modern World.* Chicago: University of Chicago Press.

Chadwick, Owen. 1975. *The Secularisation of the European Mind in the Nineteenth Century.* Cambridge: Cambridge University Press.

Chakrabarty, Dipesh. 2000. *Provincializing Europe: Postcolonial Thought and Historical Difference.* Princeton: Princeton University Press.

Chandar, Krishan. 2004. *Ghaddar* [Traitor]. Lahore: Book Home Publishers.

Chandavarkar, Rajnarayan. 1998. *Imperial Power and Popular Politics: Class, Resistance and the State in India, c.1850–1950.* Cambridge: Cambridge University Press.

Chatterjee, Nandini. 2007. *State, Christianity, and the Public Sphere in India, 1830–1950.* PhD diss., University of Cambridge.

Chatterjee, Partha. 1989. "Colonialism, Nationalism, and Colonized Women: The Contest in India," *American Ethnologist* 16(4): 622–33.

———. 1993. *The Nation and Its Fragments: Colonial and Post-Colonial Histories.* Princeton: Princeton University Press.

———. 1998. "Secularism and Tolerance," in Rajeev Bhargava, ed., *Secularism and ts Critics.* Delhi: Oxford University Press.

Cohn, Bernard. 1996. *Colonialism and Its Forms of Knowledge: The British in India.* Princeton: Princeton University Press.

Collier, Jane. 1996. "Intertwined Histories: Islamic Law and Western Imperialism," Contested Polities: Religious Disciplines and Structures of Modernity, special issue of *Stanford Humanities Review* 5(1): 162.

Commission on Student Problems and Welfare. Report. Headed by Justice Hamood-ur-Rehman, Government of Pakistan, 1965.

Connolly, William. 1999. *Why I Am Not a Secularist.* Minneapolis: University of Minnesota Press.

———. 2006. "Europe, a Minority Tradition," in David Scott and Charles Hirschkind, *Powers of the Secular Modern: Talal Asad and His Interlocutors.* Stanford: Stanford University Press.

"Constitution/Dastoor Muttahida Majlis-e-Amal." 2002. No publisher.

Cook, Michael. 2000. *Commanding Right and Forbidding Wrong in Islamic Thought.* Cambridge: Cambridge University Press.

Cooley, John. 2000. *Unholy Wars: Afghanistan, America and International Terrorism.* London: Pluto.

Corbin, Juliet, and Anselm Strauss. 1998. *Basics of Qualitative Research: Techniques and Procedures for Developing Grounded Theory.* Thousand Oaks, CA: Sage.

Crush, Jonathan. 1995. *Power of Development.* London: Routledge.

Dabashi, Hamid. 1989. *Authority in Islam: From the Rise of Muhammed to the Establishment of the Umayyads.* New Brunswick: Transaction Publishers.

Davie, Grace. 2002. *Europe: The Exceptional Case.* London: Darton, Longman and Todd.

Davis, Eric. 1984. "Ideology, Social Class, and islamic Radicalism in Modern Egypt," in *From Nationalism to Revolutionary Islam,* ed. Said Amir Arjomand. Albany: University of New York.

Devji, Faisal. 2007. "Apologetic Modernity," *Modern Intellectual History* 4(1): 61–76.

Dorronsoro, Gilles. 2002. "Pakistan and the Taliban: State Policy, Religious Networks and Political Connections," in Christophe Jaffrelot, ed., *Pakistan: Nationalism without a Nation*. London: Zed.

Downs, Anthony. 1957. *An Economic Theory of Democracy*. New York: Harper.

Eickelman, Dale F., and James Piscatori. 1996. *Muslim Politics*. Princeton: Princeton University Press.

Eickelman, Dale. 1992. "Mass Higher Education and the Religious Imagination in Contemporary Arab Societies," *American Ethnologist* 19(4): 643–55.

Eisenstadt, S. N. 1999. *Fundamentalism, Sectarianism and Revolution: The Jacobian Dimension of Modernity*. Cambridge: Cambridge University Press.

Engineer, Asghar Ali (Uday Mehta). 1999. *Essays in Contemporary Politics of Identity, Religion, and Secularism*. Delhi: Ajanta Publications.

———. 2003. *Communal Challenge and Secular Response*. Delhi: Shipra Publications.

Escobar, Arturo. 1995. *Encountering Development: The Making and Unmaking of the Third World*. Princeton: Princeton University Press.

Esposito, John, ed. 1995. *The Oxford Encyclopaedia of the Modern Islamic World*. Oxford: Oxford University Press.

———, ed. 1997. *Political Islam: Revolution, Radicalism or Reform?* Boulder: Lynne Rienner.

———. 1999a. *The Islamic Threat: Myth or Reality?* Oxford: Oxford University Press.

———. 1999b. "Contemporary Islam: Reformation or Revolution?" in John Esposito ed., *The Oxford History of Islam*. Oxford: Oxford University Press.

———. 2002. *Unholy War: Terror in the Name of Islam*. Oxford: Oxford University Press.

Euben, Roxanne. 1997. "Premodern, Antimodern or Postmodern? Islamic and Western Critiques of Modernity," *Review of Politics* 59(3): 429–59.

———. 1999. *Enemy in the Mirror, Islamic Fundamentalism and the Limits of Modern Rationalism: A Work of Comparative Political Theory*. Princeton: Princeton University Press.

Faruki, Kemal. 1987. "Pakistan: Islamic Government and Society," in John Esposito, ed., *Islam in Asia: Religion, Politics, and Society*. Oxford: Oxford University Press.

Ferguson, James. 1994. *The Anti-Politics Machine; "Development," Depoliticization and Bureaucratic Power in Lesotho*. Minneapolis: University of Minnesota Press.

Filali-Ansary, Abdou. 1996. "Islam and Liberal Democracy: The Challenge of Secularization." *Journal of Democracy* 7(2): 76–80.

Flores, Alexander. 1993. "Secularism, Integralism and Political Islam," *Middle East Report* 183:32–38

Frank, Andre Gunder. 1998. *ReOrient: Global Economy in the Asian Age*. Berkeley: University of California Press.

Freitag, Sandria B. 1991. "Introduction", special issue on Aspects of the "Public" in Colonial South Asia, *South Asia*, n.s. 14(1): 1–13.

Fuller, Graham. 2003. *The Future of Political Islam*. New York: Palgrave.

Gardezi, Hassan. 1991. *A Reexamination of the Socio-Political History of Pakistan*. Lewiston. NY: Edwin Mellen Press.

Gardezi, Hassan, and Jamil Rashid, eds. 1983. *Pakistan: The Roots of Dictatorship: The Political Economy of a Praetorian State*. London: Zed.

Gauchet, Marcel. 1997. *The Disenchantment of the World: A Political History of Religion*. Princeton: Princeton University Press.

Geertz, Clifford. 1968. *Islam Observed: Religious Development in Morocco and Indonesia*. Chicago: University of Chicago Press.

Gellner, Ernest. 1991. "Islam and Marxism: Some Comparisons," *International Affairs* 67(1): 1–6.

Gibbons, Michael. 2006. "Hermeneutics, Political Inquiry and Practical Reason: An Evolving Challenge to Political Science," *American Political Science Review* 100(4): 563–71.

Gilani, Asad. 1969a. *Socialiston kay siyasi harbay*. Sarghodha: Idara Adab Islami, May.

———. 1969b. *Socialism ki Nakamiyan*. Sarghodha: Idara Adab Islami, January.

———. N.d. *A'alam-e-Islam aur Socialism ka Challenge*. No publisher.

Gilmartin, David. 1979. "Religious Leadership and the Pakistan Movement in the Punjab," *Modern Asian Studies* 13(3): 458–517.

———. 1988. *Empire and Islam: Punjab and the Making of Pakistan*. London: I. B. Tauris.

———. 1991. "Democracy, Nationalism and the Public: A Speculation on Colonial Muslim Politics," *South Asia* 14(1): 123–40.

———. 1998. "A Magnificient Gift: Muslim Nationalism and the Election Process in Colonial Punjab," *Comparative Studies in Society and History* 40(3): 415–36.

Gilmartin, David, and Bruce Lawrence, eds. 2000. *Beyond Turk and Hindu: Rethinking Religious Identities in Islamicate South Asia*. Gainesville: University Press of Florida.

Glover William. 2007. *Making Lahore Modern: Constructing and Imaging a Colonial City*. Minneapolis: University of Minnesota Press.

Goffman, Erving. 1972. *Interaction Ritual: Essays on Face-to-Face Behaviour*. London: Allen Lane.

Gole, Nilufer. 1996. *The Forbidden Modern, Civilization and Veiling*. Ann Arbor: University of Michigan Press.

Guha, Sumit. 2003. "The Politics of Identity and Enumeration in India c.1600–1990," *Comparative Study of History and Society* 45(1): 148–67.

Habermas, Jürgen. 1989. *The Structural Transformation of the Public Sphere: An Inquiry into a Category of Bourgeois Society*. Cambridge: Polity Press.

———. 2002. *Religion and Rationality: Essays on Reason, God and Modernity*. Cambridge, MA: MIT Press.

Haddad, Yvonne Yazbeck, and John L. Esposito, eds. 1998. *Islam, Gender and Social Change*. New York: Oxford University Press.

Hale, Sondra. 1996. *Gender Politics in Sudan: Islamism, Socialism, and the State*. Oxford: Westview Press.

Hallaq, Wael. 2001. *Authority, Continuity and Change in Islamic Law*. Cambridge: Cambridge University Press.

Hamza, Amir. 2002. *Qafila Da'wat au Jihad* [Caravan of Proselytizing and Martyrdom]. Lahore: Dar Al-Andulus.

Hansen, Thomas Blom. 1999. *The Saffron Wave: Democracy and Hindu Nationalism in Modern India*. Princeton: Princeton University Press.

Haqqani, Hussain. 2005. *Pakistan: Between Mosque and Military*. Washington DC: Carnegie Endowment for International Peace.

Harding, Susan. 1991. "Representing Fundamentalism: The Problem of the Repugnant Cultural Other," *Social Research* 58(2): 373–93.

Hatem, Mervat. 1998. "Secularist and Islamist Discourses on Modernity in Egypt and the Evolution of the Postcolonial Nation-State," in Yvonne Yazbeck Haddad and John L. Esposito, eds., *Islam, Gender and Social Change*. New York: Oxford University Press.

Hefner, Robert. 2000. *Civil Islam: Muslims and Democratization in Indonesia*. Princeton: Princeton University Press.

———, ed. 2005. *Remaking Muslim Politics: Pluralism, Contestation, Democratization*. Princeton: Princeton University Press.

Hobart, M., ed. 1993. *An Anthropological Critique of Development: The Growth of Ignorance*. London: Routledge.

Hobsbawm, Eric, and Terence Ranger, eds. 1983. *The Invention of Tradition*. Cambridge: Cambridge University Press.

Hodgson, Marshal. 1974. *The Venture of Islam: Conscience and History in a World Civilization*. Chicago: University of Chicago Press.

Holyoake, George. 1896. *The Origins and Nature of Secularism*. London: Watts & Co.

Hunter, Shireen, ed. 1988. *The Politics of Islamic Revivalism, Diversity and Unity*, Bloomington: Indiana University Press.

Huntington, Samuel P. 1993. "The Clash of Civilizations?" *Foreign Affairs* 72(3): 22–28.

Hurd, Elizabeth Shakman. 2008. *The Politics of Secularism in International Relations*. Princeton: Princeton University Press.

Iqtidar, Humeira. 2002. "Higher Education Privatization: A Retrograde Step" (parts 1 and 2). *Dawn Newspaper* (Karachi). May 12 and June 12.

———. 2006. "Radical Times: Student Politics in the 1960s," in *At the Crossroads: Research, Policy and Development in a Globalized World*, Sustainable Development Conference anthology. Islamabad: Sama Publications.

———. 2008. "Terrorism and Islamism: Difference, Dynamics, and Dilemmas," *Global Business and Economic Review* 10(2): 216–28.

———. 2009. "Collatoral Damage from the Afghanistan War: Jamaat ud Dawa and Lashkar-e-Tayyaba Militancy," *Middle East Report* 251: 28–31.

———. 2010a. "Colonial Secularism and Islamism in North India: A Relationship of Creativity," in Ira Katznelson and Gareth Stedman Jones, *Religion and the Political Imagination*. Cambridge: Cambridge University Press.

———. 2010b. "Jamaat-e-Islami Pakistan: Learning From the Left," in Naveeda Khan, ed., *Beyond Crisis: Re-evaluating Pakistan*. Delhi: Routledge.

———. 2011. "Secularism beyond the State: 'State' and 'Market' in Islamist Imagination," *Modern Asian Studies*.

Jahan, Raunaq. 1972. *Pakistan: Failure in National Integration*. New York: Columbia University Press.

Jalal, Ayesha. 1985. *The Sole Spokesman: Jinnah, the Muslim League, and the Demand for Pakistan*. Cambridge: Cambridge University Press.

———. 1991. "The Convenience of Subservience: Women and the State in Pakistan," in Denize Kandiyoti, ed., *Women, Islam and the State*. Basingstoke: Macmillan.

———. 2001. *Self and Sovereignty: Individual and Community in South Asian Islam since 1850*. Lahore: Sang-e-Meel Publications.

———. 2002. "Negotiating Colonial Modernity and Cultural Difference: Indian Muslim Conceptions of Community and Nation, 1878–1914," in Leila Tarazai Fawaz and C. A. Bayly, eds., *Modernity and Culture, From the Mediterranean to the Indian Ocean*. New York: Columbia University Press.

———. 2008. *Partisans of Allah: Jihad in South Asia*. Cambridge, MA: Harvard University Press.

Jamal, Amina. 2005. "Feminist 'Selves' and Feminism's 'Others': Feminist Representations of Jamaat-e-Islami Women in Pakistan," *Feminist Review* 81:52–73.

Jones, Gareth Stedman. 1983. *Languages of Class: Studies in English Working Class History, 1832–1982*. Cambridge: Cambridge University Press.

Jones, Philip E. 2003. *The Pakistan People's Party: Rise to Power*. Oxford: Oxford University Press.

Kabbani, Rana. 1994 (1986). *Imperial Fictions: Europe's Myths of Orient*. London: Pandora.

Kandiyoti, Deniz. 1991. *Women, Islam and the State*. Basingstoke: Macmillan.

———. 1996. *Gendering the Middle East: Emerging Perspectives*. New York : Syracuse University Press.

Katznelson, Ira, and Gareth Stedman Jones. 2010. *Religion and the Political Imagination*. Cambridge: Cambridge University Press.

Kaviraj, Sudipta. 1997. "The Modern State in India," in Martin Doornbos and Sudipta Kaviraj, eds., *Dynamics of State Formation: India and Europe Compared*. Delhi: Sage Publications.

———. 2010. "On Thick and Thin Religion: Some Critical Reflections on Secularization Theory," in Katznelson and Stedman-Jones, *Religion and Political Imagination*.

Keddie, Nikki. 1997. "Secularism and the State: Towards Clarity and Global Comparison," *New Left Review* 226:21–40.

———. 2007. *Women in the Middle East: Past and Present*. Princeton: Princeton University Press.

Kepel, Gilles. 1995. *Revenge of God: The Resurgence of Islam, Christianity and Judaism in the Modern World*. Cambridge: Polity Press.

———. 2002. *Jihad: The Trail of Political Islam*. London: I. B. Tauris.

Khan, Naveeda. 2003. *Grounding Sectarianism: Islamic Ideology and Muslim Everyday Life in Lahore, Pakistan, circa 1920s–1990s*. PhD diss., Columbia University.

Khan, Nighat Said. 1993. *Voices Within: Dialogues with Women on Islam*. Lahore: ASR Publications.

Kitschelt, Herbert. 1989. *The Logics of Party Formation: Ecological Politics in Belgium and West Germany*. Ithaca: Cornell University Press.

Kugle, Scott Alan. 2001. "Framed, Blamed and Renamed: The Recasting of Islamic Jurisprudence in Colonial South Asia," *Modern Asian Studies* 35(2): 257–313.

Kurin, Richard. 1993. "Islamization in Pakistan: The Sayyid and the Dancer," in Dale Eickelman, ed., *Russia's Muslim Frontiers*. Bloomington: Indiana University Press.

Kuru, Ahmet. 2007. "Passive and Assertive Secularism: Historical Conditions, Ideological Struggles and State Policies towards Religion," in *World Politics* 59 (4): 568–94.

Laver, Michael, and W. Ben Hunt. 1992. *Policy and Party Competition*. London: Routledge.

Lawrence, Bruce. 1990. *Defenders of God: The Fundamentalist Revolt against the Modern Age*. London: I. B. Tauris.

———. 1998. *Shattering the Myth: Islam beyond Violence*. Princeton: Princeton University Press.

Leghari, Iqbal. 1979. *The Socialist Movement in Pakistan: An Historical Survey, 1940–1974*. PhD diss., Laval University.

Lehmann, David. 2006. "Secularism and the Public-Private Divide: Europe Can Learn from Latin America," *Political Theology* 7(3): 273–93.

Lehmann, David, and Batia Siebzhener. 2006. *Remaking Israeli Judaism: The Challenge of Shas*. London: Hurst.

Lewis, Bernard. 2002. *What Went Wrong? The Clash between Islam and Modernity in the Middle East*. New York: Oxford University Press.

Lewis, Martin, and Karen Wigen. 1997. *The Myth of Continents: A Critique of Metageography*. Berkeley: University of California Press.

Luckmann, Thomas. 1967. *Invisible Religion: The Problem of Religion in Modern Society*. New York: Macmillan.

MacIntyre, Alasdair. 1964. "Secularization and Moral Change." The Riddell Memorial Lectures delivered at the University of Newcastle upon Tyne on November 11, 12, and 13.

Madan T. N. 1998. "Secularism in Its Place," in Rajeev Bhargava, ed., *Secularism and Its Critics*. Delhi: Oxford University Press.

Mahmood, Saba. 1994. "Islamism and Fundamentalism," *Middle East Report* 191: 29–30.

———. 2005. *Politics of Piety: Islamic Revival and the Feminist Subject*. Princeton: Princeton University Press.

———. 2006. "Secularism, Hermeneutics and Empire: The Politics of Islamic Reformation," *Public Culture* 18(2): 323–47.

Malashenko, Alexei V. 1993. "Islam versus Communism: The Experience of Coexistence," in Dale Eickelman, ed., *Russia's Muslim Frontiers*. Bloomington: Indiana University Press.

Malik, Abdullah. 1985. *Punjab ki Siyasi Tehreek, 1920–1940 Tek* [Political Movements in Punjab, 1920–1940]. Lahore: Kausar Publications.

Malik, Iftikhar. 1997. *State and Civil Society in Pakistan: Politics of Authority, Ideology, and Ethnicity*. Basingstoke: Macmillan.

———. 1999. *Islam, Nationalism, and the West: Issues of Identity in Pakistan*. Basingstoke: Macmillan.

Mamdani, Mahmood. 2004. *Good Muslim, Bad Muslim: America, the Cold War, and the Roots of Terror.* New York: Pantheon/Random House.

Mandaville, Peter. 2001. *Transnational Muslim Politics: Reimaging the Umma.* London: Routledge.

———. 2007. "Globalization and the Politics of Religious Knowledge: Pluralizing Authority in the Muslim World," *Theory, Culture & Society* 24:101–15.

Mani, Lata. 1998. *Contentious Traditions: The Debate on Sati in Colonial India.* Berkeley: University of California Press.

Manuel, Frank. 1983. *The Changing of the Gods.* Hanover: University Press of New England.

Marsden, Magnus. 2005. *Living Islam: Muslim Religious Experience in Pakistan's Northwest Frontier.* Cambridge: Cambridge University Press.

Martin, David. 2005 [1978]. *A General Theory of Secularization.* Aldershot: Ashgate.

Marty, Martin E., and R. Scott Appleby, eds. 1993. *Fundamentalisms and the State: Remaking Polities, Economies, and Militance.* Chicago: University of Chicago Press.

Masud, Mohammed Khalid. 1993. "The Limits of Expert Knowledge," in Dale Eickelman, ed., *Russian Muslim Frontiers: New Directions in Cross Cultural Analysis.* Bloomington: Indiana University Press.

———, ed. 2000. *Travellers in Faith: Studies of the Tablighi Jama'at as a Transnational Islamic Movement for Faith Renewal.* Lieden: Brill.

———. 2005. "The Construction and Deconstruction of Secularism as an Ideology in Contemporary Muslim Thought," *Asian Journal of Social Science* 33(3): 363–83.

Masud, Mohammed Khalid, Brinkley Messick, and David Powers. 1996. *Islamic Legal Interpretation: Muftis and Their Fatwas.* Cambridge, MA: Harvard University Press.

Maududi, Humaira. 2005. *Shajr hai Sayadar.* Lahore: Manshoorat.

Maududi, Syed Abul A'ala. 1937, 1942. *Musalman aur Maujooda Siyasi Kashmakash* [Muslims and the Current Political Struggle]. Pathankot: Maktaba Jama'at-e-Islami.

———. 1962 (1926). *al-Jihad fil Islam: Islami jihad ki haqiqat aur uss ki zaroorat aur ahmiyat aur uss kay mut'aliq tamam usuli mubahis par mufasil guftagu* [Jihad in Islam: The Reality of Islamic Jihad and Its Need and Importance and a Detailed Exploration of All Related Discussions of Principles]. Karachi: Islamic Publications.

———. 1971. *Main Abul Ala Maududi Hoon* [I Am Abul A'ala Maududi]. *Zindagi* (January): 21–30

———. 2000. *Islam ka Nazariya Siyasi* [The Political View of Islam]. Lahore: Manshoorat.

———. 2004. *Qur'an ki char bunyadi istilahat: Allah, rab, Ibādat aur din* [Four Basic Terms in the Quran: Allah, God, Worship and Religion]. Lahore: Islamic Publications.

———. N.d. *Islam: Daur-e-Jadid Ka Mazhab* [Islam: A Religion for Modern Times]. Lahore: Manshoorat.

———. N.d. *Islam Kiya Hai!* [What Is Islam!]. Lahore: Manshoorat.

McLeod Hugh. 2000. *Secularisation in Western Europe, 1848–1914*. New York: St. Martin's Press.

Mehdi, Rubya. 1993. *The Islamization of the Law in Pakistan*. Richmond: Curzon.

Mehta, Uday Singh. 1999. *Liberalism and Empire: A Study in Nineteenth Century British Liberal Thought*. Chicago: University of Chicago Press.

Menon, Dilip. 2007. "An Inner Violence: Why Communalism in India Is about Caste," in T. N. Srinivas, *The Future of Secularism*. New Delhi: Oxford University Press.

Mernissi, Fatima. 1985. *Beyond the Veil: Male-Female Dynamics in Modern Muslim Society*. London: al-Saqi.

———. 1993. *Forgotten Queens of Islam*. Cambridge: Polity.

Metcalf, Barbara. 1982. *Islamic Revival in British India: Deoband 1860–1900*. Princeton: Princeton University Press.

———. 1994. "'Remaking Ourselves': Islamic Self-Fashioning in a Global Movement of Spiritual Renewal," in Martin E. Marty and R. Scott Appleby, eds., *Accounting for Fundamentalisms: The Dynamic Character of Movements*. Chicago: University of Chicago Press.

———. 2002. "'Traditionalist' Islamic Activism: Deoband, Tablighis and Taliban," International Institute for the Study of Islam in the Modern World (ISIM) paper.

———. 2004a. "Hakim Ajmal Khan, Rais of Delhi and Muslim 'Leader,'" in *Islamic Contestations; Essays on Muslims in India and Pakistan*. Delhi: Oxford University Press.

———. 2004b. *Islamic Contestations: Essays on Muslims in India and Pakistan*. Delhi: Oxford University Press.

Mir-Hosseini, Ziba. 2000. *Islam and Gender: The Religious Debate in Contemporary Iran*. London: I. B. Tauris.

Misra, K. P. 1972. "Intra-State Imperialism: The Case of Pakistan," *Journal of Peace Research* 9(1): 27–39.

Mitchell, Timothy. 1988. *Colonising Eypt*. Cambridge: Cambridge University Press.

———. 2000. *Questions of Modernity*. Minneapolis: University of Minnesota Press.

Modood, Tariq, and Fauzia Ahmad. 2007. "British Muslim Perspectives on Multiculturalism," in Bryan Turner and Frederic Volpi, eds., special issue on Authority in Islam, *Theory, Culture & Society* 24(2): 187–213.

Moghissi, H. 1999. *Feminism and Fundamentalism: The Limits of Post-Modernist Analysis*. London: Zed Press.

Mohammed, Mian Tufail. 1974. *Jama'at-e-Islami Pakistan: An Introduction*. Lahore: Ripon Press.

Monshipouri, Mahmood. 1998. *Islamism, Secularism and Human Rights in the Middle East*. London: Lynne Rienner.

Moten, Abdul Rashid. 2003. "Mawdudi and the Transformation of Jama'at-e-Islam in Pakistan," *Muslim World* 93(3–4): 391.

Mufti, Amir. 1995. "Secularism and Minority: Elements of a Critique," *Social Text* 45:75–96.

Mumtaz, Khawar, and Farida Shaheed. 1987. *Women in Paksitan: One Step Forward, Two Steps Back?* London: Zed Press.

Murad, Khuram Jah. 1988. "*Inquilab ka Rasta: Eeman, Jihad, Da'wat*" [The Path of Revolution: Belief, Jihad, and Proselytizing]. Lahore: Manshoorat.

———. 1994. *Lamhat* [Moments]. Lahore: al-badr publications.

———. N.d. *Itikhabat aur Qaum ki Zimadari* [Elections and the Nation's Responsibility]. Lahore: Manshoorat.

"Muttahida Majlis-e-Amal Manifesto/Manshoor." 2002. No publisher.

Naim, C. M. 2003. "Ghalib's Delhi: A Shamlessly Revisionist Look at Two Popular Metaphors," *Annual of Urdu Studies* 18:3–24.

Najmabadi, Afsaneh. 1991. "Hazards of Modernity and Morality: Women, State and Ideology in Contemporary Iran," in Deniz Kandiyoti, *Women, Islam and the State*. Basingstoke: Macmillan.

Nandy, Ashis. 1998. "The Politics of Secularism and the Recovery of Religious Tolerance," in Rajeev Bhargava, *Secularism and Its Critics*. Delhi: Oxford University Press.

Narayanan, Vasudha. 2000. "Religious Vocabulary and Regional Identity: A Study of the Tamil *Cirappuranam*," in David Gilmartin and Bruce Lawrence, *Beyond Turk and Hindu: Rethinking Religious Identities in Islamicate South Asia*. Gainesville: University Press of Florida Press.

Nasr, S. V. R. 1993. "Islamic Opposition to the Islamic State: The Jama'at-I-Islami, 1977–1988," *International Journal of Middle East Studies* 25(2): 261–83.

———. 1994. *The Vanguard of the Islamic Revolution: The Jama'at-I-Islami of Pakistan*. Berkeley: University of California Press.

———. 1996. *Mawdudi and the Making of Islamic Revivalism*. New York: Oxford University Press.

———. 2000. "The Rise of Sunni Militancy in Pakistan: The Changing Role of Islamism and the Ulama in Society and Politics," *Modern Asian Studies* 34(1): 139–80.

———. 2001. *Islamic Leviathan: Islam and the Making of State Power*. Oxford: Oxford University Press.

———. 2002. "Islam, the State and the Rise of Sectarian Militancy in Pakistan," in Christophe Jaffrelot, ed., *Pakistan: Nationalism without a Nation?* London: Zed Books.

Nasr, Seyyed Hossein. 1975. *Islam and the Plight of Modern Man*. London: Longman.

———. 1987. *Traditional Islam in the Modern World*. London: KPI.

Navaro-Yashin, Yael. 2002. *Faces of the State*. Princeton: Princeton University Press.

Niazi, Kausar. 1973. *JI awam ki adalat main* [Jama'at in the Court of the People]. Lahore: Kausar Publications.

Noman, Omar. 1988. *The Political Economy of Pakistan*. London: KPI.

Nussbaum, Martha. 2000. *Sex and Social Justice*. Oxford: Oxford University Press.

Paidar, Parvin. 1995. *Women and the Political Process in Twentieth-Century Iran*. Cambridge: Cambridge University Press.

Papaneck, Gustav. 1967. *Pakistan's Development: Social Goals and Private Incentives*. Cambridge, MA: Harvard University Press.

Pateman, Carole. 1988. *The Sexual Contract*. Cambridge: Polity.

Pirzada, Sayyid. 2000. *The Politics of the Jamiat Ulama-i-Islam Pakistan, 1971–1977*. Oxford: Oxford University Press.

Piscatori, J. 1983. *Islam in the Political Process*. Cambridge: Cambridge University Press.

———. 1986. *Islam in a World of Nation States*. Cambridge: Cambridge University Press.

———. 1994. "Accounting for Islamic Fundamentalisms," in Martin E. Marty and R. Scott Appleby, eds., *Accounting for Fundamentalisms: The Dynamic Character of Movements*. Chicago: University of Chicago Press.

———. 2000. "Islam, Islamists and the Electoral Principle in Middle East," International Institute for the Study of Islam in the Modern World (ISIM) paper.

Platts, John. 1994 (1911). *A Dictionary of Urdu, Classical Hindi and English*. Oxford: Oxford University Press.

Poya, Maryam. 1999. *Women, Work and Islamism: Ideology and Resistance in Iran*. London: Zed Press.

Qazi, Samiya Raheel. N.d. *Qatl-e-Ghairat* [Honour Killing]. Lahore: Women's Commission Jama'at-e-Islami.

Rahman, Fazlur. 1958. "Muslim Modernism in Indo-Pakistan Sub-Continent," *Bulletin of the School of Oriental and African Studies* 21(1/3): 82–99.

———. 1982. *Islam and Modernity*. Chicago: University of Chicago Press.

Rashid, Ahmed. 2000. *Taliban: Islam, Oil and the New Great Game in Central Asia*. London: I. B. Tauris.

Rashid, Tehmina. 2006. *Contested Representation: Punjabi Women in Feminist Debate in Pakistan*. Lahore: Oxford University Press.

Rashiduzzaman, M. 1970. "The National Awami Party of Pakistan: Leftist Politics in Crisis," *Pacific Affairs* 43(3): 394–409.

Raz, Joseph. 1986. *The Morality of Freedom*. Oxford: Clarendon Press.

Robinson, Francis. 1998. "The British Empire and Muslim Identity in South Asia," *Transactions of the Royal Historical Society* 6(8): 271–89.

———. 2001. *The 'Ulama of Farangi Mahal and Islamic Culture in South Asia*. Delhi: Permanent Black.

Roemer, John E. 2001. *Political Competition: Theory and Application*. Cambridge, MA: Harvard University Press.

Rostami-Povey, Elaheh. 2001. "Feminist Contestations of Institutional Domain in Iran," *Feminist Review* 69:44–72.

Roy, Olivier. 1994. *The Failure of Political Islam*. Cambridge, MA: Harvard University Press.

———. 2002. "The Taliban: A Strategic Tool for Pakistan," in Christophe Jaffrelot, ed., *Pakistan: Nationalism without a Nation*. London: Zed.

Said, Edward. 1978. *Orientalism*. London: Routledge and Kegan Paul.

———. 1995. *Politics of Dispossession: The Struggle for Palestinian Self-Determination, 1969–1994*. New York: Vintage Books.

Salvatore, Armando. 2005. "The Euro-Islamic Roots of Secularity: A Difficult Equation," *Asian Journal of Social Science* 33(3): 412–37.

———. 2007. "Authority in Question: Secularity, Republicanism and 'Communitarianism' in the Emerging Euro-Islamic Public Sphere," *Theory, Culture & Society* 24(2): 135–60.

Salvatore, Armando, and Dale Eickelman, eds. 2004. *Public Islam and the Common Good*. Lieden: Brill.

Samad, Yunus. 1996. "Pakistan or Punjabistan: Crisis of National Identity," in Gurharpal Singh and Ian Talbot, eds., *Punjabi Identity: Continuity and Change*. New Delhi: Manohar.

Sarkar, Tanika. 1993. "Women's Agency within Authoritarian Communalism: The Rashtasevika Samiti and Rajanmabhoomi," in Gyanendra Pandey, ed., *Hindus and Others: The Question of Identity in India Today*. New Delhi: Viking.

———. 2001. "Aspects of Contemporary Hindutva Theology: The Voice of Sadhvi Rithambhara," in *Hindu Wife, Hindu Nation: Community, Religion and Cultural Nationalism*. New Delhi: Permanent Black.

Sayeed, Khalid bin. 1980. *Politics in Pakistan: The Nature and Direction of Change*. New York: Praeger.

———. 1997. *Western Dominance and Political Islam: Challenge and Response*. Oxford: Oxford University Press.

Scott, David. 1996. "The Aftermaths of Sovereignty: Postcolonial Criticism and the Claims of Political Modernity," *Social Text* 48: 1–26.

———. 2003. "Culture in Political Theory," *Political Theory* 31(1): 92–115.

Scott, James C. 1985. *Weapons of the Weak, Everyday Forms of Peasant Resistance*. New Haven: Yale University Press.

———. 1998. *Seeing Like a State: How Certain Schemes to Improve the Human Condition Have Failed*. New Haven: Yale University Press.

Shafqat, Saeed. 2002. "From Official Islam to Islamism: The Rise of Da'wat-ul-Irshad and Lashkar-I-Jhangvi," in Christophe Jaffrelot, ed., *Pakistan: Nationalism without a Nation*. London: Zed Books.

Shahabuddin, Elora. 2008. *Reshaping the Holy: Democracy, Development, and Muslim Women in Bangladesh*. New York: Columbia University Press.

Shaikh, Farzana. 1989. *Community and Consensus in Islam: Muslim Representation in Colonial India, 1860–1947*. Cambridge: Cambridge University Press.

Shamsul, A. B. 2005. "Making Sense of the Plural-Religious Past and the Modern-Secular Present of the Islamic Malay World and Malaysia," *Asian Journal of Social Science* 33(3): 449–72.

Shepard, William E. 1987. "Islam and Ideology: Towards a Typology," *Journal of Middle East Studies* 19(3): 307–35.

Sikand, Yoginder. 2003. "The Politics of the Tablighi Jama'at," *International Institute for the Study of Islam in the Modern World (ISIM) Review*.

Singerman, Diane. 1995. *Avenues of Participation: Family, Politics and Networks in the Urban Quarters of Cairo*. Princeton: Princeton University Press.

Sivan, Emmanuel. 1985. *Radical Islam: Medieval Theology and Modern Politics*. New Haven: Yale University Press.

Skuy, David. 1998. "Macaulay and the Indian Penal Code of 1862: The Myth of Inherent Superiority of the English Legal System Compared to India's Legal System in the Nineteenth Century," *Modern Asian Studies* 32(3): 513–57.

Spivak, Gayatri Chakravarty. 1988. "Can the Subaltern Speak?" in Cary Nelson and Lawrence Grossberg, eds., *Marxism and the Interpretation of Culture*. Urbana: University of Illinois Press.

Starrett, Gregory. 1998. *Putting Islam to Work*. Berkeley: University of California Press.

Strathern, Marilyn. 1988. *The Gender of the Gift: Problems with Women and Problems with Society in Melanesia*. Berkeley: University of California Press.

———. 2006. "A Community of Critics? Thoughts on New Knowledge," *Journal of Royal Anthropological Institute* 12:191–209.

Sulehria, Farooq. N.d. *History of the Left in Pakistan*. Pakistan Labour Party.

Talbot, Ian. 2002. "The Punjabization of Pakistan: Myth or Reality?" in Christophe Jaffrelot, ed., *Pakistan: Nationalism without a Nation*. London: Zed Books.

Tamimi, Azam. 2000. "The Origins of Arab Secularism," in Azam Tamimi and John Esposito, eds., *Islam and Secularism in the Middle East*. London: Hurst and Co.

Tamimi, Azam, and John Esposito, eds. 2000. *Islam and Secularism in the Middle East*. London: Hurst and Co.

Tarik, Jan, ed. 1998. *Pakistan between Secularism and Islam: Ideology, Issues and Conflict*. Islamabad: Institute of Policy Studies.

Tarrow, Sidney. 1998. *Power in Movement: Social Movements and Contentious Politics*. Cambridge: Cambridge University Press.

Taylor, Charles. 1989. *Sources of the Self: The Making of the Modern Identity*. Cambridge: Cambridge University Press.

———. 1998. "Modes of Secularism," in Rajeev Bhargava, ed., *Secularism and Its Critics*. Delhi: Oxford University Press.

———. 2004. *Modern Social Imaginaries*. Durhan: Duke University Press.

Tharu, Susie, and Tejaswini Niranjana. 1994. "Problems for a Contemporary Theory of Gender," *Social Scientist* 22(3–4): 93–111.

Thompson, David. 2010. "The Enlightenment: The Late Eighteenth Century Revolutions and Their Aftermath: A Protestant Perspective," in Gareth Stedman Jones and Ira Katznelson, *Religion and the Political Imagination*. Cambridge: Cambridge University Press.

Tibi, Bassam. 1988. *The Crisis of Modern Islam: A Preindustrial Culture in the Scientific-Technological Age*. Salt Lake City: University of Utah Press.

———. 1998. *The Challenge of Fundamentalism: Political Islam and the New World Disorder*. Berkeley: University of California Press.

Tilly, Charles. 1990. In *Coercion, Capital and European States, AD 990–1900*. Oxford: Blackwell.

Tjomsland, Marit. 1993. *The Educated Way of Thinking: Individualisation and Islamism in Tunisia*. Working paper D, Development Research and Action Programme, Michelsen Institute.

Tully, James, ed. 1988. *Meaning and Context: Quentin Skinner and His Critics*. Cambridge: Polity.

Turner, Bryan. 1974. *Weber and Islam: A Critical Study*. London: Routledge.

Turner, Bryan, and Frederic Volpi. 2007. "Making Islamic Authority Matter" *Theory, Culture & Society* 24(2): 1–19.

Usmani, Mufti Taqi. 2000. *Taqlid ki Sharai Hasiyat*. Maktaba Darul-uloon: Karachi.

———. 2003. *Akabar-e-Deoband Kiya thay?* Maktaba Ma'arifulqur'an: Karachi.

———. N.d. *Hakeem ul Ummat kay Siyasi Afkar* [Political Thoughts of Maulana Ashraf Ali Thanvi]. Maktaba al-Ashrafiya.

Vanaik, Achin. 1997. *The Furies of Indian Communalism: Religion, Modernity, and Secularization*. London: Verso.

van der Veer, Peter. 2001. *Imperial Encounters: Religion and Modernity in India and Britain*. Princeton: Princeton University Press.

———. 2004. "Secrecy and Publicity in the South Asian Public Arena," in Armando Salvatore and Dale Eickelman, eds., *Public Islam and the Common Good*. Lieden: Brill.

van der Veer, Peter. 1999. "The Moral State: Religion, Nation and Empire in Victorian Britain and British India," in *Nation and Religion: Perspectives on Europe and Asia*. Princeton: Princeton University Press.

van der Veer, Peter, and Hatmut Lehmann. 1999. *Nation and Religion: Perspectives on Europe and Asia*. Princeton: Princeton University Press.

Verkaaik, Oskar. 2004. *Migrants and Militants: Fun and Urban Violence in Pakistan*. Princeton: Princeton University Press.

Wald, Kenneth, and Clyde Wilcox. 2006. "Getting Religion: Has Political Science Rediscovered the Faith Factor?" *American Political Science Review* 100(4): 523–29.

Waseem, Muhammed. 1987. *Pakistan under Martial Law, 1977–85*. Lahore: Vanguard.

Washbrook, David. 1998. "The Rhetoric of Democracy and Development in Late Colonial India," in S. Bose and A. Jalal, eds., *Nationalism, Democracy and Development: State and Politics in India*. Delhi: OUP.

Weber, Max. 1950 [1904]. *The Protestant Ethic and the Spirit of Capitalism*. Trans. Talcott Parsons. London: George Allen and Unwin Ltd.

Weinbaum, Marvin G. 1996. "Civic Culture and Democracy in Pakistan," *Asian Survey* 36(7): 639–54.

Weiner, Myron. 1987. "Political Change: Asia, Africa and the Middle East," in Myron Weiner and Samuel Huntington, eds., *Understanding Political Development*. Boston: Little Brown and Company.

Weiss, Anita. 1986. *Islamic Reassertion in Pakistan: The Application of Islamic Laws in a Modern State*. Syracuse: Syracuse University Press.

———. 2002. *Walls within Walls: Life Histories of Working Women in the Old City of Lahore*. Oxford: Oxford University Press.

Weiss, Bernard. 1991. "Law in Islam and the West, Some Comparative Observations," in Wael Hallaq and Donald Adams, *Islamic Studies Presented to Charles J. Adam*. Lieden: Brill.

White, Jenny. 2002. *Islamist Mobilization in Turkey: A Study in Vernacular Politics*. Seattle: University of Washington Press.

Wiethman, Paul. 1991. "Separation of Church and State: Some Questions for Prof. Audi" *Philosophy and Public Affairs* 20(1): 52–65.

Wilcox, Wayne. 1970. "Pakistan in 1969: Once Again at the Starting Point," *Asian Survey* 10(2): 73–81.

Wilder, Andrew. 1999. *The Pakistani Voter: Electoral Politics and Voting Behaviour in the Punjab.* Oxford: Oxford University Press.

Wilson, Jon. 2007. "Anxieties of Distance: Codification in Early Colonial Bengal," *Modern Intellectual History* 4(1): 7–23.

Winter, Timothy. 2004. "Bombing Without Moonlight: The Origins of Suicidal Terrorism," *Encounters* 10(1–2): 85–118.

———. N.d. "Understanding the Four Madhabs." http://www.masud.co.uk/ISLAM/ahm/newmadhh.htm.

"Women's Rights Charter." N.d. Islamabad: Women's Commission Jama'at-e-Islami.

World Bank. 2002. "Poverty in Pakistan: Vulnerabilities, Social Gaps and Rural Dynamics." October.

Zafar, Fareeha, ed. 1991. *Finding Our Way: Readings on Women in Pakistan.* Lahore: ASR Publications.

Zaidi, Akbar. 1999. *Issues in Pakistan's Economy.* Karachi: Oxford University Press.

Zaigham, Sibt'l Hasan. 2004. *"Punjab ki Aik Gumshuda Awaz: Mian Iftikharuddin Ahmed"* [A Lost Voice of Punjab: Mian Iftikharuddin Ahmed]. *Awami Jamhoori Forum* 10 (April): 14–21.

———. 2005. Interview, *Awami Jamhoori Forum* 24 (September): 15.

Zaman, Mohammed Qasim. 1998. "Sectarianism in Pakistan: The Radicalization of Shi'I and Sunni Identities," *Modern Asian Studies* 32(3): 689–716.

———. 2000. "The Rise of Sunni Militancy in Pakistan: The Changing Role of Islamism and the Ulama in Society and Politics," *Modern Asian Studies* 34(1): 139–80.

———. 2002. *The Ulama in Contemporary Islam: Custodians of Change.* Princeton: Princeton University Press.

———. 2008. *Ashraf Ali Thanawi: Islam in Modern South Asia.* Oxford: One World.

Žižek, Slovaj. 1994. *Mapping Ideology.* London: Verso.

Zubaida, Sami. 1997. "Religion, the State and Democracy: Contrasting Conceptions of Society in Egypt," in Joel Benin and Joe Stork, eds., *Political Islam.* Berkeley: University of California Press.

———. 2005. "Islam and Secularisation," *Asian Journal of Social Science* 33(3): 438–48.

Newspapers and Magazines

A'ain Jama'at sponsored political monthly, Lahore

Al-Tayyabat Monthly magazine for women by the Jama'at-ud-Da'wa, Lahore

Asia Monthly current-issues magazine published by the Jama'at-e-Islami, Lahore

Awami Jamhoori Forum Monthly left magazine started in 2002, Lahore

Batool Monthly women's magazine published by the Jama'at-e-Islami

Dawn Pakistan's leading national English-language daily, Karachi

Jung Leading national Urdu daily, Karachi/Lahore

Maj'ala Al-Da'wa Monthly magazine of the Jama'at-ud-Da'wa, Lahore

Pakistan Times National newspaper owned by left-leaning Mian Iftikharuddin

Raftar Newsletter of the Women's Circle, Jama'at-e-Islami, Islamabad

Tarjuman-al-Qura'an Monthly magazine and key organ of the Jama'at-e-Islami

Zindagi Weekly magazine sympathetic to the Jama'at-e-Islami, popular during the 1960s and 1970s and defunct since 1984

Index

Abu Lughod, Lila, 9, 78, 133
Afghanistan: Hijrat movement to, 64;
    invasion of, 131; Islamism and, 25;
    JD in, 6, 104–6, 111, 123; JI in, 4, 5,
    95, 162
Ahl-e-hadīs: differences between "fun-
    damentalists" and, 101–2; JD and,
    109, 114, 118, 123–27, 171n18
Ahmad, Irfan, 14, 55, 57, 99
Ahmed, Aziz ud din, 54, 69–70, 82
Ahmed, Qazi Hussain, 91–95, 143
Al-Fatah (magazine), 80, 178n74
America: Allan Bloom on, 89; JI and,
    74, 85, 89, 93, 96, 144, 164nn8–9,
    183n115; resistance against, 102,
    107–9, 125, 166n21, 171n15; secu-
    larization theory and, 15–17, 138,
    165n14; wars in Afghanistan/Paki-
    stan and, 3–5, 25, 156, 161, 184n13
Aron, Raymond, 153
Asad, Talal, 14–15, 21, 25, 35–38, 40
Asdar Ali, Kamran, 131, 134, 177n49
atheism, 7, 17, 74, 85, 104
Awamification, 60
Awami Fikrī Mahaz, 70, 81

Ba'az, Shaikh Abdul Aziz, 123
Baloch, Liaqut, 151
Bangladesh (also East Pakistan), 2, 61,
    75, 122, 165n20
Barēlvīs, 109, 114, 164n10, 171–72n18
Basic Democracy Scheme, 187n45
Bayat, Asef, 99, 163n2
Bayly, Chris, 39, 42, 46
Bhashani, Maulana, 55, 66, 81–83,
    175n26

Bhutto, Benazir, 71, 76, 181n92
Bhutto, Zulfiqar Ali, 62, 70–76, 80–83,
    87, 92, 176n30
Bruce, Steve, 17, 165n14
Butt, Hafiz Salman, 77, 120

Casanova, Jose, 6, 16–18, 138, 153
Central Intelligence Agency (CIA), 5,
    103–5
Chakrabarty, Dipesh, 11–12, 24, 79
Chandar, Krishan, 65
Closing of the American Mind, 89
communism, 174n7; collapse of USSR
    and, 162; Islamism and, 25, 58, 65
    (*see also* Leninist Party, JI as)
Communist Party: in India, 64; in
    Pakistan, 61–66, 69, 75, 82, 84; in
    Punjab, 64, 65, 80; students and,
    67, 72
Connolly, William, 16, 19, 165n15

democracy: Islamic socialism and,
    55–56; Islamism relationship with,
    47, 162, 163n2; JD and, 3, 108, 122,
    124–25; JI and, 51, 57–59, 91–92,
    95, 124–25, 183n116; Mohammed
    Iqbal on, 171n16; secularization
    and, 16, 20
Deoband, 40, 101–2, 111, 123, 164n10
Devji, Faisal, 170nn6–7

Eickelman, Dale, 25, 128; Piscatori and,
    23, 25, 105, 126, 128, 152
elections: implications of for national-
    ism, 47–48, 171n16; JD and, 99,
    109, 122; JI and, 5, 27, 29, 66, 85, 94,

elections (*cont.*)
120, 147, 164n8, 190n24; Left and,
64–68, 76, 92; Muslim League and,
61, 64; political parties and, 99
Enlightened Moderation, 8, 145, 159
Enlightenment: influence of, on Islamist
thought, 11; postcolonial critique
and, 11, 158; religion and, 19,
129–30, 165n15, 166n24
Euben, Roxanne, 10, 11, 128, 169n2

feminism: and colonialism, 131–32;
Iranian writers on, 130; religion and,
131–49

Gilmartin, David, 45–47, 49, 51, 61
Goffman, Erving, 18, 142

Habermas, Jürgen, 18
Hallaq, Wael, 40, 115, 117, 152, 164n10,
186n36
Hamza, Abu/Amir, 104, 109–10,
185n28
Hashmi, Farhat, 104, 127, 184n16,
188n64
Hefner, Robert, 25, 152
honor killings, 144–50
Hussain, Munawar, 151

imaginary, 165n20, 167n34
imperialism, 58–59, 70, 89, 91, 95, 113,
174n12
Inter Services Intelligence (ISI), 108
Iqbal, Mohammed, 50, 65, 117, 171n16,
172nn22–23
Islahi, Maulana, 93
Islamia College, 69, 75, 169n52, 176n36
Islamic socialism, 55–56, 81–84
Islami Jamhuri Ittehad (IJI), 5
Islami Jami'yat Tulaba (IJT), 57, 72–78,
91, 93, 104; Hafiz Saeed and, 5, 122

Jalal, Ayesha, 46–47, 51, 61, 131
Jami'yat Ulema Islam, 82, 102–3,
179n78, 180n87

Jami'yat Ulema Pakistan, 102, 103,
179n78
Jewish Question, 51
jihad: in Afghanistan, 3, 77, 95, 103, 106;
centrality of, in JD narrative, 104–9,
123, 185n24; CIA support for, 103,
164n9; debate about types of, 106,
112, 186n33; Islamic socialism and,
82; Maududi on, 112–13; traditionalist view of, 113–14

Kashmir, xi, 3, 77, 107–8, 122, 171n17,
184n17, 187n48
Kaviraj, Sudipta, 42, 43, 47, 170n4
Khaksar movement, 81
Khan Ayub, 62–63, 66–71, 80, 81,
87, 92
Khyber Pakhtunkhwa, 4, 33, 93, 107

labor unions, 2, 58, 68, 76, 87–93,
143
Lail-o-nahar (magazine), 80, 175n23
Lashkar-e-Tayyaba (LT), 2, 6, 102–7,
163n6
Latifi, Danyal, 64, 88
Lehmann, David, 125, 166n27
Leninist Party, JI as, 48, 52, 66
liberalism, 11, 20, 159–62, 163n2

MacIntyre, Alasdair, 16, 159–60
Madrasa, 73, 84, 108, 146
Mahmood, Saba, 20, 25, 105, 133–39
Maki, Abdul Rehman, 109, 124, 187n50
Maoism, 69, 71, 85–86
Maslak, 6, 101, 123, 164n10
Masroor, Hajra, 80
Masud, Mohammed Khalid, 13, 20, 44,
48, 105, 106, 152, 166n27, 168n38,
171n17
Maududi, Abul A' la: America and,
74; break from traditionalists, 48,
52–56, 113–16; career, 4, 44, 59; Hi-
jrat movement and, 174n9; IJT and,
72; land reforms, 78, 86; the Left
and, 58, 65, 66, 83, 93, 94; Pakistan

movement, 50, 171n11; ulama and, 114, 117

Maududi, Humaira, 184n17

Metcalf, Barbara, 45, 48, 54, 100, 156, 170n9, 172n18

modernity: Islamism and, 9, 13, 35, 39, 53, 58, 65, 128; problems with definition of, 38, 40, 48, 116, 155, 158, 170n3; secularism and, 13, 17, 41, 48, 138, 159

modernization theory: feminism and, 134; secularization and, 8, 15–17, 137, 150

mufti, 186n36

Mufti, Amir, 51

Murad, Khurram Jah, 73, 176n37, 190n24

Murad, Shaikh, 115, 186n35

Musharaf, Pervez, 8, 58, 76, 88, 91, 107, 119, 145, 159, 164n8, 187n45, 191n1

Muslim League, 32, 61–67, 92, 109

Muttahida Majlis-e-'Amal (MMA), 4, 95, 102, 164n8

Nasr, Syed Hossein, 113, 130

Nasr, Syed Vali Reza, 52–66, 75, 101–4, 156, 164n9, 172n23, 174n15, 179n78

National Awami Party (NAP), 66, 69

National Students' Federation, 81

NGOs (nongovernmental organizations), 79, 142–43

"Objectification," 6, 23, 31, 36, 54, 125–27, 157

Orientalism, 9, 79, 165n19

Pakistan People's Party (PPP), 60, 71, 75, 80–85, 92

Pakistan Times, 81

parda: among Islamists, 3, 26–28, 135; piety and, 126–27, 140–42; variations in, 53, 125–27

piety, 28, 111, 115; belief and, 139–51; dress and, 125–28; *Politics of Piety*, 134–38; Weber on, 153–54

Piscatori, James, 168n39, 173n26; Eickelman and, 23, 25, 105, 126, 128, 152

political science: methodology in, 24–25, 37; religion and, 24

Professors' Group, 69, 70, 83

Protestant Church, 6–7, 16, 153, 154

Punjab University, 2, 57, 68–69, 75–78, 122, 184n16

Qazi, Samiya Raheel, 144, 145

Qur'an ki char bunyadi istilahain: Allah, rab, ibadat aur din, 114

Qutb, Syed, 11, 59, 115

religious authority, 16, 23, 39, 120, 151–55

Robinson, Francis, 54, 171n13

Roy, M. N., 64

Roy, Olivier, 2, 22–24, 34, 59

Russia: in Afghanistan, 25, 77, 104; communist literature from, 69, 179n82; Islamists campaign against, 74, 84–85

Saeed, Hafiz Mohammed: career, 3, 104, 107, 109, 122–23, 185n20, 188n54; family, 28, 139, 185n26; in IJT, 5, 122

Scott, David, 158, 161, 162

Scott, James C., 21, 25, 42, 133

secularism: agency and, 129–30, 149–50; "Archemdian" secularism, 20; atheism and, 7, 164n12; colonial secularism, 38, 41–49; definitions of, 7, 12–14, 20–21; Islam and, 13–17, 34–35; Islamist opposition to, in Pakistan, 55–59, 85, 97, 104; political science and, 24; as a project, 8, 12, 19–22, 38–41; public sphere and, 17–20; tolerance and, 159–61

secularist, difference from secularizing, 22

secularization theory, 15–23, 138, 152–55

Seeing Like a State, 21

Shahadat, 100, 104, 106–7, 109
shari'a: colonial rule and, 44, 172n20; Islamists and, 6, 85–86; traditionalists and, 111, 114, 185n30
Sharif, Nawaz, 5, 76, 109, 181n92
social movements, 29, 78, 92, 99–100
Spinoza, Baruch, 166n24
Stedman Jones, Gareth, and Ira Katznelson, 21, 165n15
student unions, 2, 57–58, 67–69, 72–78, 91
sufi, 54, 100, 111, 114, 173n28, 186n31

Tablighi Jama'at, 34, 44, 48, 101, 102, 183n8, 188n63
Taliban, 135, 131–32
Tarjuman ul Qur'an, 65, 177n45, 179n84
Tarrow, Sidney, 92–93
Taylor, Charles, 10, 39, 159–60, 167n34
Thanavi, Ashraf Ali, 111–12
Tilly, Charles, 35
Toba Tek Singh, 80–83, 95
tolerance: Islamists and, 78; secularism and, 159–61
tradition, 9, 15, 24–25, 39–41, 52–54, 111–16 ; of democratic politics, 61; legal, 48–49
traditionalists, 111–18. *See also* shari'a, Islamists and; shari'a, traditionalists and
Tufayl, Mian, 78, 93–95
Turner, Bryan, 13, 152

Umm Hammad, 136, 137
Umm Talha, 139, 140
United States: Allan Bloom on, 89; JI and, 74, 85, 89, 93, 96, 144, 164nn8–9, 183n115; resistance against, 102, 107–9, 125, 166n21, 171n15; secularization theory and, 15–17, 138, 165n14; wars in Afghanistan/Pakistan and, 3–5, 25, 156, 161, 184n13
University of Eastern Toilers, 64
Usmani, Taqi, 53, 111, 186n31

van der Veer, Peter, 13, 43, 48, 167n29, 170n10
veiling, 53, 140–42, 173n29. *See also parda*
violence: IJT and, 72–77, 90, 159, 161–62, 163n3; JD and, xi, 122, 135

"war on terror," 156
Weber, Max, 13, 21, 153–55
World Bank, 88, 91, 107–10, 173n4, 183n118

Zaman, Mohammed Qasim, 39–40, 44, 101–3, 112, 116, 152
Zia-ul-haq: Islamization and, 102, 156–57, 169n56, 185n19; JI and, 5, 55–57, 75–78, 94–95, 164n9; Left and, 80, 180n89; unions and, 2, 87–88
Zindagi (magazine), 74–75, 83, 87